Red Flags in Psychotherapy

This book delves into risks that can easily bedevil any psychotherapist and what can happen if they are ignored. Dramatic storytelling, based on actual incidents from the author's experiences as a member of ethics committees and as an ethics teacher and consultant, explores actions that may prompt clients to file formal complaints. Set in the context of an ethics committee meeting over the course of a weekend, twelve psychologists face their peers who will stand in judgment. Issues include the fallout from losing one's temper with a difficult client, a personal disclosure gone terribly wrong, a bartering arrangement that literally falls apart, a private life revealed in a most public way, a vengeful act that sullies the reputation of an entire department, breaking confidentiality when a client threatens harm, and the slippery slope to sexual exploitation.

The stories are absorbing, enlightening, sometimes shocking, and often stranger than fiction. Narrative nonfiction puts human faces and emotions on what would otherwise be cursory statistics. What led to the formal complaint, from the vantage point of both the complainant and the psychologist, offers insights not otherwise available unless the challenges agitating their lives leading up to the conflict are revealed. An author's commentary and discussion questions follow every story. Both new and seasoned practitioners, as well as those still in training, will find this to be an invaluable resource.

Patricia Keith-Spiegel, Ph.D., is the Voran Honors Distinguished Professor of Social and Behavioral Sciences Emerita at Ball State University, where she was the director of the Center for Teaching Integrity. She was a member of the Ethics Committee of the California State Psychological Association and was also on the Ethics Committee of the American Psychological Association for six years, serving two terms as Chair.

Red Flags in Psychotherapy

Stories of Ethics Complaints
and Resolutions

PATRICIA KEITH-SPIEGEL

Routledge
Taylor & Francis Group

NEW YORK AND LONDON

First published 2014
by Routledge
711 Third Avenue, New York, NY 10017

and by Routledge
27 Church Road, Hove, East Sussex BN3 2FA

Routledge is an imprint of the Taylor & Francis Group, an informa business

Library of Congress Cataloging in Publication Data
Keith-Spiegel, Patricia.
Red flags in psychotherapy : stories of ethics complaints and resolutions /
    Patricia Keith-Spiegel. pages cm
ISBN 978-0-415-83338-7 (hardcover : alk. paper) — ISBN 978-0-415-
83339-4 (pbk. : alk. paper) 1. Psychotherapists—Professional ethics.
2. Psychotherapy—Moral and ethical aspects. 3. Therapist and patient.
I. Title.
RC455.2.E8K45 2014
174.2'9689—dc23
2013012103

ISBN: 978-0-415-83338-7 (hbk)
ISBN: 978-0-415-83339-4 (pbk)
ISBN: 978-0-203-50611-0 (ebk)

Typeset in Minion
by Cenveo Publisher Services

Please visit the eResources website at
www.routledge.com/9780415833394

To the spirited and wise colleagues with whom I have served on ethics committees.

Contents

About the Author

Patricia Keith-Spiegel is a winner of the California State University Trustee's Outstanding Professor Award across all campuses and disciplines and of the American Psychological Foundation's Distinguished Professor Award. She credits these honors largely to the power of storytelling, a technique she used throughout her 34 years of teaching ethics classes to both university students and professional psychotherapists. Although she has authored many books and articles on ethical standards and practice, this is her first work sharing full-length stories about how ethics complaints arise between psychotherapists and clients or others with whom they work, and how they are eventually resolved. The stories are adapted from actual incidents.

Dr. Keith-Spiegel is the Voran Honors Distinguished Professor of Social and Behavioral Sciences Emerita at Ball State University where she was Director of the Center for Teaching Integrity. She was also Professor of Psychology at the California State University, Northridge, and a Visiting Professor of Psychology at Harvard Medical School. She was a member of the Ethics Committee of the California State Psychological Association and served six years, two terms as Chair, on the Ethics Committee of the American Psychological Association. She and her husband currently reside in San Jose, California.

Foreword

"No way that's true!"

"No sane person would ever do that, especially a psychologist."

"She must have made that stuff up."

"Well, maybe *some* psychologists really do such stupid things."

These are some of the thoughts that will run through your mind as you read this book, and that is most certainly one of Professor Keith-Spiegel's key motives. Part of the message to follow is indeed: truth is (much) stranger than fiction. The deeper message in telling these stories involves informing the reader about how some mental health practitioners seem oblivious to ethical transgressions, stumble into them, or calculatedly charge ahead regardless of their vulnerable clients' well-being. You will also get a good feel for the way those who breach ethical codes are viewed by their colleagues and the way professional associations and licensing boards try to enforce ethical standards and make things right, when possible. All will unfold through artfully disguised renderings of actual ethical problems, discussed through the eyes of the psychologists called upon to investigate and resolve complaints.

Having known and collaborated with Professor Keith-Spiegel for nearly four decades I have consistently marveled at her skills as a consummate award-winning teacher, storyteller, and ethical humanist. I have sat with her on committees where some of the stories you are about to read unfolded. She has carefully crafted each chapter to detail a different fascinating case with sensitive attention to unpacking the perspectives of the clients who complained, the practitioners called to account, and the members of the ethics committee attempting to adjudicate fairly. Whether you seek insight into the confidential inner workings of professional disciplinary panels, or understanding how a case can go horribly wrong, or simply a fascinating read, you are in for a real treat.

Gerald P. Koocher, Ph.D., ABPP
President of the American Psychological Association, 2006

Preface

"Ethical standards of practice" sounds cold, detached, and dry as old bones. The flesh and the fury underlying most allegations of unethical conduct against mental health professionals—be they psychologists, marriage and family therapists, social workers, psychiatrists, or counselors—are best told as stories. The cases herein are adapted from actual incidents gleaned from years as a member of ethics committees and as a consultant to those seeking information or just someone to listen.

As a much younger psychologist and newly elected to the Ethics Committee of the American Psychological Association I was astonished by how many of my colleagues judged to be guilty of ethics violations appeared to have committed them with neither intent nor full awareness. I even wrote an article about my discernments (Keith-Spiegel, 1977). Over 30 years later, this is the book I needed to write, putting human faces on both the mental health professionals who stumbled as well as those who were harmed in the process. Telling their stories is the best way I know to fully communicate how intelligent, highly-educated, and often otherwise competent mental health professionals fall from grace.

Why Narrative Nonfiction Instead of Traditional Case Histories?

Ethics case presentations are popular, and the richer the content the more effective they are as teaching tools (Harkrider et al., 2012). And yet the telling of engaging stories has long been known as *the* most powerful method of increasing moral awareness and learning (e.g., Hensel & Rasco, 1992; Tappan & Brown, 1989; Tappan & Packer, 1991; Vitz, 1990). Arousing our emotions along with our intellects improves retention and performance (Immordino-Yang & Damasio, 2007).

Neurological research confirms what those of us who integrate vivid stories into our teaching style have always suspected. Stories are processed differently in our brains compared to presentations of straight facts and data (Mar, 2011). Recent neuroimaging studies reveal how reading stories stimulates many of the same brain areas as when we encounter actual experiences (Paul, 2012). Thus, reading absorbing narratives creates a deep and immersive simulation of social interactions, almost as if learning through experience (Mar & Oatly, 2008).

My Ethics Committee

The Ethics Committee of the California League of Psychologists—a fabricated name allowing me to present a collection of hearings taking place in a single venue over a weekend—decides twelve cases. Readers are privy to what the members of the committee do not and could not know: the back stories of those who complained as well as those accused. What else was going on in the lives of the clients and psychotherapists provides a far deeper understanding of how, why, and what went wrong before the matter entered a formal arena.

Most of the story plots, including cases referred to during the Ethics Committee discussions, are based on material originally shared in confidence. Identities were protected using the precautions required for the presentation of case studies (Gavey & Braun, 1997; Patterson, 1999). Names, places, genders, and physical descriptions of the characters were altered as well as other possibly identifying features. Elements of similar cases were sometimes merged into a single story. What I created reflects the emotions upset clients and colleagues shared with me resulting in narratives as intense as any fictional tale of anguished, frightened, and sometimes angry individuals entering into moral combat. None of the dialog betrays an actual ethics committee discussion.

A few caveats are in order. My ethics committee interactions honor an era when an informal and collegial approach to resolving cases was valued over the current copious and tight legalistic requirements. To keep my characters animated and to tell stories with a minimum of minutiae, I condensed or eliminated altogether many features of ethics committee procedures. These include the additional investigative steps taken and information made available to members before any group meeting. I offer a quick and partial glimpse into the process of discussing cases where evidence may be sparse or conflicting, given that psychotherapy is usually conducted behind closed doors. The types of cases that arise, the kinds of the questions and discussions in which ethics committees engage, the sanctions and directives available, and the final decisions reached remain realistic, though substantially abbreviated.

It is far less common for those facing an ethics inquiry (known as respondents) to appear in person before an ethics committee as they do in all of my stories. Currently respondents may even be offered an opportunity to resign from the professional organization rather than face a formal inquiry at all. "Resignations under ethics investigation," as this option is called by the American Psychological Association, are made known to others, leaving the reason why up to the imagination.

Today few state level ethics committees investigate complaints against its members. Instead, most state associations, such as the California Psychological Association, provide educative and consulting roles focusing on prevention (Donner, 2006). The investigative and sanctioning process is increasingly methodical and complex, due in part to more public exposure of violators in recent years, creating a motivation for respondents to contest the charges or appeal the findings. State and smaller organizations have neither the staff nor monetary reserves to defend against legal actions, leaving the burden of case adjudication of psychotherapists largely to the professional organizations at the national level, state licensing boards, and the courts. Appendix A provides lists of websites for the major national mental health professional organizations' current ethics codes, rules and procedures for processing and hearing complaints, and licensing laws for psychologists in California. Appendix B presents the available sanctions and directives for members of the American Psychological Association found guilty of an ethics code violation.

Finally, what is it like to serve on an ethics committee? Wright (1989) characterized the structure of ethics committees as "defensive and self-righteousness." I never found that to be the case. Our meetings were lively, occasionally intense, but I never thought I joined an armored tribunal. The members are volunteers from the ranks of their peers, complete with distinct personality styles and specialties within the field, making for a varied group determined to do its very best to uphold both the profession's values and the public trust. The membership diversity is very much by design to ensure representation and to avoid groupthink (Lo, 1987). Members sometimes disagreed, even squabbled, but almost always arrived at reasonable conclusions given available evidence and resources.

References

Donner, M. B. (August/July, 2006). California Psychological Association Ethics Committee: A new mission. *The California Psychologist*, n.p.n.

Gavey, N., & Braun, V. (1997). Ethics and the publication of clinical case material. *Professional Psychology, 28*, 399–404.

Harkrider, L. N., Thiel, C. E., Bagdasarov, Z., Mumford, M., Johnson, J. F., Connelly, S., & Devenport, L. D. (2012). Improving case-based ethics training with codes of conduct and forecasting content. *Ethics & Behavior, 22*, 258–280.

Hensel, W. A., & Rasco, T. L. (1992). Storytelling as a method for teaching values and attitudes. *Academic Medicine, 67*, 500–504.

Immordino-Yang, H., & Damasio, A. (2007). We feel, therefore we learn: The relevance of affective and social neuroscience to education. *Mind, Brain, and Education, 1*, 3–10.

Keith-Spiegel, P. (1977). Violation of ethical principles due to ignorance or poor professional judgment versus willful disregard. *Professional Psychology, 8*, 288–297.

Lo, B. (1987). Behind closed doors: Promises and pitfalls of ethics committees. *New England Journal of Medicine, 317*, 46–50.

Mar, R. (2011). The neural bases of social cognition and story comprehension. *Annual Review of Psychology, 62*, 103–134.

Mar, R. A., & Oatly. K. (2008). The function of fiction. *Perspectives on Psychological Science, 3*, 173–192.

Patterson, A. (1999). The publication of case studies and confidentiality—an ethical predicament. *Psychiatric Bulletin, 23*, 562–564.

Paul, A. M. (2012). Your brain on fiction. *New York Times*. Retrieved from http://www.nytimes.com/2012/03/18/opinion/sunday/the-neuroscience-of-your-brain-on-fiction.html?tntemail0=y&emc=tnt&pagewanted=all&_r=0

Tappan, M. B., & Brown, L. M. (1989). Stories told and lessons learned: Toward a narrative approach to moral development and more education. *Harvard Educational Review, 59*, 182–206.

Tappan, M. B., & Packer, M. J. (Eds.). (1991). Narrative and storytelling: Implications for understanding moral development. *New Directions for Child Development, No. 54.* San Francisco, CA: Jossey-Bass.

Vitz, P. C. (1990). The use of stories in moral development: New psychological reasons for an old education method. *American Psychologist, 45*, 709–720.

Wright, R. (1989). On ethics committees: Happiness and the pursuit of life and liberty. *Psychotherapy in Private Practice, 7*, 1–18.

Additional Reading

Coles, R. (1989). *The call of stories*. Boston, MA: Houghton Mifflin.

Coles, R. (2004). *Teaching stories*. New York, NY: Modern Library (Random House).

Frank, F. (2010). *Letting stories breathe: A socio-narratology*. Chicago. IL: University of Chicago Press.

Josselson, R. (1996). *Ethics and process in the narrative study of lives*. Thousand Oaks, CA: Sage.

Lewis, B. (2011). *Narrative psychiatry: How stories can shape clinical practice*. Baltimore, MD: John Hopkins University Press.

Acknowledgements

Too many good friends and students to name here listened to me reflect on stories over the years, and some of them looked over early drafts once I settled down to write. I appreciate each and every one. As the writing firmed up, I owe considerable gratitude to those colleagues who reviewed some or all chapters just prior to finalizing them: Drs. Whitney Gordon, Gerald P. Koocher, Marci Gaither, Barbara Goza, D. Louise Mebane, Baron Perlman, Dee Sheperd-Look, and Don Spiegel. Their suggestions were invaluable in making final content decisions. I offer special thanks to my husband, Rich Racimora, who remained close by to discuss the characters and what they may have actually said to each other. Stan Davis, a much appreciated friend with a distinct flair for grammar and detail, edited the manuscript as it neared its final phases. Sadly, Stan passed away before seeing the published project.

Dr. George Zimmar, my editor at Routledge Mental Health, was a delight to work with. Every author should be so lucky. I also thank the anonymous (to me) reviewer of my initial proposal for understanding my purpose, namely to sensitize readers to the early stages of risk and then to reflect on their own practice. Chris Tominich, Senior Editorial Assistant at Routledge Mental Health, is deeply appreciated for his competence and diligence in keeping the publishing process in motion. Finally, Ruchika Agarwal and Gayathri Bellan, Project Managers for Cenveo Publisher Services, were extremely helpful, patient, and a pleasure to work with as the manuscript headed into print.

Introduction
SELF-DECEPTION
AND RED FLAGS

The worst deluded are the self-deluded.

Christian Nestell Bovee

The stereotype of unethical psychotherapists inspires images of unsavory characters misusing, abusing, or harming vulnerable clients. In my experience, however, most psychotherapists charged with professional misconduct were neither sociopaths nor purposely exploitive, nor did they ever set out to commit an ethical violation.

Lying to Ourselves

We humans have a remarkable ability to deceive ourselves. How people stumble with their eyes seemingly wide open and believe they are morally justified while engaging in unethical behavior has long captured the attention of theorists and social scientists. Self-deception, according to Burton (2012) is common, universal, and responsible for the vast majority of human tragedies.

Often enough what we want to be true we see as true, even though impartial assessments would indicate our beliefs are radically out of line with the facts (Mele, 2001). When self-interest is superimposed it functions in an automatic, compelling, and often unconscious manner (Moore, 2004), allowing us to engage in an "internal con game," while minimizing guilt by believing that we have acted morally (Epley & Caruso, 2004;

Kieffer & Sloane, 2009; Tenbrunsel & Messick, 2004). Deluding ourselves often operates under subtle and seemingly harmless circumstances, sometimes for convenience or to justify action or inaction. Related processes are known by various names: rationalization, moral dissonance, moral fading, moral credentialing, moral self-licensing, moral hypocrisy, denial, repression, perceptual distortion, intellectualization, neutralization, confirmation bias, moral disengagement, and egocentric ethics (Bandura, 1999; Batson & Collins, 2011; Brown, Tamborski, Wang, et al, 2011; Detert, Trevino, & Sweitzer, 2008; Epley & Caruso, 2004; Lowell, 2012; Mele, 2001; Merritt, Effron, & Monin, 2010; Monin & Miller, 2011).

Upon a more careful analysis of cases that baffled me because the psychotherapists seemed to be such unlikely ethics violators I uncovered early warning signs—red flags, sometimes waving ever so gently at first—that went unheeded. Miscommunications or overlooked cues accelerated a potentially perilous process until it was too late to turn it around. Stressors, insecurities, emotional problems, burnout, physical ailments, financial worries, relationship issues, or other deficits in psychotherapists' personal lives sometimes overwhelmed the sacred obligation to focus on clients' well-being. In some cases opportunities for personal advantage or gratification overshadowed professional responsibilities. A few cases revealed psychotherapists who were uninformed or practicing beyond their level of competence without realizing how poised they were to make mistakes. Occasionally they simply made an unintended slip by becoming distracted. Often enough an unethical act was the fateful culmination of tidy rationalized steps. By the time awareness of possible danger ahead kicked in, usually followed by frantic efforts to reverse course, the harm was already done.

Clear and consistent awareness of self is a hallmark of an effective and ethical mental health professional (Bazerman & Banaji, 2004; Schwebel & Coster, 1998). In most of the stories we see psychotherapists who experienced—sometimes only minimally or for an instant and sometimes intensely and over an extended period—loss of sight of self. Abandonment of self-awareness, allowing for extraneous influences in concert with personal agendas unrelated to professional commitments to sway decisions and actions, sets one up for unexpected consequences.

The High Price of Being Sanctioned by an Ethics Committee

Ethical mistakes can be costly beyond potential harm to clients. Facing an ethics or licensing board inquiry and awaiting an outcome is intensely anxiety arousing and embarrassing, sometimes to the point of jeopardizing the mental and physical health of the accused (Koocher & Keith-Spiegel, 2008) as well as their livelihoods (Grenier & Golub, 2009). Sanctions and directives vary from warnings to severe penalties. Such punitive measures can stop a career in its tracks when a member is expelled from a professional association and the licensing board suspends or pulls the license to practice. Regardless of the severity of the infraction, a finding by an ethics committee must be reported to insurance panels and on HMO contracts, review boards, and other professional disclosure requests.

A thoughtful research article by Warren and and Douglas (2012) offers insights rarely discussed in the open about the stigma attached to being sanctioned by an ethics committee. The shame and silence often results in isolation, stunting the healing process. It is difficult to know who to confide in and who will turn away, perhaps in disgust, and who might sympathetically engage. In a case presentation, Warren and Douglas offer a painful segment from a participant's diary:

> The day the letter came from the licensing Board was not unlike the day I received the call of my father's death. Something permanently ended, the pain visceral, deep, unrelenting, and the regret of not doing things differently is unforgiving. Not only is the pain unending, the fears are immobilizing. What will others think of me? Will I lose my job?…I wish there was a cave of solitude and safety I could escape to…I do not want to be seen.
>
> (p. 137)

My own experiences with psychotherapists who have endured ethics or licensing board scrutiny also reveal intense shame, guilt, fear, loss of self-worth, unrelenting anxiety, suicidal thoughts, and even onset of physical ailments, such as high blood pressure. Whereas some guilty mental health professionals have earned harsh judgments, most who stumble deserve second chances coupled with support and empathy from colleagues. Prevention is the primary purpose of my cautionary stories, helping to recognize those often subtle clues otherwise competent and decent psychotherapists miss or ignore, much to their later regret.

The Parade of Red Flags

It is important to note upfront that not all red flags are unethical indicators in and of themselves. Nor does their existence automatically lead to poor decisions with regrettable results. Many items in the line-up of red flags seem like simple common sense. But once a matter signaling potential risk becomes apparent, careful consideration and any necessary accommodations in one's next steps are imperative. This assessment requires clear-minded self-awareness.

The groupings below offer examples of potentially risky conditions ripe for encouraging unfortunate decisions that could result in ethical mistakes, sometime serious ones. Many of the individual items are adapted from Epstein and Simon (1990), Koocher and Keith-Spiegel (2008), Pope, Sonne and Greene (2006), Pope and Vasquez (2011), and Walker and Clark (1999).

A Desire for a Different Relationship from Client/Psychotherapist

- Disclosing considerable, irrelevant detail about your own life to a client.
- Thinking often about a client outside of sessions.
- Attempting to influence a client's hobbies, political, or religious views, outside relationships, or other personal choices that have no direct therapeutic relevance.
- Instigating communications with a client between sessions for reasons you contrive or that are unrelated to treatment issues.
- Daydreaming that a client is not a client but, instead, in some other type of relationship with you (e.g., your friend or business partner).
- Noticing interactions with a client are becoming unrelated to the therapeutic goals.
- Actively seeking opportunities to spend time with a client outside of a professional setting.
- Anticipating, with excitement, a certain client's appointment.
- Flirting with a client.
- Feeling sexually attracted to, or aroused by, a client.
- Wanting to touch a client.
- Finding yourself paying more attention to grooming and dress on a certain client's appointment day.
- Daydreaming about having a sexual relationship with a client.
- Moving a client's hour to accommodate a personal agenda (e.g., the last client of the day so that a personal two-way conversation or other activity could occur afterwards).

Rationalizing the Acceptability of a Contemplated Boundary Crossing or Deviation from Standard Practice

- Hearing yourself thinking, "This time it's different," "Everyone does it," "No one will get hurt," "No one will know," "I can still be objective," "It's such a minor thing," "Nobody else will care," or "Just this one time."
- Allowing clients to run up a bill that will be difficult for them to pay back.
- Taking on an individual as a psychotherapy client with whom you had a pre-established close relationship (e.g., close family member, close friend, or ex-lover).
- Seeing clients outside of a professional setting that has no relevance to the client's therapeutic needs.
- Adding additional roles on to the therapeutic relationship (e.g., employing a client).

Concerns about Personal Ambition and Financial Gain

- Viewing a certain client as being in a position to advance your own career or fulfill one of your extraneous needs.
- Being exceedingly ambitious to "make it big" as a psychotherapist.
- Bartering with clients for services or tangible objects in lieu of collecting fees.
- Accepting clients while aware that your training and experience are likely insufficient to provide competent treatment.
- Failing to refer clients when it becomes clear that they are not benefitting from your treatment or that their issues are outside your level of training and expertise.

Needs for Enhancing One's Own Self-esteem

- "Showing off" to clients beyond revealing the usual dissemination of credentials and achievements relevant to the services you render.
- Relying on a client's presence or praise to elevate how you feel about yourself.
- Believing that you are the only psychotherapist who can help a particular client

- Indulging in rescue fantasies.
- Bragging about high-profile clients to others (even if not identifying them).
- Feeling entitled to *all* of the credit when a client improves, especially if a marked achievement is attained while under your care.

Expecting the Client to Fulfill your Personal or Social Needs

- Anticipating that a client will offer favors (e.g., use of a beach house or getting you a better deal from her furniture store).
- Viewing one or more clients as among the central people in your life.
- Feeling jealous or envious of a client's other close relationships or life circumstances.

Fear of being Rejected or Client Terminating Therapy for Financial or Other Reasons

- Giving into a client's requests and perspectives on issues based on fear that he or she would otherwise quit therapy.
- Experiencing a feeling of dread on sensing that a client may decide to quit therapy.
- Resisting the process of terminating a client despite clinical indicators that termination is appropriate.
- Frequently allowing the therapy session to go overtime.

Negative Feelings Towards a Client

- Resenting a noncompliant client.
- Feeling upset if a client is uncomplimentary towards you.
- Realizing a client's values, politics, and opinions deviate markedly from your own.
- Resenting what you experience as unreasonable demands placed on you by a client.
- Feeling put off by a client for strongly resembling someone else you detest or fear.
- Disliking a client.
- Dreading a certain client's appointment.

Signs that the Client is the More Powerful Individual in the Relationship

- Allowing a client to take undue advantage without confronting him or her (e.g., allowing many missed appointments without calling to cancel).
- Failing to confront a client when doing so would be therapeutically appropriate and justified.
- Accepting a gift that is exorbitant, inappropriate, or, even if it is modest, beyond the client's ability to afford.
- Giving gifts or offering to do favors unrelated to the client's therapeutic needs.

Personal Life Contaminating Professional Performance

- Failing to monitor how what is going on in your private life could negatively affect your professional life (e.g., marital difficulties, crises at home).
- Having trouble paying attention during therapy sessions.
- Taking your own personal frustrations out on a client.
- Being so stressed or feeling burned out that your attention is diverted from professional responsibilities.
- Suffering from an emotional disorder (e.g., depression) that interferes with delivering competent services.
- Suffering from a physical ailment causing you to cancel many scheduled appointments or to cut sessions short.
- Failing to seek professional help with a medical or psychological problem that affects the quality of client services.

General Red Flags

- Allowing a problematic relationship with a colleague to fester and accelerate.
- Feeling uncomfortable discussing looming "red flags" that pertain to you with a trusted colleague for fear of being negatively judged.
- Being ignorant or misinformed with regards to the ethical expectations and standards of your profession or resources in your community in case of an emergency.
- Thinking the issues raised in this book would never apply to you.

This list is a mere skeleton. Memorizing the bones, however, is hardly a fool-proof method for avoiding ethical snags. The chapters that follow illustrate how these potential traps ensnare psychotherapists with unfocused attention or who acted impulsively, overrated their own competence, or failed to moderate their own needs or other personal issues. We start off by introducing the members of the Ethics Committee whose daunting job it will be to sort out the actions of those brought before it. Then let the stories begin!

References

Bandura, A. (1999). Moral disengagement in the preparation of inhumanities. *Personality and Social Psychology Review, 3*, 193–209.

Batson, C. D., & Collins, E. C. (2011). Moral hypocrisy: A self-enhancement/self-protection motive in the moral domain. In M. D. Alicke, & C. Sedikides (Eds.). *Handbook of self-enhancement and self-protection.* New York, NY: Guilford Press.

Bazerman, M. H., & Banaji, M. R. (2004). The social psychology of ordinary ethical failures. *Social Justice Research, 17*, 111–115.

Brown, R. P., Tamborski, M., Wang, X., Barnes, C. D., Mumford, M. D., Connelly, S., & Davenport, L. D. (2011). Moral credentialing and the rationalization of misconduct. *Ethics & Behavior, 21*, 1–12.

Burton, N. (2012). *Hide and seek: The psychology of self-deception.* Oxford, England: Acheron Press.

Detert, J. R., Trevino, L. K., & Sweitzer, V. L. (2008). Moral disengagement in ethical decision making: A study of antecedents and outcomes. *Journal of Applied Psychology, 93*, 374–391.

Epley, N., & Caruso, E. M. (2004). Egocentric ethics. *Social Justice Research, 17*, 171–187.

Epstein, R. S., & Simon, R. I. (1990). The exploitation index: An early warning indicator of boundary violations in psychotherapy. *Bulletin of the Menninger Clinic, 54*, 450–465.

Grenier, J. R., & Golub, M. (2009). American Psychological Association and State Ethics Committees. In S. F. Bucky, J. E. Callan, G. Striker (Eds.). *Ethical and legal issues for mental health professionals.* (pp 189–220). New York, NY: Routledge.

Kieffer, S. M., & Sloan, J. J. (2009). Overcoming moral hurdles: Using techniques of neutralization by white-collar suspects as an interrogation tool. *Security Journal, 22*, 317–330.

Koocher, G. P., & Keith-Spiegel, P. (2008). *Ethics in psychology and the mental health professions.* New York, NY: Oxford University Press.

Lowell, J. (2012). Managers and moral dissonance: Self-justification as a big threat to ethical management? *Journal of Business Ethics, 105*, 17–25.

Mele, A. R. (2001). *Self-deception unmasked.* Princeton, NJ: Princeton University Press.

Merritt, A. C., Effron, D. A., & Monin, B. (2010). Moral self-licensing: When being good frees us to be bad. *Social and Personality Psychology Compass, 4*, 344–357.

Monin, B., & Miller, D. T. (2011). Moral credentials and the expressions of prejudice. *Journal of Personality and Social Psychology, 81*, 33–43.

Moore, D. A. (2004). Self-interest: Automaticity, and the psychology of conflict-of-interest. *Social Justice Research, 17*, 189–202.

Pope, K. S., Sonne, J. L., & Greene, B. (2006). *What therapists don't talk about and why: Understanding taboos that hurt us and our clients.* Washington, DC: American Psychological Association.

Pope, K. S., & Vasquez, M. J. T. (2011). *Ethics in psychotherapy and counseling: A practical guide.* New York, NY: Wiley.

Schwebel, M., & Coster, J. (1998). Well-functioning in professional psychologists: As program heads see it. *Professional Psychology, 29,* 284–292.

Tenbrunsel, A. E., & Messick, D. M. (2004). Ethical fading: The role of self-deception in unethical behavior. *Social Justice Research, 17,* 223–236.

Walker, R., & Clark, J. J. (1999). Heading off boundary problems: Clinical supervision as risk management. *Psychiatric Services, 50,* 1435–1439.

Warren, J., & Douglas, K. I. (2012). Falling from grace: Understanding an ethical sanctioning experience. *Counseling and Values, 57,* 131–146.

Additional Reading

Bersoff, D. M. (1999). Why good people sometimes do bad things: Motivated reasoning and unethical behavior. *Personality and Social Psychology Bulletin, 25,* 28–39.

Golman, D. (1985). *Vital lies, simple truths: The psychology of self-deception.* New York, NY: Simon & Shuster.

Katsavdakis, K. A., Gabbard, G. O., & Athey, G. I. (2004). Profiles of impaired health professionals. *Bulletin of the Menninger Clinic, 68,* 60–72.

Lewis, M., & Saarni, C. (1993). *The enigma of self-deception in everyday life.* New York, NY: Guilford.

McLaughlin, B. P., & Rorty, A. M. (Eds.). (1988). *Perspectives on self-deception.* Berkeley, CA: University of California Press.

Murphy, G. (1975). *Outgrowing self-deception.* New York, NY: Basic Books.

Shermer, M. (2011). *The believing brain: from ghosts to gods to politics and conspiracies: How we construct beliefs and reinforce them as truths.* New York, NY: Times Books.

Twerski, A. J. (1997). *Addictive thinking: Understanding self-deception.* Center City, MN: Hazelden.

Vazire, S., & Wilson, T. D. (Eds.). (2012). *Handbook of self-knowledge.* New York, NY: Guilford Press.

one
SAMMY MEETS THE WOLF

Among the most endearing individuals to grace my life are those with whom I served on ethics committees. Somehow, often after a period of lively discussion and occasional flying sparks, we were able to make decisions we believed to be fair while maintaining respect for due process as well as protecting the public to the limits of our authority.

The setting for weaving the stories together is a weekend meeting of the League of California Psychologists Ethics Committee. Dr. Sammy Halsey, the newly elected member, has much to learn about how accusations of unethical conduct play out. We follow Sammy and his vivacious and more experienced colleagues as they grapple with complaints lodged against twelve psychologists. In that short period Sammy emerges with an increased understanding of ethics, his profession, the human condition, and himself.

The anticipated message was aglow in Sammy Halsey's email inbox. He crossed his fingers on both hands, leaned his head back and closed his eyes tight for a few seconds before opening the message from Dr. Victor Graham.

Dear Dr. Halsey,

We are pleased to inform you of your election to the LCP Ethics Committee. The next meeting will be held on March 16th and March 17th at our headquarters in Reseda. Please plan to arrive the previous evening as we start early the next morning. Details will be sent soon from Mrs. Peggy Aldridge, our LCP office administrator.
    Congratulations! We look forward to meeting you.

Sincerely,
Victor Graham, Ph.D.
Chair, Ethics Committee
League of California Psychologists

Sammy hoisted both arms in a victory salute while a thrill trickled down his spine like a bamboo rain stick.

"I can help root out the bad apples, the clever psychopaths who cheated their way in, and those once-whole practitioners who slid down a slope into debauchery," he declared out loud.

Sammy proudly announced his new position as a watchdog to Wesley Huntsman, a psychologist with whom he shared an office in downtown Santa Cruz.

"Sammy, you've been in California for only a year," Wesley said, laughing. "You have no idea what's in store for you. Things are not always as you expect them to be."

Wesley's response was not quite what Sammy expected. Vulnerable clients who come for emotional healing only to be gored instead must be avenged. He would willingly commit to becoming a zealous adjudicator of careers deserving to falter, his way of serving God and country.

March 15, 7:35 p.m.

Sammy settled into his seat on the 8 p.m. commuter flight out of the Monterey Peninsula Airport destined to arrive in Los Angeles forty minutes later. He opened his briefcase and scrambled for a magazine. A small stash of business cards tumbled into the aisle, only to be quickly retrieved by an attractive young woman who was about to take the seat across from his.

"Dr. Samuel Halsey, Psychologist," she said, glancing at the cards before passing them back. "That's quite a racket, getting paid a buck fifty a minute to be entertained by loons." Her disarming smile let Sammy know it was a friendly barb. But she did seem familiar with psychotherapy, though not apparently in a good way.

"Are you a mental health professional?" Sammy asked, knowing her answer would unlikely be in the affirmative.

"No, but I went through a rough spot a while back and saw a shrink. A psychiatrist. Didn't help me at all. He was so distracted and cancelled our appointments often. I decided to dump him. His name is Dr. Lettman. Do you know him?"

Sammy did indeed know Alvin Lettman, M.D. Al and his wife were among the first to welcome Elizabeth and him into the Santa Cruz mental health community soon after they arrived from Indiana to be closer to their two adult sons in San Jose. Al was ill even then, but his remarkable spirit kept him more active than many of his physically-fit peers. Now gone for six months, Sammy recalled how Al became pale, almost translucent, as the chemo wore him down. Sammy even suggested Al suspend his practice to enjoy friends and the beach until he regained his strength, knowing deep down his vitality would never return. But Al adamantly refused, insisting his patients needed him whenever he was able to make it into his office.

"Yes," Sammy said to the pretty woman across the aisle. "I knew Al Lettman rather well. You must have been seeing him when he was very ill. He passed away last September."

"Oh, my God!" she gasped. "He never said anything. I thought he was naturally skinny with pasty skin," her voice breaking. "I just imagined he had better things to do than to care about me. I left a message saying I was done with him, and I wasn't polite. Now I feel guilty."

Sammy assumed Al had been forthright with his patients, even preparing them for the inevitable and referring those who required longer-term therapy to colleagues.

"He should have said something," Sammy muttered as the American Eagle commuter plane revved its engines and sputtered towards the runway.

This brief interlude with the pretty woman whose name he never caught made him aware of what he could confront over the next couple of days. A psychotherapeutic relationship requires the clarity of mutual understanding. Yet sometimes the client and therapist might as well be speaking in languages neither fully comprehends.

March 15, 9:05 p.m.

After an uneventful flight into the Los Angeles International Airport, Sammy stood on the busy island in front of the terminal. The endless stream of vehicles zipping by created a foul-smelling draft. "Nothing like Muncie, Indiana" he thought to himself, wondering how people could adapt to such unrelenting traffic and the stench of exhaust fumes. Almost half an hour later the Flyaway Service bus lumbered up to the curb to take passengers into the San Fernando Valley. Dr. Zev Levin, an Ethics Committee member who lived near the LCP office, would meet him at the Van Nuys terminal and drive him to a motel.

As Sammy stepped off the bus, he couldn't help but spot a small man with a large grin and a hand-printed sign reading "Looking for Sam" taped to a Dodger's baseball cap. Sammy waved and smiled, although he had expected to meet a far more austere-looking individual.

"Welcome to the land of cars and smog—our slogan is 'If you can't see it, don't breath it,'" chirped Dr. Levin, slapping Sammy gently on the back. "Let's get your baggage and go for a drink. I'll fill you in before dropping you off at the Midnight Roach Motel where we so generously store our out-of-town members."

"Sounds good, Dr. Levin, or do I call you Zev?" Sammy asked, hoping Dr. Levin was kidding about infestation.

"Call me Wolf. Zev means wolf in Hebrew. I like having the name of a wild animal. Makes me look taller."

Wolf pulled up to the Blue Bubble Bar, a small pub on Ventura Boulevard. Inside were plastic spheres stuck to the ceiling and blue lighting that made everyone look seriously ill. Wolf wriggled his way up onto a stool.

"I like this place," Wolf said glancing up at the ceiling. "The drinks aren't mostly water. Sam, name your poison and save us a place in the back where we can talk."

"Gin and tonic. With ice."

"Got it. My treat. You pay next time."

Sammy settled into a small booth farthest from the buoyant chatter of patrons perched at the bar. He instantly liked Dr. Wolf Levin, even though he was almost the opposite of how he imagined an ethics committee member to be. Wolf was unceremonious and chatty and didn't seem to take himself too seriously. He guessed Wolf to be 45 or so, about the same age as himself. And despite his short stature, maybe five feet three inches, his personality created a much larger presence.

"Here ya go Sam." Wolf hoisted up his glass of whiskey neat as if preparing a toast. "Welcome to the keepers of the rules. I thought you might want to know a little more about who will be in the bullpen tomorrow. Yes?"

"Absolutely," replied Sammy, wincing upon taking the first sip. "Yikes, you are right about the drinks. Do they even put in tonic?" Wolf smiled as if to say "I told you so." Sammy knew he dare not finish it lest he wake up with a headache or worse. He needed to be prepared to impress the others who protect the public from wrongdoers.

"OK, here goes," said Wolf, licking his lips. "Let's start with our fearless leader, Dr. Victor Graham. He's a rock, keeps us on task, or at least tries to. We sometimes get like fish floating about aimlessly, bumping into each other, not going up for air. But Victor reels us in when we become swept up in some off-topic current or act like piranhas."

"Sounds good," said Sammy, reflecting back to Wesley Huntsman's warning about what was in store for him. "How about the others?"

"OK, next the ladies," Wolf responded. "Stella Sarkosky is the grand old dame. You can figure her out just by her white hair piled high enough to make her look like the tallest person in the room, well now except for you. That you must be over six feet will piss her off. Be nice. She comes up from Del Mar. When she speaks, she expects us to listen. She's a wise soul, trained as a lay analyst. Sigmund Freud's daughter, Anna, was apparently one of her friends. We will be lucky if she reminds us of that only once."

"Looking forward to meeting Stella. Should I stand stooped over?" Sammy asked in jest.

"Wouldn't hurt," Wolf chuckled. "Next, Charlotte Burroughs is the kid of the group with no more than 32 birthdays to her name. She's a staff psychologist at a big clinic in San Bernardino. I forget the name. She became a new member last year and picked up on this role fast. She is a good soul but has a mouth on her if riled up, which is advantageous because Stella would take her over otherwise."

Sammy nodded. "OK so far," although he was already getting a different picture from what he expected of his new colleagues.

"Next, Ted Bates is our token humanistic psychologist. He's our own Rodney King, just wants everyone to get along. He usually gives both the accuser and the accused the benefit of the doubt, which can work out well *when* it works. But the debates can get sharp when one or the other has clearly been wronged. Thankfully we almost always reach a consensus, although most of the time someone has to compromise their position. Often enough it's Ted."

"Finally, Archie Wittig is an African American in his early sixties I would guess. He doesn't speak up as often as the others, but when Archie chimes in he's always on target. He has a private practice linked up with a health maintenance organization."

"Sounds like a good group," said Sammy, wishing he could find a more inspiring response while struggling to realign the apparent reality with his preconceived notion of joining a board of stern, solemnly-focused individuals.

"You'll see soon enough. Let's finish our drinks and get you to the motel. We meet for breakfast at 7:30 a.m. sharp at Ting's Cafe on Reseda Boulevard, just a block from your room and a stone's throw from the LCP office. You'll get acquainted with the whole gang, then off to our first case."

two
I'M NOT YOUR MONKEY

All psychotherapists will experience at least one client they find abrasive. The psychologist in the first story fails to set early limits on his client's hostilities and mismanages his negative feelings, resulting in a furious climax.

Dr. Roger Pegoris could not have received the letter requiring him to justify his fitness as a psychotherapist on a worse day. The washing machine overflowed the night before. He had yet to dry out the cat's bed and gather up the soaked contents of three slumped-over paper bags containing a week's worth of garbage. No soothing hug awaited him after a long day of listening to clients' spill out their emotional anguish. Jeannie would be in Missouri for yet another week tending to her terminally ill mother. Worse still, their 18-year-old son would walk through the door any minute after what was originally planned as a six-month crusade through the mid-section of South America despite his parents' apprehension. But Alex had a vision and was old enough to ignore being told what to do. Only three weeks later, the young man's passionately-held conviction—to know an American would be to love America—shattered with the tepid reception to his attempts to proselytize. The frantic phone call yesterday from the El Alto International Airport in La Paz meant Alex would require his father's ear and consolation well into the night.

Roger sank deep into his leather recliner, half wishing it would swallow him up. With shaky hands he delicately removed the envelope's contents a second time, as if it were written on decaying parchment.

Dear Dr. Pegoris,

We received a letter of complaint from your previous client, Miss Loranna Birch. The content raises questions about your competence and lack of concern for her well-being. Therefore we are opening an inquiry.

Miss Birch appears to be extremely upset. She may be contacting law enforcement authorities, believing your actions to be criminal. As ill-advised as her proposed actions may be, this matter requires the earliest possible resolution.

You must make an appointment with the LCP administrator, Mrs. Peggy Aldridge, to appear before the Ethics Committee at its March meeting, unless there is a highly compelling reason to request a postponement. We expect you to respond to Miss Birch's allegations. She has signed a release allowing you to discuss the matter with us. Failure to contact us within 10 days of the receipt of this letter will constitute an act of noncompliance, which is itself an ethics violation.

Sincerely,

Victor Graham, Ph.D.
Chair, Ethics Committee
League of California Psychologists

"Couldn't they be just a little more congenial?" Roger thought. After all, he was one of them. Loranna Birch was not. He placed the envelope on his lap and sighed before reaching for it again, picking out the letter with fingers poised like tweezers, as if another reading would reveal more agreeable content.

This time Roger shoved the letter back into the envelope with sufficient disregard to tear off a corner. He slumped back into the leather lounge chair. There had been occasional days like this when Roger wished he had fulfilled his father's ardent dream to take over the family's used-car dealership. Knowing the Ethics Committee had no authority to put him behind bars offered only minimal relief. But if found guilty, he could be reported to the California Board of Psychology. He could be barred from practicing for an extended period of time. Maybe forever.

Roger pondered what he would do if he was no longer a psychologist. He had spent five years in graduate school and another two years of internship and residency, costing over a hundred thousand dollars to qualify him for what he had been doing for 19 years. He prided himself on helping his clients restore their sense of worth and purpose, sometimes even their sanity. But had he become too cocky, too sure of himself in believing he could chase away any client's demons? He didn't know how to do anything else, including how to sell old cars. Even that option closed when his father passed away two years ago, and the dealership was sold to his father's best friend who drove it into the ground six months later.

"Why did I take on this unsettling woman in the first place?" he whispered through set jaws, pounding both fists on the arms of the recliner. After all, a gut feeling only five minutes into their first session told him Loranna Birch might not be a good fit with how he worked. She swaggered into his office wearing black tights revealing slightly bulging hips, an equally tight pink sequined tank top barely containing huge augmented breasts, gold sandals with five inch heels, and gold-tone filigree earrings the size of saucers. Her bleached blonde hair piled high and held up with several randomly placed rhinestone-studded combs looked as if it would be brittle to the touch. Although her thick makeup made it impossible to know for sure, she appeared to be in her mid-thirties. Roger thought her best features were her large, wide-set hazel eyes, but false eyelashes sprinkled with gold glitter diminished them. And before Roger could begin his customary introductory comments to first-time clients, Loranna announced why she was there, revealing an annoying squeak in her voice.

"I am an actress, possibly the best in the world," she said with dramatic bravado, shoving a resume in Roger's face. "I need someone who knows how to get inside people's heads, someone to help me fight the evildoers."

"Evildoers?" Roger inquired, startled by Loranna's boldness as well as her curious pronouncement. "And who might you be referring to?"

With eyes flashing she bellowed, "It's the inability of those Hollywood asshats to appreciate my unique talent, of course."

"And how do you think I can be of help to you, Miss Birch?" he asked calmly in hopes of eliciting a more composed response. "I'm a psychologist. I would like to tell you about how I work and what I think we can…"

"I know who you are," she interrupted. "I check everyone out on Google. I see you wrote an article in 1999 on narcissistic personality disorders. All of these Hollywood moguls only care about themselves. So you know how they think. Then I checked Yelp, and you have pretty good reviews from other clients. One even said you helped him get a guest appearance on *NCIS Los Angeles*. That definitely caught my attention. I figure you have what it takes to help me even the score with those mucky-mucks who pissed on me."

Roger was well aware that Hollywood is brutally unforgiving. A number of his current and past clients were in "The Business," or wanted to be. They understood the statistical odds of landing movie and television roles. They sought professional counsel to maintain an inner determination to show up for an unending stream of cattle calls followed by the interminable wait for callbacks that rarely materialized. They benefited from Roger's soft, sympathetic support while surviving disappointments and continuing to pursue their yet-to-be realized dreams. But Loranna Birch sought out Dr. Pegoris neither for comfort from rejection nor to consider alternative ways of coping. Loranna sought nothing short of retribution. And she wanted a sharp tool she could wield to do it.

Despite his early assessment that this client would be difficult, Roger remained determined to help her. After all, his calling was to assist clients in finding their most adaptive selves, and he felt disdain for those colleagues who only accepted clients with excellent insurance coverage or could pay full fees and were going to be "easy" or, better yet, "fun and easy." But the first session with Loranna was discouraging. He tried to engage her in conversation about what psychotherapy can and cannot accomplish, but Loranna would not connect. Instead she focused on her self-proclaimed destiny to win an Oscar and what battles needed waging to do it. Nevertheless, Roger remained optimistic. Maybe her first session was about letting off steam. Loranna would surely be ready to delve into the hard work of psychotherapy next week.

In the meantime Roger researched Loranna's resume, digging for clues to better understand her background and aspirations. The glamour shots were obviously taken when she was much younger. The films in which she claimed to have roles either did not exist or were never commercially released.

When Loranna arrived for the second session, she wore a strapless gold lamée dress with a hemline barely covering black lace panties, tall black boots with gold buckles, huge rimmed Gucci sunglasses, and large red plastic earrings in the shape of roses. Her yellow hair was worn down and loose this time, which Roger thought resembled a haystack.

"Those blind bastards will pay someday for treating people like turds," Loranna shouted before Roger could greet her, her face turning noticeably flushed even through heavy makeup. "That rat-faced little queer didn't let me finish my monologue on Thursday. I'd like to hide outside his office, and when he ventures out I'll grab him from behind and relieve him of his remaining manhood."

"Loranna, how would accosting anyone be helpful?" Roger said softy, angling for a productive back-and-forth conversation.

"What a stupid question!" she angrily responded with both arms flying in wide half circles. "Look here doctor, therapy is about supporting your patients. That's what I pay you for. I can't count on others. They are jealous of me. So, if I need to scream, it needs to be OK with you. If I need to plan how to deal with those knuckle-dragging trolls, that needs to be OK with you. CAPICHE?"

Roger tried to disregard her commands and outbursts. But the second session progressed much like the first, with Loranna hurling accusations and demanding Roger's compliance with her position. Nevertheless, Roger kept trying to refocus the conversation.

"Loranna, I want to know more about your life. About your family. Tell me first about your father."

"Well, Daddy would be mad as hell if he could know how that slimy toad treated me yesterday."

Roger quietly sighed. "Is he still alive?"

"Is who still alive? Oh, you mean Daddy. Left me 12 years ago. Lung cancer. He created a trust fund so I can at least pay the bills while fighting the earth's scummiest scum. He must have known what I would have to go through."

"What about your mother? And do you have siblings or other family?"

"My mother didn't make it through childbirth. Preeclampsia. A bunch of nannies, or maybe they were his lovers—I never knew for sure—raised me. No brothers or sisters. No other family I talk to. Daddy always bought me everything I wanted. He was all I ever needed."

Roger took a small measure of satisfaction in eliciting some factual data about Loranna. He now knew how she paid her bills and that her relationship with her father was apparently both indulgent and distant.

The third session went about as badly as the first two. As always Loranna was garishly dressed and made up. Roger again gently nudged her away from demanding him to help her take on Hollywood. This time she issued a specific marching order.

"Call Benjamin Glickman at this number right now and use your persuasion skills to make him understand how he has caused me considerable psychic pain by refusing to see me. He's missing out on the best talent since Marilyn." She tossed a business card down on the desk.

"That's not what psychotherapy is, Loranna," he tried to softly explain. "I would like to help you, but our relationship exists only between you and me in this office."

"Well then what the hell good are you? I mean seriously! I don't need someone hiding behind a door in a high-rise. I need you to get with the program." Loranna looked almost maniacal while squirming in the armchair.

Roger thought he had managed to successfully filter out the impact of her histrionic assaults on him, at least on an intellectual level based on what he was originally taught in graduate school. When clients express negative emotions towards their therapists, it's not really personal. Such acting out can have therapeutic advantages. It creates a window to more clearly see what is going on and to work directly with it. Nevertheless, Roger spent the rest of the third session trying to steer Loranna towards more realistic alternatives, but she seemed to enjoy informing him of the gross errors in his thinking.

The next four sessions broke no new ground. In fleeting exchanges Roger learned Loranna had been briefly married at 22, had no children and no extended family members who remained in touch with her, and no one else to turn to for support. She collected teddy bears. She had three cats. She liked anchovies on her pizza. Roger was also obligated to ascertain whether Loranna had any plans to actually assault anyone physically. She often made bizarre threats to submit certain individuals who ignored or brushed her off to stealth attacks. She claimed she wanted to hang one casting agent from the rafters of the Egyptian Theater. She also expressed a desire to ambush a director on his *Shogun Vendetta* movie set with a Samurai sword. If Roger thought she was capable of following through with any of her threats, he would be legally mandated to warn the identifiable intended victims. However, he concluded she was too scattered and self-absorbed to do actual harm to anyone.

Roger had come to dread Tuesday mornings. He could not undo the knot in his stomach until Loranna left his office after her 10 a.m. appointment. He would go to the window, push the shade slightly aside, and visually track her to her car. He relaxed only after he saw her make a right turn onto Sunset Boulevard. Looking back, Roger realized his therapy with Loranna had devolved into a total calamity by the seventh session. Loranna now blamed him for not understanding who and where she should be. He had joined her long list of foes.

Something snapped in Roger during their eighth and final session. Loranna plopped down in the chair across from him and screamed, "You are as bad as those bastards who run this crappy movie business," after he simply asked how she was doing. "Why don't you do anything I want?" she continued with her usual squeaky voice rising to an ear-piercing howl. "I pay you good money, and you just sit there like a fucking lump!"

This time Roger felt his face flush and his heart race. "I'M NOT YOUR MONKEY," he roared in a thunderous voice, forcing Loranna to slide back in her chair, her mouth opening wide in astonishment. "We can't do this anymore, Loranna," he continued at only a somewhat lower volume. "I don't know who could help you, but I know for sure it's not me! NEVER, EVER, EVER ME!" his voice rising again. Roger was shaking and on the verge of hyperventilating.

Loranna went still. For a moment Roger thought he pierced a new and perhaps more reasonable place in her. Maybe she needed to finally hear the impact of her abusiveness and attempts to manipulate him. Instead she rose up slowly from her chair and inched towards him with small unsteady steps, circling with her forefinger inches from his face and shrieking, "YOU! YOU ARE A SNAKE, A FLESH-EATER, A DESTROYER OF GREATNESS." She whipped around and stomped out of the office, slamming the door so hard that Roger was sure she had broken it.

***

"Did that creep actually say that to me? Did I hear that Judas correctly?" Loranna Birch blurted out loud, gripping the steering wheel with both hands, her heart pounding like a jungle drum. She lurched back against the headrest. "I don't dare drive quite yet," she whispered. "Sit for a few minutes. Breathe. 1…2…3…You've been betrayed before. You know how to take care of people like him. OK, let's do this."

Loranna arrived at her apartment not remembering getting there. Her mind was occupied by plotting to discredit Dr. Roger Pegoris. She recalled a memo with directions for registering a complaint against psychologists tacked on a small cork board over the water cooler in his reception area. She even asked him about it.

"We're required to post it," Dr. Pegoris had responded.

"Do you expect someone to sue you?" she had playfully asked.

"Hasn't happened yet," he answered with a toothy smile.

But that was then. Now was different. He needed to experience what happens to those who let people down, who turn on them, and then drop them into a pond as if they were a burlap sack of unwanted kittens. She congratulated herself on her good sense to take down the information needed to make her move.

Once inside her apartment Loranna searched frantically for the scrap of paper containing directions for filing a complaint, finally spotting it in a stack of mail on her breakfast table. She grabbed a piece of stationery from the hutch drawer and scrawled out her grievances. If she hurried she could make it to the post office for the noon pickup.

***

Roger decided he might as well deal with the letter from the Ethics Committee before Alex arrived home from his ill-fated trek through Bolivia. He picked up the phone and entered the number on the letterhead to confirm an appointment with the Ethics Committee meeting in March. Peggy Aldridge's voice was business-like yet had a pleasing ring to it. Roger was grateful for this small mercy. Just as he hung up, Alex opened the door, his backpack dragging on the floor and looking utterly defeated. "Hey, Dad," he almost whispered. Roger went to his son and hugged him tighter and longer than he ever had before.

The Ethics Committee:
Roger Pegoris, Ph.D. March 16, 8:37 a.m.

Dr. Roger Pegoris was already sitting on a folding chair outside the meeting room when Sammy and the other Committee members filed past him. A couple of them nodded his way but were otherwise expressionless. Roger hadn't slept all night, flopping in his bed like a jumping bean. He was thankful the drive to Reseda took only 20 minutes. "Maybe my droopy eyes will make me look more sympathetic," he thought. But then a wave of panic washed over him. A restless night might interfere with his ability to think clearly. He might come off as confused, influencing the Committee's assessment of his competence.

Dr. Victor Graham, the Chair of the Ethics Committee and the last to head into the conference room, paused to face Roger. "Dr. Pegoris?"

"Yes…sir," Roger replied in a deferent tone.

"We have to review the minutes from our previous meeting, but will call you in soon." Roger's palms went cold and clammy. He prayed he would not have to shake anyone's hand.

***

Sammy Halsey took notice as he passed by Roger Pegoris, anticipating a burly, cruel-looking man with shifty eyes. He expected all of the accused to bear at least some resemblance to the poster images of wanted felons. Instead this noticeably anxious man dressed conservatively in a light grey suit with a white dress shirt and navy blue tie was slightly built, appearing almost bird-like with his undersized triangular face, pointy nose, circular eyes, and black hair combed up and back like small wings. He didn't appear to be at all evil, just tired and unhappy.

Once inside the meeting room Victor Graham took his place at the head of the table. "The accused sits here," he said, looking directly at Sammy and pointing at the chair to his right. After a reminder to refer to each other and the accused as "Doctor" instead of using first names and a quick review of the minutes from the last meeting, Victor read Loranna Birch's hand printed complaint letter aloud.

Dear Ethics People,

Let me tell you about a psychologist who will destroy the reputation of your profession if left to run free. Dr. Roger Pegoris charged me good money to crush my self-esteem and make me feel less than nothing. He did not listen to anything I was trying to tell him. He tortured me mercilessly with his screaming. Then he sent me packing out the door for no reason. I accuse him now of committing emotional terrorism on the people of Los Angeles County. I will also be seeking assistance from the local police in Silverlake.

I demand you hold a tribunal and give him a dishonorable discharge from your profession and help arrange for a criminal trial by serving as witnesses.

Sincerely,

Loranna Birch, Professional Actress

"What did he do to her?" asked Charlotte Burroughs.

"Or what does she *think* he did to her," added Wolf Levin.

This was Sammy's first case, and the charges against this psychologist sounded even more serious than what Sammy expected, even though the nature of the charges remained unclear. He wondered if everyone who complained was this livid. And is the bird-like man sitting in a chair outside a criminal? Yet this *is* what he signed up for after all. He blurted out, "Is this typical of the letters the Ethics Committee receives?"

"She's angry," answered Wolf, "and almost all of those who write to us are upset about how they believe they were wronged."

"It's where the fuel to complain comes from," added Ted Bates. "I often worry about those who were treated poorly or exploited but are too fragile, too struck down, to find us. We'll never know who they are."

"True, but let's get to what we're here for today," said Victor. "Normally we talk a little about the charge before we bring the accused in," Victor added, looking directly again at Sammy. "But why Miss Birch is so upset remains nebulous, so I think it best if we just start by asking Dr. Pegoris for his perspective."

Victor led an uneasy Roger Pegoris into the conference room. Perfunctory introductions were made around the table with no hand shaking.

"Dr. Pegoris, would you recount your interactions with Loranna Birch as they pertain to what she described as an uncaring attitude followed by an abrupt termination? Victor asked. "And, would you like a cup of coffee?"

Roger relished consuming anything capable of perking him up, but politely signaled a pass. Should his trembling hands cause him to spill, he worried he would appear a buffoon.

After clearing his throat twice, Roger spoke. "My therapeutic link with Miss Birch is best described as an unsuccessful alliance from the start, not unlike a train wreck," a description Sammy found curiously refreshing. Sammy had expected accused colleagues to vigorously deny any therapeutic errors and blame the complaining clients as lacking credibility due to their mental state. But Roger Pegoris quickly and genuinely acknowledged failure.

"My approach to confronting Miss Birch on her unconstructive way of living her life was counterproductive," Roger continued. "Unfortunately, it only resulted in hostility directed towards me. At first I thought I could use her anger to therapeutic advantage, but it seemed she only wanted someone with a Sunset Boulevard office address to confirm her destiny for success on the big screen. Those unable to accept her presupposition were, as she put it, 'smaller than bacteria.' I finally realized I wasn't getting anywhere. I wasn't the right one to be treating her, which is why I terminated my services." Roger took a deep breath,

"Did you at least try to help her find another therapist?" Wolf asked.

"To be truthful, I don't know who I would have referred her to. Maybe a psychiatrist to get her on some medication, Paxil perhaps. But she still needed to explore her issues. Chemistry might alleviate some of her histrionics, but would not be the complete answer. I didn't bill her for the last session, of course, and I never heard from her again, well, until… you know…your letter."

Wolf nodded and continued, "So my other question is, if this client was so challenging and you appear to have determined a poor fit early on, why didn't you terminate her sooner by explaining why someone else might be better suited to counsel her?"

"In retrospect I should have. I have treated clients with far more serious problems, although no one so flamboyant or profane. Improvement can be slow. Sometimes persistence in working with a client on challenging feelings will strengthen a therapeutic relationship. Miss Birch was functioning, getting to every open call she came across, imposing herself on anyone who had even a remote connection to the movie or television business, sending out endless though highly deceptive resumes, and living within her means from a trust set up by her father. I thought if I just gave it more time."

"Thank you," Wolf replied flatly.

Ted Bates signaled it was his turn. Ted often came down on the side of the clients, seeing them as especially vulnerable and in need of unconditional acceptance no matter how angry or seductive they became.

"Tell me this," Ted said. "What did you say to set Miss Birch off during your last session when you, as she put it, 'sent her packing?' She seems to think you didn't try to understand her."

"I swear she's a one trick pony," Roger answered, sounding defensive now. "I tried to steer the discussion to other areas of her life, and she may have interpreted that as me not listening. But she herself offered up only one theme; the Hollywood players—virtually every one of them—somehow schemed to stifle her rise to stardom. I tried to get her off an emotional treadmill. But when I would simply inquire as to her well-being she would say something like, 'I have a migraine, thanks to the vile rubbish running this town.' Always back to the same place. I pride myself on staying controlled when clients get upset."

"So why did you fail this time?" Ted asked.

"I just lost it," Roger answered, bowing his head slightly downward. "I felt like she saw me as one of those old organ grinders with a monkey on his shoulder wearing a tiny red suit and a little fez on its head. No more than a prop to manipulate others into giving her what she wanted. I told her I wasn't her puppet...her monkey...and I was done with her. I guess I got loud, but she finally struck a raw nerve."

Ted nodded, but said nothing.

Stella Sarkosky spoke up. "How do you feel about what happened, Dr. Pegoris? I hear you saying your loss of control is uncharacteristic. So do you view this as a one-time event or have you thought about what this might mean for the future?"

"I like to think I learned from Loranna...Miss Birch. I'm human, even if that's not an excuse for what happened at the end. I need to monitor my own emotional reactions instead of shoving them down and risking another rupture."

"How do you think Loranna feels?" Stella continued. "Despite her outwardly disparaging assessment of you, do you think she was harmed in any way? Or do you think she is tough as nails?"

"She comes across as hard. But I never got to a different place in her. I know I didn't help her, but I'm not sure about hurting her. I am just one more disappointment."

Stella's nose twitched suggesting dissatisfaction with the answer, but she said nothing.

Sammy wished he had a good question to ask Dr. Pegoris. But this was his first case, and he feared asking something injudicious or off-limits. He worried the others might think him unprepared. But Archie Wittig didn't ask any questions either, yet as the official note taker Archie had an excuse. Sammy vowed to find something to contribute to the discussion after Roger Pegoris was excused.

After a short silence Victor asked, "Does anyone have any other questions? Or do you have anything else to add. Dr. Pegoris?" Roger shook his head. No one else spoke.

"Thank you for coming in, Dr. Pegoris. You will hear from us within two weeks. I'll show you out."

Once in the hallway, Roger felt relief and anxiety, an odd mixture of emotions. What would the Committee decide? How did he come off? He had cancelled plans for the rest of the day and looked forward to getting home to Jeannie and a nap.

***

"OK, people," Victor bellowed loud enough to be heard over the cranky voices of Stella and Ted complaining about the coffee going cold. "Let's see what you think about Dr. Pegoris' side of the story."

"I have to admit," said Wolf, "as much as I care for my clients I have had a couple who sent me clinging to the ceiling. One fellow came in for stress reduction, but all he did was increase mine. I had to take a Lorazapam an hour before his appointments. I swear to God it's true. He would fidget and bite on his nails with this terrified look on his face as I spoke. When it was his turn to speak it was like fingernails on a chalkboard—all rattled and screechy. His voice pierced my brain like a stake. We finally arranged to get him on some meds and worked on a couple of his issues, but I couldn't do my best work. He moved out of town, so I got off the hook."

"You think that's bad? I had a client who would win the international title of Mr. Odious," chimed in Charlotte. "He was bigoted and arrogant. Hated Blacks and Mexicans. And Jews. And gays. Said they were all mistakes but that God kept trying until he finally got it right and created white Christian people. I think I helped him with why he came in, how to relate better with his daughter. I was relieved when he thanked me and quit on his own after five unpleasant sessions…well, unpleasant for me."

"I think it's wrong to keep working with clients we don't like or who don't share our values," added Wolf. Charlotte nodded her head in agreement, although she rarely had the option in her own practice. The clinic administration decides who sees whom, and Charlotte had to take on whoever came through her door.

"It would even be better for the clients," said Ted. "How can you help someone who is yanking hard on your tail? Thank God most clients are pleasant to work with."

"Let's get to the business at hand people. And that would be Dr. Roger Pegoris," Victor said sternly. "The clock keeps moving even when we don't."

Sammy had remained quiet. He wanted his first statement to the Ethics Committee to be satisfying to the other members, although impressing them would be even better. But Victor prematurely forced the issue.

"What do you think, Sammy? As the new man on our team, we'd be interested in your take."

"Well…," Sammy drawled, hoping the right words would come out next. "I have to say I was impressed when Dr. Pegoris didn't try to make a lot of excuses."

"Good point, Sam. And you are right." said Victor. "We respect an expression of guilt or at least blame-sharing. Those who press ethics charges against their therapists are vulnerable to a 'the client is crazy' defense by the very nature of why they consult us in the first place. We're never impressed by attempts to discount the client as incompetent or delusional. It makes things easier all around when those who make ethical errors take some responsibility, especially if they also have insights or misgivings and are already working to ensure no repetitions in the future."

Sammy felt an inner glow. He had pleased the Ethics Committee's chairperson.

"Yeah, I agree," chimed in Wolf. "Pegoris is not a bad guy. I met him a couple of times at conventions. Seems like a solid sort. But why in the hell did he keep her on for so long if he wasn't getting anywhere?"

"Maybe he would see himself a failure. Or maybe he didn't know what to say. It's hard to tell clients you don't want to work with them," added Archie.

"I don't get the feeling it was about money" Wolf continued. "Some therapists will hang on to a client forever no matter what's going on just for the coin. I don't sense that happening here. But I would've cut the woman loose around the second or third session, but more gently, of course." Wolf put on a bogus sweet smile.

"Well, maybe he thought he could get somewhere if he just hung in there long enough to pierce through her armor," said Ted. "She's got to be hurting deeper down. Eight sessions is only two months. If it had been two years, well that would be a whole different enchilada."

"The major problem isn't keeping her for eight sessions," said Stella, sounding perturbed. "We are dodging the larger picture here. Dr. Pegoris was the only personal relationship she had, and he knew that, even though she was paying him for it. He still rejected her outright and then abandoned her. This is precisely where this woman was already deeply wounded. He should have better understood her underlying vulnerability and held himself together."

"Just how human do we have to be?" Wolf asked, staring Stella right in the eye as if baiting for an argument. "Pegoris apparently took a lot of abuse himself, you know."

Stella frowned. "Think about it seriously, Wolf. If she only wanted revenge, she could have hired a hit man. But she chose a psychologist and showed up for every session. She knew at some level she needed help."

"And he said he learned a good lesson to not let things build up to where they boil over," Archie quietly interjected. "But I'm not sure he ever perceived the injured individual underneath."

"Enough interpretation I think," said Victor, thumbing through the LCP Ethical Standards. "Our ethics code has two principles to consider. First, 'Clients must always be treated with respect regardless of gender, sexual identity, race, color, religion, or creed.' Second, 'If a client is not benefitting from one's services, he or she should be terminated while preserving the individual's sense of self-worth and referred, if appropriate, to another practitioner who may be able to provide more effective treatment.'"

Sammy felt ambivalent as well as inadequate in the face of his admission to himself that he didn't know how he would work with a fiery and demanding client like Loranna Birch. There weren't any similar clients in Muncie, Indiana, and the most flamboyant client he had in Santa Cruz was a young man with hair dyed turquoise, multiple pierced earrings, and a metal rod though his nostrils. Otherwise he was a sweet kid struggling with depression set off by a friend's death in a head-on crash on

Highway 1, sending both cars off a cliff and onto the sands of Monterey Bay. But Victor's recitation of the ethics code as it applied to Roger Pegoris impressed him. He decided to share his observation.

"I must say I am struck by the difference between just reading the ethics code—which I did scores of times to prepare for my committee duties—and applying it to an actual real-life situation. The code feels animated now, like a living, breathing guide to the right answers." Sammy sounded elated, as if he had just discovered a diamond under a rock.

Victor smiled at Sammy's enthusiastic interjection of vitality into the ethics code, but added, "This time it works, Sammy. Don't hold your breath though. Sometimes things slip through the cracks. Sometimes the code is silent when we think it shouldn't be. Occasionally it's in there, but it doesn't seem to apply to a particular case. You'll see what I mean soon enough. OK, let's close this one up."

Decision and Dispositions

The Committee issued a stern reprimand to be placed into Roger Pegoris' file. The members agreed that Roger's outburst to a client, especially one with no outside support system, was improper and he used deficient judgment in continuing to see her when he was fully aware that the therapy had stagnated. Still, his actions fell short of deserving a severe penalty.[1]

Roger had hoped the LCP Ethics Committee would view his behavior as understandable, given such an abrasive client. But he also felt a measure of relief. He would not be publicly censured or reported to the licensing board. It remained disconcerting to know fifteen esteemed colleagues— the Ethics Committee members and the LCP Board of Directors that reviews all findings—would now know he had not lived up to ethical expectations, although he took some comfort in knowing his sanction remained confidential.

Loranna Birch received a letter containing no specifics about the deliberation or outcome, but confirming appropriate action was taken. The Committee members wanted her to know she had been heard. A week later, a letter with a return address from Loranna Birch arrived at the LCP office. Peggy Aldridge tilted the envelope upside down and removed its contents. Stationery with images of bouncing cats and strewn-out yarn around the margins read, "Thanks for having some balls. Sincerely, Loranna

---

1 To illustrate various levels of sanctions and directives, see Appendix B.

Birch, Professional Actress." Then Mrs. Aldridge spent the next 10 minutes picking gold glitter out of the reception area carpet.

Case Commentary

It is ironic to note that Dr. Pegoris might have prevailed had he claimed Loranna Birch was delusional, given the bizarre nature of her complaint letter. However, the Committee had a major advantage in this care; the psychotherapist did not attempt to wriggle out of responsibility. Ethics committees tend to view more favorably the accused who accept fault, who have no previous complaints, who act respectfully during the hearing (or are civil in their written responses), and where no substantiated harm befell the complainant or others (Koocher & Keith-Spiegel, 2008).

In truth, it remains unclear whether or how much Loranna Birch's emotional condition was further compromised as a result of the psychologist's outburst and abrupt termination. It appears, however, that Dr. Pegoris failed to form an alliance with the wounded, vulnerable part of this outwardly abrasive client as Wepman and Donovan (1984) recommend. Should a psychotherapist become counter-abrasive, serious consequences for the client's mental health can ensue (Warner, 1984). An ethics committee, however, is not in a position to make such a finding.

Finally, I must remind my readers that ethics committees are empowered to engage in far more preliminary or additional follow-up information-seeking than was illustrated in this and the other stories. For example, the committee could have requested additional detail from Miss Birch regarding her actual session experiences than was apparent in her peculiar complaint letter. The American Psychological Association ethics office maintains legal and investigatory staff, obviously affordable only to large organizations.

Notes on Difficult Clients

Psychotherapists are vulnerable to a range of uncomfortable feelings brought on by clients' disturbing verbal comments and inappropriate behavior (Wolf, Goldfried, & Muran, 2012), and such negative responses are not necessarily an artifact of countertransference (Bongar, Markey, & Peterson, 1991). There will be times when the fit is mismatched, personalities don't engage, or deeply-held values clash (Baker, 2009). In one survey, the vast majority of psychologists admitted feeling anger towards their clients for being verbally abusive, uncooperative, or overly demanding. One-third even admitted feeling hatred towards a client. Almost half admitted doing something with their anger that they later regretted (Pope & Tabachnick, 1993). With only rare exceptions (e.g., Knapp & Gavazzi, 2011) the ethical implications of managing difficult clients are missing from the literature.

In a classic article published in 1978 in the *Journal of British Psychiatry*, psychiatrist James Groves forthrightly offers four categories of hateful patients: the dependent clingers (who evoke feelings of aversion in the clinician); the entitled demanders (who evoke a wish to counterattack); the manipulative help-rejecters (who evoke feelings of depression); and the self-destructive deniers (who evoke feelings of malice). Groves is quick to point out that these are not patients with whom one experiences an occasional upsetting moment or disappointment, but rather those whose very presence is dreaded. The story in this chapter focuses on an entitled demander, a client who uses intimidation, guilt induction, and devaluation in an attempt to create what Groves called "an inexhaustible supply depot," and her psychologist who became goaded to breaking point.

Groves believes that those who treat difficult patients often do not recognize how the patient's hostility stems from a fear of abandonment. Koven (2012) illustrates this seemingly illogical strategy on the part of the complaining, insulting, and demeaning client by sharing the old joke; "The food in this restaurant is terrible, and the portions are so small."

Discussion Questions

1. Do you think Dr. Pegoris did about as well as any psychotherapist could with Miss Birch up until his volatile outburst? If not, what would you have done differently?

2. Albert Ellis (1984) asserted that psychotherapists who believe they can successfully treat *any* client are their *own* most difficult client. Ellis reasoned that holding such an irrational belief about oneself could lead to poor therapeutic decision-making compared to those who are realistic about their competence and personal limitations. Dr. Pegoris seems to have fallen into the former category. Do you agree that unquestioning confidence in one's own abilities can harm clients? If so, how and why?

3. Imagine you found a client annoying or unlikeable during the initial session. What would you do?

4. Imagine a client says to you, "Your therapy sucks. Did you get your license to practice from the bottom of a cereal box?" How do you think you would you respond on the spot?

5. Your client expresses his (her) deepest feelings, but uses heavy profanity and ethnic slurs. Do you just ignore this language? Why or why not?

6. If it hasn't happened yet, you will more likely than not become extremely angry or frustrated with a client. Do you feel prepared? (Or, if you have already become angry or frustrated with a client, how did you respond? What did you do right, or how could the incident have been handled better?)

References

Baker, B. (2009). Deal with clients you don't like. *APA Monitor, 40,* 58.

Bongar, B., Markey, L. A., & Peterson, L. G. (1991). Views on the difficult and dreaded patient: A preliminary investigation. *Medical Psychotherapy: An International Journal, 4,* 9–16.

Ellis, A. (1984). How to deal with your most difficult client — You. *Psychotherapy in Private Practice, 2,* 25–35.

Groves, J. E. (1978). Taking care of the "hateful" patient. *The New England Journal of Medicine, 298,* 883–887.

Knapp, S. J., & Gavazzi, J. (2011). Ethical issues with patients at a high risk for treatment failure. In Knapp, S. J. (Ed.). *APA handbook of ethics in psychology* (pp 401–415). Washington, DC: American Psychological Association.

Koven, S. (Feb. 25, 2012). The hateful patient revisited. *The Boston Globe.* Retrieved from http://www.boston.com/lifestyle/health/articles/2012/02/27/the_hateful_patient_revisited/

Pope, K. S., & Tabachnick, B. G. (1993). Therapists' anger, hate, fear, and sexual feelings: National survey of therapists' responses, client characteristics, critical events, formal complaints, and training. *Professional Psychology, 24,* 142–152.

Warner, S. J. (1984). The defeating patient and reciprocal abrasion. In E. M. Stern (Ed.). *Psychotherapy and the abrasive patient.* New York, NY: Haworth Press.

Wepman, B. J., & Donovan, M. W. (1984). Abrasiveness: Descriptive and dynamic issues. In E. M. Stern (Ed.). *Psychotherapy and the abrasive patient.* (pp. 11–19). New York, NY: Haworth Press.

Wolf, A. W., Goldfried, M. R., & Muran, J. C. (Eds.). (2012). *Transforming negative reactions to clients from frustration to compassion.* Washington, DC: American Psychological Association.

Additional Reading

Hanna, F. J. (2001). *Therapy with difficult clients.* Washington, DC: American Psychological Association.

Koekkoek, B., van Meijel, B., & Hutschemaekers, G. (2006). "Difficult patients" in mental health care: A review. *Psychiatric Services, 6,* 795–802.

Stern, E. M. (Ed.). (1984). *Psychotherapy and the abrasive patient.* New York, NY: Haworth Press.

three
JUNK YARD
THERAPY

Tangled nonsexual multiple role relationships between clients and their psychotherapists account for a large percentage of ethics complaints. Every psychotherapist is at risk for a boundary violation, often crossing into hazardous territory without intent or awareness. The psychologist in this story imposes her self-justified multiple roles on to her clients to an alarming extreme.

A clutter of get well and sympathy cards covered the front room mantle of the Cohen family home. Sophie was ill for 10 months before succumbing to non-Hodgkin's lymphoma. Jacob had not changed anything in the house since that day.

"No one ever died from a broken heart," Jacob's best friend Henry Bornstein often said in his attempts to cheer Jacob up during his frequent check-in calls. But Jacob wished he could succumb to grief. He would gladly desert this life if he felt certain about reuniting with Sophie, this time forever. Henry stopped calling when he was unable to pierce through Jacob's unshakable gloom.

Jacob's loneliness was unrelenting, a raging river washing away his smiles and drowning the laughter once typifying the ebullient owner of Jake's Deli in Encino. Without Sophie at his side he could no longer face the endless parade of customers lining up for his pastrami on rye that ɔod a full six inches tall. Most days he sat in the family home flipping the TV remote control searching for reruns of the shows he and Sophie enjoyed together with their three children. *I love Lucy. Leave it to Beaver. Gunsmoke.* Now the children were scattered around the country raising families of their own. Jacob's only regular visitor was his sister Rachel, not because he wanted to see her but because she pounded on the front door until he relented and let her in.

"You must go to counseling," Jacob's sister insisted during her last visit. "I lie awake worrying about you. Sophie would not have wanted this."

At first Jacob declined her advice for financial reasons. Sophie's medical bills had absorbed most of the Cohen's reserves. Jake's Deli was sold within three months of her death for far less than it was worth. Finally, though begrudgingly, he conceded to Rachel's persistence if she could locate someone nearby and affordable.

Rachel soon became disillusioned after calling over a dozen psychotherapists around the greater San Fernando Valley. Those sounding appropriate for Jacob were charging $120 or more a session. His private insurance would pay for less than half, and Rachel was sure the policy's limit of ten sessions was insufficient to restore Jacob's willingness to move on in this life.

On the verge of giving up, Rachel spotted an ad in a local paper for a woman who claimed 25 years of grief counseling experience. Dr. Eve Pilcher charged less than half the going rate; the ad read *50 dollars for 50 minutes.* Furthermore, Rachel thought someone in Jacob's age range would be a plus. After all, what could younger counselors know about losing someone to whom he had been married since before they were born? After a quick check on the legitimacy of Eve Pilcher's credentials, Rachel set up the appointment with the stolid-sounding person who answered the phone. The next Saturday Jacob begrudgingly drove to the Canoga Park location for a 3 p.m. session.

***

"This can't be the right address," Jacob said to himself, pulling up to the curb. Instead of an office building on busy Corbin Avenue, a bright pink ranch-style house was nestled in a mixed zoning area. The large front yard bustled with people sorting through piles of mismatched dishes, vases, picture frames, and every imaginable kind of chotskie littered across a dozen folding tables. Ladders, old furniture, portable TVs, air conditioners, exercise bikes, and other not immediately identifiable large-sized hunks were strewn on the ground. Pausing at the short wrought iron gate looking totally lost, Jacob caught the eye of a thick-hipped woman in her later fifties wearing jeans and a blue plaid shirt, her graying hair pulled back into a long pony tail. As she approached him with a spritely gait Jacob spotted what appeared to be several stop watches attached to a belt around her waist

"Jacob Cohen?" she asked in a hospitable tone, giving him a bear hug. "Welcome to our family!"

***

Thus began Jacob's year-long relationship with Dr. Eve Pilcher. Rachel had not seen Jacob for months despite living only five miles apart. She often made a point of driving past Jacob's home, noting how the yard had steadily declined through neglect. Tending his garden had been the sole activity Jacob maintained after Sophie's passing. His prize-winning dahlias, once his pride and joy, were now brown and droopy. The lawn was yellowing and mottled with crabgrass and dandelions.

Jacob expressed feeling better the few times he answered the phone, but Rachel remained uneasy. Her gentle probes about counseling resulted in vague, abrupt responses.

"Good," was Jacob's usual reply, offering no further detail.

When Rachel asked where he spent most days, "Out and about," was his standard response.

Rachel found such perfunctory replies unsatisfying. The time had come to follow Jacob surreptitiously to his next Saturday counseling appointment. Parked across the street and down the block to avoid detection, Rachel expected to find only Jacob's 1998 Cadillac Deville in front of the pink house. Instead, many cars were parked on the street and scores of people were milling around tables in front of the house. A big sign reading "YARD SALE" explained what was going on, but why Jacob was helping shoppers carry purchases to their cars baffled her. Rachel watched for an hour as Jacob worked the yard, pausing only for a few minutes when no customers were present to talk to a woman with a graying pony tail. The two looked as though they were sharing secrets, leaning close in as one spoke and the other listened intently.

Rather than confronting her brother about this strange scene, Rachel chose instead to check out where Jacob spent his weekdays. On the following Wednesday she followed him again to the same address. No yard sale was in progress. Instead Jacob was warmly welcomed by the same woman with the pony tail and ushered into the house. Within minutes Jacob reappeared alone, entered the garage, dragged out a ladder and some tools, and climbed cautiously on to the roof. A young woman emerged from the house and started watering the rose bushes lining the fence. A third person, a man older than Jacob, stumbled out the door yanked by two enthusiastic labradors through the gate and down the sidewalk towards Victory Boulevard. Now Rachel was totally baffled. She wanted to remain longer to see what her brother would do after he came down off the roof, but she was already running late for an appointment.

Rachel needed to meet with Jacob face-to-face. What was going on? Had Jacob taken a full-time job? Had he found a girlfriend and feared criticism for dating too soon after Sophie's passing? Who were those other people in the house? Mostly, where was he all day and sometimes into the night seven days a week? After considerable nudging, Jacob agreed to meet her for coffee.

**

Rachel waved as Jacob entered the Blackbird Cafe. She arrived early to order coffee and save a booth way in the back so they could speak privately.

"I'll get right to the point, Jacob. Where are you all the time? I confess I was worried enough to follow you a couple of times, and you went to the address I gave you for counseling. Instead I watched you schlepping old stuff around and risking your life up on the roof."

"You followed me?" Jacob roared, turning the heads of the other patrons at the counter.

"Not following really," she whispered, trying to lower the volume. "You won't talk to me. You haven't given me any information about what you are doing. I'm still worried about you."

Jacob's face hardened to a scowl. "Rachel, it's my life and it's enough for you to know I'm doing fine. You need to butt out!" Incensed and feeling violated, Jacob rose from his seat and stomped out, leaving his steaming coffee cup untouched.

**

Rachel's small real estate office sat directly across the street from the *Valley Outlook*. She met with Denise Ross, a reporter she knew slightly, to tell her about the strange happenings on Corbin Avenue. Denise was looking for an opportunity to do an investigative report and found Rachel's story intriguing. She promised to find out more.

Two weeks later Denise Ross invented a dead husband and became a "mystery client" to observe first-hand what went on inside the pink house on Corbin Avenue. Her first appointment with Dr. Pilcher was on a Wednesday afternoon. No yard sale was in progress, but she did notice two individuals washing windows. A bashful, dejected looking woman led her into a small empty room. From the window she observed three more people, two appearing to be teenagers and another too old to be in the sun without a hat, tending to what appeared to be a vegetable garden. Dr. Pilcher entered the room a few minutes later carrying a tray.

"Hello my dear. Denise? Yes? What brings you to my little family today? Here, I brought us some cookies and lemonade." After setting the tray on the small table she approached Denise with outstretched arms.

Dr. Pilcher's friendly energy and broad smile impressed Denise. This woman whose operation she was investigating looked and acted like a traditional grandmother; a little plump, rosy cheeks, cheery disposition, and bearing goodies. Denise poured out the tragic story she had concocted. Dr. Pilcher's sympathetic responses felt like how Denise imagined the conversation would go had she actually lost "Fred" in a small plane crash. If anything was awkward, it was Denise's occasional stammering while trying to answer questions about a spouse that never existed.

Denise's next session was also scheduled for Wednesday afternoon, but without lemonade and cookies. It was going well—well enough to make Denise wonder if Rachel had it all wrong. Then, with 15 minutes remaining, Dr. Pilcher abruptly ceased reassuring Denise about how proud "Fred" would be of the initial steps she was taking to announce a need to discuss a different matter.

"Denise, dearest, to remain at fifty dollars a session you can take advantage of one of my fee reduction plans. You can perform some additional service, one full day a week to help pay for one 50-minute session. There's a lot to do around here and also at my private home in Northridge. Or you can bring in items, either things you own or find somewhere, and I will personally credit you at 50 percent of what they bring at my weekend yard sales. Or you can help with yard sales, stocking merchandise and helping customers. I will provide counseling until you are needed to help with the next customer."

Dr. Pilcher pulled a wide brown belt from a cabinet drawer. Five stopwatches were affixed with thin leather straps. Each watch had a sticky label with a name on the back.

"I keep time this way, so I know for sure when my clients reach fifty minutes," Dr. Pilcher chirped, raising the belt in the air as if she was proud of such an ingenious method of keeping her clients and their earned minutes straight. "When the time adds up to 50 minutes, you are free to leave. Other clients are helping out, so I do have to take turns. These are the options. Otherwise you will need to pay my full fee, $125 an hour from now on. Any questions, dear?"

"Uh, well, I guess," Denise stammered, stunned by such an abrupt shift from tender support to a brusque financial proposition. But she had more questions. "So, if I do one of the alternatives, I still also pay fifty dollars?"

"Yes, of course. But that's less than half my regular price. I allow you to work off the seventy five dollars. That's the beauty of it. You actually make more than I charge you. Any other questions?" Dr. Pilcher asked in a tone signifying she wanted the session to be over.

Denise thought the logic convoluted and she had trouble processing what she was hearing. She had to find out more. "If I work on a yard sale, about how long will it take to earn 50 minutes of counseling? Would I ever be able to get home before noon? I like to drive to my mother's in Apple Valley on Saturday afternoons."

"I never promise what time you will be allowed to leave," Dr. Pilcher responded sternly. "It depends on how many other clients are working, how many shoppers come by and if I have to fit in a private client in my office. Usually all my clients earn their full session by 3 or 4 in the afternoon, enough time to get on the road and have dinner with your mother. Or you can work the yard sale on Sundays instead."

"What time do we start on Saturday or Sunday mornings?" Denise asked, finally getting sufficient control of her thoughts to ask better questions.

"Seven thirty sharp. The merchandise must be removed from the garage and storage buildings and set out to display. Shoppers are allowed in a little after eight. We have lots of fun. In fact, some of my clients work more than one day because they want to. One man, a widower, is around almost all the time. Poor fellow. His life was over until he found a home here." Denise suspected she was referring to Rachel Cohen's brother.

Denise now understood why the advertised fee appeared to be such a good deal. A new wrinkle on bait-and-switch. She had to ask more questions.

"What are the weekday jobs I could do," Denise asked, trying to sound as if she was seriously considering this option.

"This place takes a lot of care. The produce gardens in the back, the orchid greenhouse, the flowers in front. I bring the dogs with me, and they need walking twice a day. Then inside there's always plenty to do. Even though I have a home in Northridge, I want this place kept nice for clients. I do my private and group sessions here. Oh, you could be one of my receptionists to help keep the books and client records in order. I need clients to help on Wednesdays through Fridays, and someone to answer the phone on weekends. This place is closed on Mondays and Tuesdays."

"I notice that a couple of the people working outside are quite young. So you counsel teenagers also?"

"No, their parents are my clients. I do them a favor and let their kids fill in for them."

"Some favor," Denise thought to herself. But she had to find out more. "You said you have a home in Northridge. What happens there?" Denise asked, swallowing hard.

"A lot of the same as far as yard work goes. The pool must be maintained twice weekly. The inside needs cleaning. I have little things to dust or polish. And meal preparation, but only if you are a good cook."

"I wish I could cook, but I'm not very good. Any other assignments?"

"Well, small repairs, running errands, that sort of thing. My husband is homebound. He suffers from advanced Parkinson's, which is why I am able to empathize with the difficult circumstances of others. My best clients care for him until he goes to bed, reading him books, bringing his meals, whatever he wants done. I match clients up with their skills. And I keep hoping I will get a client who is a talented seamstress. Finding off-the-rack clothes that fit me right isn't easy."

"Sorry, I don't sew," Denise said, her mind still spinning. She suspected she might find something odd going on after hearing Rachel's concerns, but Dr. Pilcher was running a sweat shop with grieving psychotherapy clients as her labor force! She decided to stick with "counseling" for a couple more sessions to learn more for the article she knew she had to write.

"I'll be at the yard sale next Saturday," Denise said.

"That will be fine, dear. Bring a sack lunch with your name on it. I provide cold drinks and cookies. Oh, and remember to wear a hat. Sometimes clients forget." Eve Pilcher rose up from her chair and left the room.

***

It was a warm Saturday, even for early morning. Denise arrived at the pink house at 7:15 a.m. Dr. Pilcher and two other "sales staff," as Dr. Pilcher called them, were busily setting up tables and moving merchandise into the front yard. Denise pitched in, already feeling exhausted by the time the first customers came crashing through the gate. So much stuff.

Denise couldn't help but be impressed with how nice many of the items were. The prices were reasonable, which explained why Dr. Pilcher's weekend operation drew many shoppers off the street.

Denise attempted to strike up conversations with two of the other client helpers, although she was always cut short. When Dr. Pilcher noticed such tête-à-têtes, she would yell, "Hey, back to work!" always with a sweet smile. Denise did manage to capture one troubling piece of information from a man who introduced himself as Jacob Cohen. "Rachel's' brother!" she said to herself.

"Where do these nicer things come from?" she asked Jacob, as he busily ordered the glassware a customer had messily rearranged.

"I'm not sure," he replied, "but one woman told me she doesn't have anything, so she steals from other residents at her assisted living facility. Another old guy like me told me he shoplifts."

"Did you inform Dr. Pilcher about this?" Denise asked.

"I did, and she said not to worry. But these two geezer bandits still bring in really first-rate stuff. The shoplifter doesn't even remove price tags. But I'm sure Dr. Pilcher is taking care of it."

Jacob Cohen was clearly hooked on Dr. Pilcher, Denise thought. His response was not logical.

By noon Denise had racked up only 19 minutes on the stop watch tag bearing her name, consisting of three separate interactions before being interrupted. By the late afternoon Denise thought she would faint from the intense heat. Only 41 minutes were earned from a total of seven short exchanges. Dr. Pilcher explained how sometimes it was necessary to make up minutes the next time and reminded Denise to write out a check for fifty dollars.

***

Denise had pages of notes for her expose of Dr. Eve Pilcher's counseling operation and had taken several photos covertly with the mini-camera concealed in her shirt pocket. But she wanted to play out one more session. She negotiated with a client-receptionist to serve time at the Pilcher home in Northridge.

The following week Denise drove into the hills above Northridge and parked in front of the address printed on a sheet along with a list of her assigned duties. The lavish Spanish style home with graceful arches and lush flowering gardens of Bougainvillea and Aster boasted a spectacular view of the entire San Fernando Valley and the skyline of downtown Los

Angeles. A three-tier fountain edged with colorful Mexican tile greeted guests coming up an adobe brick pathway to a massive carved oak entry door.

"This gal does alright," Denise thought to herself. She estimated Dr. Pilcher's take from the yard sales to be at least a couple thousand dollars every week, probably more when higher end items were available, all the while also being paid $50 by each of her helpers. Then other paying clients were also doing her work including home care for Eve Pilcher's husband, a service that would cost well over $5,000 a month at the current going rate for in-home care.

Denise's assignments were to do a week's worth of laundry and sweep the pathways in the front and back while the washer and dryer were going. She could leave when the clothes and bedding were folded, remembering the client-receptionist's warning that she may not get credit if Dr. Pilcher wasn't satisfied with her work. Because Denise knew she would never return, her performance was superficial, just decent enough to avoid raising suspicion. She was far more interested in what else was happening in the house—a frail woman with thick glasses in the kitchen scrubbing a large pan and another sturdily-built woman stooped over the stove, a spry older man running up and down the stairs retrieving things for the invalid husband, and another man, probably still in his forties, outside trimming deadheads off flower bushes. She would go home and finish writing her article.

***

The following Sunday morning, Dr. Pilcher arrived to prepare for the yard sale. The newest merchandise needed to be appraised and tagged. At 7:30 a.m. a frantic call came from one of her clients. Had Dr. Pilcher seen today's *Valley Outlook*? If not, she needed to get hold of a copy now. Dr. Pilcher ran to a newspaper rack in front of the drug store a block away and back again to her office. She sat down to read the six column story exposing her counseling operation, complete with a photograph of a yard sale in progress.

"I knew there was something sneaky about that Denise," she hollered loud enough for one of her clients who had since arrived to come see if Dr. Pilcher was all right.

"After everything I do to help people pay for services they need but can't afford, she does this to me," she wailed to the client. "I work so hard every week, only taking two days off. I have more clients than anyone else.

Over 45 regulars at any point in time. That should tell them how good I am, how much I put into my profession." She then asked to be left alone.

Eve Pilcher was determined to fight back. She would ask Jane, a client with a pleasant manner and voice, to call her entire client list and insist they write letters to the *Valley Outlook* lauding her services and disparaging the reporter. She would then sue Denise Ross and the *Valley Outlook* for defamation.

Two weeks later, she received a letter from the League of California Psychologists' Ethics Committee. "This will give me another chance to make this go away," she sighed. "My colleagues will understand everything once I explain what I do. The Committee will be my best defense in the law suit."

Dear Dr. Pilcher,

The LCP Ethics Committee received a copy of a newspaper article by Denise Ross (see enclosed) about your practice. Several features, if accurate, raise questions with regards to exploitation, boundary violations, and failure to maintain the confidentiality due to your clients

We need to hear your side before taking any action. Please make an appointment with the LCP administrator, Mrs. Peggy Aldridge, to appear before the Ethics Committee at its March meeting unless a compelling reason requires a postponement. Failure to contact us within 10 days of the receipt of this letter will constitute an act of noncompliance, which is itself an ethics violation.

Sincerely,

Victor Graham, Ph.D.
Chair, Ethics Committee
League of California Psychologists

The Ethics Committee:
Eve Pilcher, Ph.D. March 16, 10:15 p.m.

"I've never seen one quite like this," announced Victor Graham, bringing the Committee back to the table after a stretch break. "We received a copy of an article featured in the *Valley Outlook*. The reporter sent it with her letter, but Wolf saw it the day it came out. I made copies."

"It appears this woman thinks professional boundaries have the consistency of H_2O," said Wolf Levin. "She doesn't just dribble occasionally like some therapists who disclose too much about themselves or take clients out to dinner. This lady is Niagara Falls."

"I'll read the reporter's letter aloud," said Victor.

Dear LCP Ethics Committee Members,

My article, Junk Yard Therapy, *was featured in this week's* Valley Outlook. *I paid Dr. Eve Pilcher $200 for four counseling sessions, albeit I was under-cover and not honest with my presenting problem. However, this operation is a scam. Led to believe the fee would be only $50 a session, she abruptly increased it to $125 near the end of the second session. If clients cannot pay she attempts to conscript them into her labor force to work off the additional $75. Clients still pay $50 and then may work for as many as 8 hours to bring their total credit up to $125 for a single 50-minute session.*

My story raises additional concerns. Minors are working to help pay for their parents' counseling. Clients serving as receptionists have access to other clients' personal records. Some clients, including elderly ones, are assigned hazardous duties. Dr. Pilcher's grandmotherly demeanor creates an effective snare for people in emotional pain but they are soon shuffled into an exploitive work program.

I think your committee may want to look into this operation. I became aware of it from a woman who was concerned about her brother, a widower. He currently works for Dr. Pilcher practically full time for no pay. When I last spoke with his sister, she asked her brother to also press ethics charges against Dr. Pilcher. He told her to go to hell.

Do with my story as you see fit.

Sincerely,

Denise Ross, Reporter
Valley Outlook

The Committee members made intermittent sighs and utterances as they perused the two-page article. Stella Sarkosky muttered something about giving female psychologists a bad name.

Ted Bates, who almost always tried to find some redeeming quality in colleagues under scrutiny said, "Let's wait until we hear her side. Just because it's in print doesn't mean it's entirely factual, you know."

Eve Pilcher had called the LCP office to say she was running late. A half hour later, Peggy Aldridge escorted her into the meeting room. Dr. Pilcher's brown hair streaked with gray was done up in a tight bun. Her rosy cheeks, granny glasses, flowered cotton dress, and flat sandals reminded Sammy of the sweet widow who lives next door to his home in

Santa Cruz—except for her facial expression. Eve Pilcher looked mad as a wet cat and spoke out loudly before Victor had a chance to make the customary introductions.

"This…this Denise Ross woman caused me all sorts of problems," she bellowed, as she sat down hard on the empty chair. "I am asking you to join me in a lawsuit against her and the *Valley Observer*. My business has been trashed. I'm not getting new clients, and some of my regulars were pulled out by their despicable family members. I had over 40 clients, and now I'm down to 28."

"We can't join in on such lawsuits," Victor said calmly but sternly. "Let me ask you first what kinds of clients you counsel. Are they all experiencing grief?"

"Almost all of them, yes. Most lost someone dear to them, usually a spouse or partner, but sometimes a sibling or parent and occasionally a child or a family pet. Most feel alone. People tend to move away from those who are grieving. It reminds them of their own mortality. I give them the consistent unconditional love they need."

"Thank you," said Victor. "What we need you to do now is tell us where the article was incorrect or misleading about having clients work for you."

"Well, of course it was incorrect! She made me sound like I am bleeding them. If it wasn't for me they would not be getting any counseling at all. Most are hurting financially and can't pay the going rate for psychotherapy. Do you have complaints from any of my clients? No. I treat them all well. They have access to snacks and water or tea and a nice place to rest when they need breaks. They choose the jobs they want to reduce their fee. They are bartering their services for my service. Nothing in the ethics code forbids such exchange agreements."

"Had you considered a sliding fee scale for any who cannot afford your full fee?" Charlotte Burroughs asked.

"Absolutely not! That would be humiliating. These are proud people. They don't want charity."

"Uh, the article suggests some of your yard sale merchandise is stolen property and you knew about it and did nothing. Is that true?" asked Archie Wittig.

"I tell clients who pay off part of their fee with yard sale merchandise to make sure they are items they already owned or purchased. I'm a psychotherapist, not law enforcement."

"Do your clients do your bookkeeping and client records? And, if so, is that not a violation your clients' rights to confidentiality?" Wolf asked, confidently, thinking Eve Pilcher would stumble this time.

"Lots of therapists hire receptionists and bookkeepers. What's the difference? Do they get hauled in for violating their client's rights? I have the advantage of knowing everything about who is doing these jobs, a lot more than taking someone from the classifieds. Only my most stable and trusted clients have access to records."

"Let me rephrase the question. Do you see anything inappropriate with how you conduct your practice? Is there anything you think you should change?" Victor asked with a hint of frustration.

"No! We are family, and everyone comes of their own free will. Many clients put in more hours than are required for my fee reduction program. I keep those who are lonely or depressed busy in an active social environment."

"OK. About your ad," added Wolf. "50 minutes for 50 bucks. That seems misleading."

"Not at all. The first two sessions are $50, and clients who want to stay on still pay only $50 from their own pockets if they can't afford my full fee and join one of my alterative programs. I don't even see what you are getting at here. It seems so obvious to me!" Eve Pilcher's face was now fire engine red.

"Do you inform your prospective clients that the full fee is $125 an hour at the beginning of their initial session? How they must work their bill off starting with the third session?" Wolf prodded.

"No, I don't. And I will tell you why. These people are hurting. They only want to deal with the reasons they came to me, nothing else. They can stop after the second session if they choose. At least I gave them some consolation and relief at a bargain price."

Wolf softly cleared his throat.

Sammy had to get a question in. But what? She had an answer for everything. He would try something more general.

"So," Sammy asked, "you don't think you are taking advantage of your clients?"

"What? Of course not! Why do you ask me these questions?" Eve Pilcher was now clearly perturbed. "I'm the victim here of a reporter who lied to me and then wrote an awful story. Are you going to haul her in for a grilling?" She clenched her teeth.

Victor thought the Committee had heard enough. "Thank you for coming in, Dr. Pilcher. We will discuss the matter and contact you within two weeks."

"Good. I have to get back to the yard sale. It's Saturday you know. My clients need me. At least I set the record straight, and I trust you are smart enough to understand the unique service I provide for the grieving."

Dr. Pilcher stood up tall and marched out of the room like an Army cadet on patrol.

***

"Oy vey, where to start?" said Victor, slapping his hand on his forehead.

Sammy found Eve Pilcher to be a conundrum, unlike anything he expected. He assumed psychotherapists who broke the rules knew exactly what they were doing. They plotted their misdeeds and may even take some measure of satisfaction in their wrongdoing. Yet this woman seemed to sincerely believe everything she said. She saw herself as a savior, a keeper of broken souls who found a way to make it all work for herself as well. No amount of questioning was going to reveal a recognition of ethical improprieties.

"I think she has built up kind of a cult, though not of the creepier sort," Sammy said. "On the one hand she has an Earth Mother feel to her. She fills up her clients' empty spaces. But on the other hand, she greatly advantages herself in the process."

Charlotte broke in. "The main problem overall is this; she does nothing to help them move on with a life beyond indentured servitude. She gives her clients just enough to not complain."

"I agree," added Wolf. "The widower, for example, should be out meeting new people and forming social ties and activities, not stuck working for her for free and alienated from his sister. A competent counselor would have helped him create the next chapter of his life. Instead the poor guy is apparently a contented slave."

"Her clients are exploited. No question. Would you work all day in addition to paying her $50 for 50 minutes with her, sometimes for only a few minutes at a time?" added Archie with uncustomary vigor.

Ted had remained quiet until now. "Well, you know me. Looking for a silver lining. She has apparently been doing this for years and not a single client complained to us. They must be getting something. She slid way past those acceptable boundary crossings, and the confidentiality thing is a problem, but I believe she has actually helped people over their rough spots."

"Yes," Wolf broke in, "that's what cults do. Few lock the doors or put up barbed wire fences. Their psyches become imprisoned, mental bars as strong as steel. Dr. Pilcher is skilled in the art of manipulation, whether she realizes it or not. She created a subservient flock, grateful to be part of it."

"Right," chimed in Charlotte. "They are dependent on her. To complain or consider leaving would be disloyal."

Stella looked sternly at Ted. "Here is the critical point. Psychotherapists tend to clients' needs. Period. We benefit from getting paid for our services and from gaining satisfaction for enhancing the well-being of those who seek our services."

"Right on," said Wolf.

"And another point," Stella continued, "If her clients work for eight hours to pay off the extra $75, that adds up to $9.37 an hour. I pay the woman who helps me keep up my house over twice that. And let's not even get started on the IRS issues. She probably reports none of this."

This time Ted had no response. He knew Stella was right.

Sammy, still learning the ins and outs of how to apply the ethics code to actual situations, spoke up. "Dr. Pilcher claimed she is bartering her services for her clients' services. The current code does not prohibit bartering. Does she have a valid defense?"

"Good observation Sammy!" said Stella, smiling as if Sammy just earned a gold star. "Although the line separating bartering from engaging in multiple role relationships is not thick, Pilcher's reasoning is faulty on several grounds. First, she acts like an employer, and ethical exchanges are negotiated on a level playing field wherein each party has a clear say in fair market values. Dr. Pilcher gets far more than she gives, is in total control of what tasks are acceptable, has enforced rules, and oversees the clients' work. She even denies credit if the tasks are not completed to her satisfaction. She is both their counselor and their employer. Such an arrangement violates our ethics code."

"Enough," said Victor. "Let's pair up what we know about Dr. Pilcher and the Ethics Code. What principles has she violated? I think the most salient ones are engaging in exploitative multiple role relationships with clients and compromising confidential information. We'll toss in misleading advertising if we want."

"Can we do anything with accepting stolen property or elder abuse, like having older clients doing hard labor?" asked Sammy.

"Or child labor laws and putting clients generally at risk, given what she asks them to do?" added Charlotte.

"Or what about overall competence?" asked Wolf. "The ultimate goal of psychotherapy is to work with clients to terminate therapy when their issues have been sufficiently resolved. Pilcher strings them along indefinitely like so many pearls to adorn her neck in perpetuity."

"It's complicated," said Victor. "We cannot definitively prove some of the allegations, although, ironically, Dr. Pilcher was an effective witness against herself. The accused shooting off their own toes happens more often than you might think. The case is strong and we don't need to use every piece of evidence. We're running a little late now anyway."

Decision and Dispositions

The Committee decided that Dr. Eve Pilcher violated the ethical principles dealing with improper multiple role relationships, exploitation, and failing to maintain client confidentiality. They also concluded she was not suitable for a diversion program, supervision or psychotherapy, given her own brash testimony at the hearing. The vote was to recommend expulsion to the League of California Psychologists Board and to forward the report to the California Board of Psychology because she also violated state licensing rules.

Dr. Pilcher received a letter informing her of the Ethics Committee's actions and recommendations. She scrawled back a note indicating her intent to sue the LCP as well as Denise Ross and the *Valley Outlook*. However, no legal action materialized.

The LCP Board did vote to expel Dr. Pilcher, and she did not choose to appeal. Her license to practice psychology was later revoked.

Almost a year later Wolf Levin noticed an ad in a local throwaway paper advertising "Dr. Eve Pilcher, Grief Counselor, $40 for 40 minutes." Wolf decided to drive past the pink house on Corbin Avenue on a warm Saturday morning. The yard was dotted with people sorting through merchandise. Off in a corner Dr. Pilcher was whispering intently to a despondent-looking older woman. "She's at it again," Wolf said, shaking his head as he drove on by.

Even though Eve Pilcher lost her license, she kept on practicing using the unregulated title of "Grief Coach." By not advertising herself as a psychologist, Dr. Pilcher was beyond the reach of the LCP and California Board of Psychology. She only needed a business license to continue what she had been doing all along.

Case Commentary

My readers are surely thinking they would never let their practices lapse into such entanglements as described in this case. But we are all adept at not seeing what we don't want to see, especially if our personal needs are at issue, leaving us vulnerable to making self-serving decisions with ethical implications (Koocher & Keith-Spiegel, 2008). While this case is, indeed, at the extreme end of a continuum, I chose it because it includes variations of many of the common types of nonsexual multiple role relationship that can turn into complaints: befriending clients, employing clients, bartering items for psychotherapy services, bartering services for psychotherapy services, excessive self-disclosure, touching and hugging, conducting therapy in improper settings, and giving clients access to other clients' confidential files. The main difference between Eve Pilcher and the more ordinary boundary violation is that she orchestrated so many of them into a single operation.

This story also illustrates what can go wrong when those with personal agendas have a remarkable ability to self-delude. Eve Pilcher cast herself as savior to the bereft who creatively justified her practice, even after having errors pointed out to her by the Ethics Committee. Instead she perceived herself as a victim, complete with initial expectations of receiving LPC support.

Here's where paying close attention to red flags (e.g., "This situation is different," "No one can get hurt," "I'm actually doing my client a favor," and hundreds more) can save one from consequences down the line. Consultation with a trusted colleague is wise when a hint of doubt or confusion arises. Documenting any decisions involving a role blending that might ultimately require a defense is also recommended (Younggren & Gottlieb, 2004).

Notes on Multiple Role Relationships

The status of boundary crossings, which includes multiple role relationships, has evolved over the years (Knapp & Vande Creek, 2006; Pope & Keith-Spiegel, 2008; Zur, 2007). The risk management, "slippery slope" perspective gave way to allowing some role flexibility to serve clients' treatment needs (Barnett, 2007). As Lazarus (1994) put it, too strict boundary rules "can obstruct a clinician's artistry" (p. 255). It has also been recognized that not all multiple role relationships are avoidable, especially in small or rural communities.

The most recent Ethics Code of the American Psychological Association (2010) does not disallow all multiple role relationships (Principle 3.05). Those that "would not reasonably be expected to cause impairment or the risk of exploitation or harm are not unethical," leaving the outcome assessment up to the practitioner. Ironically, despite the relaxed rules, psychotherapists may be at increased risk of being brought up on ethics charges. Why? Because the prior rules were more forthright and specific about what was acceptable and what was not. So, if one hires a client to perform a service (or barters for same), and a disgruntled client later claims she was taken advantage of, the psychotherapist can only hope an ethics committee will disagree.

When psychotherapists contemplate layering a therapeutic alliance on another type of relationship or connection, red flags should be waving and carefully evaluated before proceeding. If the psychotherapy or the other shared role go awry, both relationships may collapse, leaving the client feeling abandoned, confused, angry, or resentful. When deviations from standard practice stem primarily from self-serving motives, ethical violations are inevitable.

Discussion Questions

1. Dr. Pilcher appears to have a defense for every charge of ethical misconduct leveled against her. Did you find yourself agreeing with any of them? Why or why not?
2. Dr. Pilcher continued her practice using an unprotected title. What advantages do clients have when they consult only licensed practitioners?
3. A psychologist invites his client to join a poker group, given the client's love of the game. What can go wrong?
4. A social worker allows her client, a talented but financially-strapped seamstress, to make her clothes instead of paying for therapy. The social worker supplies the pattern and materials one week, and the client brings the completed outfit to the next session. What could go wrong here?
5. A client who lost his job and health insurance agrees to give his therapist his second car in lieu of future psychotherapy fees.

The car is worth $5,000 and the therapist charges $100 per session. They agree that 50 sessions have been paid for in advance. What can go wrong with this deal?

6. A client is hired to do after-school babysitting for two hours every weekday day in the therapist's home for two children, ages 6 and 8. In exchange, the client receives a full session in the family's den on Thursdays. What are the possible pitfalls surrounding this agreement?

7. Can you come up with examples of bartering arrangements with clients that would be non-exploitive and explain why you believe each to be fair and ethical? What other factors (gender, treatment, and cultural issues, for example) pertain?

References

American Psychological Association (2010). *Ethical principles of psychologists.* Washington DC: Author. Retrieved from http://www.apa.org/ethics/code/index.aspx?item=3#

Barnett. J. E. (2007). Whose boundaries are they anyway? *Professional Psychology, 38,* 401–410.

Knapp, S. J., & VandeCreek, L. D. (2006). *Practical ethics for psychologists: A positive approach.* Washington, DC: American Psychological Association.

Koocher, G. P., & Keith-Spiegel, P. (2008). *Ethics in psychology and the mental health professions.* New York, NY: Oxford University Press.

Lazarus, A. A. (1994). How certain boundaries and ethics diminish therapeutic effectiveness. *Ethics & Behavior, 4,* 255–261.

Pope, K. S., & Keith-Spiegel, P. (2008). A practical approach to boundaries in psychotherapy: Making decisions, bypassing blunders, and mending fences. *Journal of Clinical Psychology, 64,* 638–652.

Younggren, J. N., & Gottlieb, M. C. (2004). Managing risk when contemplating multiple relationships. *Professional Psychology, 35,* 255–260.

Zur, O. (2007). *Boundaries in psychotherapy.* Washington, DC: American Psychological Association.

Additional Reading

Barnett, J. E., Lazarus, A. A., Vasquez, M. J. T., Moorehead-Slaughter, O., & Johnson, W. B. (2007). Boundary issues and multiple relationships: Fantasy and reality. *Professional Psychology, 38,* 401–410.

Ebert, B. W. (2006). *Multiple relationships and conflict of interest for mental health professionals: A conservative psychological approach.* Sarasota. FL: Professional Resource Press.

Gabriel, L. (2005). *Speaking the unspeakable: The ethics of dual relationships in counseling and psychotherapy.* New York, NY: Routledge.

Gutheil, T. G., & Brodsky, A. (2008). *Preventing boundary violating in clinical practice.* New York, NY: Guilford.

Gutheil, T. G., & Gabbard, G. O. (1993). The concept of boundaries in clinical practice: Theoretical and risk-management dimensions. *American Journal of Psychiatry, 150,* 188–196.

Reamer, F. G. (2012). *Boundary issues and dual relationships in the human services.* New York, NY: Columbia University Press.

Rubin, S. S. (2000). Differentiating multiple relationships from multiple dimensions of involvement: Therapeutic space at the interface of client, therapist, and society. *Psychotherapy, 37,* 315–324.

four
RATS!

A downhill spiral culminating in a shocking act by one adversary against another illustrates how collegial relationships can devolve into serious ethical misdeeds. Harm resulting from interpersonal conflicts often seeps beyond the original players, especially when in the context of an organizational setting.

The most prolific scholar in the Psychology Department at Pasadena University was the seemingly unsinkable Professor Jade Lurch. For over 25 years she held the record for the number of published papers, more than all of her colleagues in the social science division combined. And, she intended to keep it that way. When Dr. Vernon Pyle applied for an Associate Professor position with tenure possible after only two years, Jade sniffed a rival. This ebullient, impressive young man came with impeccable recommendations and 12 publications in respectable journals. He boasted ambitious plans to submit grant applications, some likely to lead to profitable university-licensed products, a most welcome boon to the university's sagging financial profile. In an attempt to pre-empt this unforeseen competition, Professor Lurch lashed out at Vernon Pyle during his initial job interview.

"The whole topic of attitudes held by frazzled people seems somewhat trivial to me. How did you arrive at this idea for a project as significant as a doctoral dissertation?" Jade asked in a superior voice, her chin tilted upwards while peering down her nose.

Vernon Pyle was taken aback by such rudeness. Stress is a major health risk, and conducting research to better understand the impact of intense anxiety and how to lower its damage attracted him even as an undergraduate. His stammered response sounded inadequate, even to him. He was sure it cost him a job offer, but much to his surprise he was hired over Jade Lurch's resolute objections.

Once on board, Jade annoyed Vernon every chance she got after Vernon published three more research-based articles and was invited to deliver the keynote address at the International Behavioral Medicine meetings in Zurich. She interrupted Vernon's presentation during a faculty seminar, challenging the choice of a control group for his study of attitude changes following stress reduction training. A student also told Vernon how she once disparaged his work in her neurobiology class. When she described his entire line of programmatic research as "below par," to a seminar audience of over 100 students and faculty members, he decided to confront her in the hallway.

"Enough with your vicious backstabbing!" he shouted directly into her face, pointing his finger at her nose.

"My dear boy," she haughtily responded, "Scholarly critique is the backbone of scientific advancement. If you attempt to squelch academic freedom, consequences will ensue."

"You should spend more time shoring up your own work," Vernon snidely snapped back, a risky retort for a still untenured professor. Witnesses spread the content of this brief fracas, much to the delight of those who regarded Jade Lurch as an insufferable prima donna.

Vernon approached the department chair several times with his complaints about Jade Lurch's nasty behavior, but nothing changed. She had tenure and also brought in grant funds—two impressive protections against censure. Vernon realized he was on his own.

So began a reign of mutual condemnation. No matter how nit-picking the point, neither one letting a chance slide to degrade the other's work. Jade rumored that Vernon exploited his graduate students by forcing them to do most of the data collection without receiving due credit. Vernon, now emboldened upon achieving tenure based on the elevated status his research brought to the university, whispered accusations that Jade deleted outlier data points to achieve desired results. New allegations raced through the grapevine on a monthly basis, but no one stepped in to mitigate.

More recently the acrimony extended beyond bashing each other's research endeavors by shifting into the realm of character assassination. The slurs often seemed based on hearsay, flimsy evidence, or groundless invention. Jade told her associates that Vernon's excessive beer-drinking was impairing his judgment and that he and a sophomore foreign exchange student were having sex on a beach towel during the lunch hour in his basement lab. Vernon whispered to those he suspected had exceptionally loose tongues that Jade likely had a brain tumor causing her to be bitchy and sometimes delusional, and she passed gas so frequently that it was best to stay clear of her.

This week was different. Vernon was dealt a blow extending well beyond the backstabbing heretofore confined to inside the hallowed walls of the academy. His formidable adversary spilled her venom into the international arena.

***

At 5:45 a.m., as was his usual early morning routine, Vernon Pyle purchased coffee from the dispenser, picked up his mail in the psychology department office, and settled into the most comfortable chair in the adjoining faculty lounge. Three pieces of mail—two advertisements for newly released scholarly books and what looked like a bill from his dentist—were quickly dismissed before spreading out the current edition of *The Behavioral Psychologist* on his lap. He took several deep breaths to enhance his arousal. Then, fumbling for the section containing letters to the editor, he felt a groundswell of confidence. He was certain his latest project on the role of individual vs. group stress-reduction therapy with male alcoholics featured in last month's issue was destined to make him renowned by clinical psychologists the world over.

Bristling with anticipation he thought to himself, "Surely I will find several laudatory letters written by experts from around the country." He would then showcase these comments to strengthen his almost completed funding application to the National Institute on Alcohol Abuse and Alcoholism. Expecting the splendid rush accompanying lofty praise, Vernon found only a single entry painting his work as resulting in misleading conclusions. The letter was signed "Jade Lurch, Ph.D."

Vernon sat motionless for a full five minutes before folding the newsletter into neat squares and placing it into his briefcase, rising up from the chair and stiffly marching back through the office. Ignoring the department secretary who had since arrived, he lumbered down the hall and into the elevator. He descended two floors to Jade Lurch's laboratory and pushed open the heavy swinging doors.

The large darkened space was unoccupied, save for the 90 Norwegian Hooded rats in rows of cages comprising the study population for Jade's ongoing research. Vernon then did what all scientists who seek nothing short of searching for the truth would consider unimaginable.

***

Professor Jade Lurch arrived at her lab at 8:45 a.m. Her research on the ability to learn a complex spatial task by varying the amount of visual stimuli was nearing completion. In three weeks she would administer a learning task to discover if her hypothesis was supported. If so, she was confident the article based on her findings would be accepted by *Science*, or maybe even *Nature*. Such a coup would trump her arch enemy, that "repellent hulk" as she often described Vernon Pyle to others. He would only appear foolish if he ever again attempted to degrade her or her work.

Jade set her lunch bag and briefcase on the table in the darkened room. Yet even before she turned on the small desk lamp, an eerie feeling that something was amiss overtook her. She flipped the switch.

A high pitched scream brought everyone within hearing range streaming through the swinging doors. "What's wrong?" a student cried out as Jade swayed back and forth before sinking to the floor. "She fainted," someone yelled out. "Call 911."

After taking a few days off to recuperate from shock, Jade Lurch launched a grievance procedure with the university. Three weeks later she sent a letter to the League of California Psychologists.

Dear Members of the League of California Psychologists Ethics Committee,

Despite my vigorous objections during the evaluation of Dr. Vernon Pyle, my colleagues offered him a position in the Psychology Department at Pasadena University. In the last three years he has been nothing but an embarrassment. I harbor many concerns about the quality of what his students are being taught, and I suspect the veracity of his research.

His behavior towards me personally has been appalling. He has not stopped with his rumor mongering, telling people I have various physical and mental problems and claiming my work is tainted. I've published 48 articles in refereed journals and possess a far more impressive reputation as a scholar and scientific investigator than does that weasel, Vernon Pyle.

However, his latest action consists of not only an ethical infraction but a criminal offense. My double-blind research requires three groups of Norwegian hooded rats, 90 altogether, to receive varying amounts of visual stimulation in a controlled environment during the four months after weaning. Data collection was well into its third month with the critical dependent variable test to be administered this Thursday.

So, what has this wretched scallywag done? He came into my lab when no one was around and left my hard work in shambles, not to mention the shock to my body and time and financial losses. Now I am forced to start anew, if I can even manage to acquire the necessary resources. Two students witnessed his despicable conduct. I have signed affidavits from them. Enclosed is a complete description of the outrageous act, including a photograph of the incident taken by a witness with an iPhone.

Sincerely,

Jade Lurch, Ph.D.
Distinguished Professor of Psychology
Pasadena University

***

Vernon Pyle's revenge hardly went unnoticed. He was the talk of the campus and on the front page of the *PU Daily Poop*. He did not welcome a letter from the LCP Ethics Committee, but it was not entirely unexpected either. He viewed it as one more hurdle to jump before things quieted down.

Dear Dr. Pyle,

We have received a complaint from Professor Jade Lurch regarding your alleged vandalism of her laboratory. We are opening an inquiry, and despite the short notice we would like you to attend the next meeting of the LCP Ethics Committee on March 16. We ask to hear your side of the story.

You must make an appointment with the LCP administrator, Mrs. Peggy Aldridge, to appear before the LCP Ethics Committee at its March meeting unless a compelling reason requires a postponement. We expect you to respond in detail to Dr. Lurch's allegations. Failure to contact us within 10 days of the receipt of this letter will constitute an act of noncompliance, which is itself an ethics violation.

Sincerely,

Victor Graham, Ph.D.
Chair, Ethics Committee
League of California Psychologists

Vernon dutifully called Peggy Aldridge to confirm his appointment on March 16th. One more jolt in a bumpy road. And, he did have his own story to tell.

The Ethics Committee:
Vernon Pyle, Ph.D. March 16, 11:20 a.m.

Victor Graham stood tall at the head of the table and read Professor Jade Lurch's letter aloud.

"Well, what did Professor Pyle do?" Wolf Levin wailed, tossing his arms high into the air and flailing them about as if drowning. "Don't keep us submerged here, man!"

"I know! I know!" squealed Ted Bates. "He shuffled the rats around to sabotage her double-blind identification system."

"Just hold on, please!" said Victor, rubbing his forehead. "I was curious myself because I could find no enclosure. So I called her. She apologized for inadvertently omitting a statement outlining the offense, saying she was still too upset to concentrate. She sent an email filling me in a little more, so I'll give you information as we go. She also attached a photo. Promise me you will not fall out of your chairs and hurt yourselves when you look at it."

"Spit it out man," cried Wolf. "Did he burn down her lab?"

"No."

"Well, *what* then?" Wolf seemed on the verge of frenzy.

"He set all of her rats loose in the university's botanical garden," Victor replied, trying to sound collected.

Wolf let out a howl imagining the scenario of rodents bouncing about amongst the flora. "How in the hell did he accomplish such a feat? Ninety of them? Norwegian hoodeds are huge, some almost as big as cats."

"It apparently took him seven trips and over an hour, according to Dr. Lurch's estimate," replied Victor. "Large carts were stored nearby. Dr. Pyle evidently used them to stack up cages and roll them into the service elevator, up to the first floor, and out a main door for a one block trek to the gardens. It was early in the morning. Not many people were around. Jade Lurch did locate two students who said they witnessed Vernon Pyle opening up cages, shaking the occupants out, sometimes yelling 'You are free, free at last' or 'Take that, you senseless bitch.'"

Victor removed a printed photo from the file and started it around the table. "Here's what one student snapped showing what appears to be Dr. Pyle dumping a cage with his mouth obviously yelling something."

No one even tried to stifle a giggle, not even Archie Wittig who was usually unflappable.

"OK," said Victor, "Archie, would you find Dr. Pyle and bring him in? And please try to maintain some measure of decorum, people."

***

Vernon Pyle, a big man still in his thirties, confirmed the physical capability to execute such an escapade. His height and bulk were crammed into a light blue polyester suit that appeared to be a size too small, as if he had outgrown it. A splash of red hair and freckled skin gave his moon-shaped face a childlike appearance that complemented his alleged choice of retaliation. He seemed squeamish during the brief introductions, like a kid caught with a forbidden cookie sticking half way out of his mouth. Victor motioned Vernon to the empty chair to his right and pointed to each committee member as he introduced them by name.

"Dr. Pyle, you know why you are here," said Victor looking too serious, as if he were trying to mask his authentic emotion. "Your colleague, Professor Lurch, has charged you with…er…disbanding her research animals. The first question is, of course, to ask if you did what she accuses you of doing."

"Yes. I did liberate her rats. The animal rights organization on campus practically made me their poster boy." A wave of pride shifted Pyle's demeanor from uncomfortable to self-righteous. "I would like to offer my defense, if I may."

"Go ahead, please," said Victor.

"The truth is any human being can take only so much. This woman has been on my case since Day One. I don't know why I crank her gears into high. Maybe I remind her of a lover who dumped her or a kid who pulled her pigtails. She is unkind to almost everyone, not just me. If you could only know how many colleagues have come up to me when no one was watching to shake my hand. She needed to be brought down a few pegs." Vernon Pyle now sounded even more sanctimonious.

"Has the university taken any action against you?" Charlotte Burroughs asked.

"Yes. I've been given an unpaid leave for a semester in lieu of involving outside authorities. I also had to pay the bill for Anderson's X-cellent

X-terminators to come trap the rats. They turn around and sell them as snake food to Shifty's Reptile Farm in the Mojave Desert. They made out on both ends. From me, then Shifty."

Sammy thought Dr. Pyle's cavalier attitude would likely be interpreted as evidence of sociopathy by the other clinicians in the room. And, it was obvious to Sammy that this scientist with a Ph.D. degree was clearly having trouble, regardless of his feelings towards his one human and 90 non-human victims, seeing his act as extreme and, at least in retrospect, regrettable. But Sammy could not help but compare Vernon Pyle to a nine-year-old client he treated in Indiana who killed his older brother's six-month-old Holstein with a sledge hammer. Because it was not initially apparent who crushed the calf's skull, the local newspaper published an article asking for anyone with leads to come forward. When Bucky Piper tearfully confessed, a follow-up article predicted Bucky would someday be a serial killer given his propensity to slaughter livestock. But Sammy knew Bucky to be a long-suffering victim of an emotionally abusive and sadistic 14-year-old brother. Sammy gave the parents credit for seeking counseling for Bucky despite their mistaken reason for doing it. The families in the surrounding farms valued independence and strength in the face of adversity above all else. Bucky's parents brought him for psychotherapy, not because of his long-standing suffering at the hands of his older brother and its consequences for the hapless calf, but for his cowardly act bringing shame and embarrassment to the family.

"What are you thinking, Dr. Halsey?" asked Victor.

Sammy snapped back into the moment. "Uh, well I was wondering if Dr. Pyle believes his actions to be justified by the treatment he alleg-edly suffered from Dr. Lurch, or whether it was an unpremeditated on-the-spot kind of thing. In other words," turning his head to look directly at Vernon Pyle, "I am trying to better understand what led you to take such a drastic action."

"Maybe both," answered Vernon after a moment's reflection. "She has hounded me for over three years now. I tried to put a stop to it. But she just kept firing at me like a battle tank with a 120 millimeter gun mounted on her ample turret. I held it together as best I could. When she made a mockery of my research in an international forum, humiliating me and putting a serious dent in my career, sirens went off."

"Do you regret what you did?" asked Charlotte.

"Only a little. Her rats didn't have much of a life in that dark lab, and they had a lot of fun for almost twelve hours before they were trapped. I hear a few got away. So I don't feel bad about them. And Dr. Lurch had to understand in no uncertain terms how it feels when one's hard work is flipped into the dumpster. We both must start all over again now, except my reputation has taken a big hit. I'll recover. She'll recover easier—just needs some time and new rats they are making me pay for. But, from now on she will know I mean business and leave me alone."

"So, no remorse?" asked Ted, giving Vernon Pyle another chance to admit wrongdoing with a sincere ring to it.

"I'm sorry because it has cost me a lot of money plus no salary for a semester. Thankfully I do maintain a small clinical practice to tide me over. But if you want me to say I feel sorry for that vicious harridan, I won't. I should've brought *her* up on ethics charges a long time ago. In fact, I think I will still do it." Vernon sat back in his chair, looking defiant.

Turning to the Committee members Victor asked, "Any other questions for Dr. Pyle?"

"Just one," said Stella Sarkosky. "Do you see the destructive relationship between you and Dr. Lurch as affecting the rest of the department? The students? Dr. Lurch's research assistants in the lab?"

"The Department Chair hauled us both in a few times asking us to be nicer to each other or to at least keep a lid on it. He gave up a year ago. One of my colleagues says our relationship lowers department morale, but another says we provide endless entertainment, so I figure it's a wash. I don't know about the students."

"Thank you," said Stella, but she didn't mean it.

Victor, sounding a little weary, concluded the discussion. "Unless you want to add anything, Dr. Pyle, we will let you go for today. We will communicate back to you within two weeks."

Dr. Pyle stood up and yanked down his suit jacket that had since hiked up to his waist. "Thanks, and have a good one. I bet it's your lunch time." He flashed a boyish smile as he walked briskly out the door.

***

The LCP Administrator Peggy Aldridge had already fetched takeout lunches from a deli down the street. As Dr. Pyle was leaving she entered the room carrying a large tray containing 12 sandwiches, 7 apples, 7 bananas, 14 cans of various diet sodas, and 12 packaged chocolate chip cookies and placed them on the back table.

"We eat lunch in, Sammy," said Victor. "This way we just keep going."

"Like snakes eating rats," added Ted. "Geesh, talking about rodents during lunch really isn't my thing."

"Man up!" said Charlotte, with a smile indicating she wasn't trying to be combative.

"OK, everyone, go pick up your lunch and then come to the table and let's do this. You will find paper plates and napkins."

"Is turkey available this time?" asked Stella. "Peggy said she would make sure of it. I don't touch red meat anymore, but I'm not about to become a vegetarian. Only if I suffer another arterial embolism will I ask for just lettuce and sprouts."

"Yep. It should be back there," answered Victor Graham.

Sammy was already a vegetarian by choice. Heart problems ran in his family. His father died suddenly at 54, and Sammy was only nine years away. He realized he should have informed Peggy of his self-imposed dietary restrictions, but didn't think about it and she didn't ask.

As the last one in the lunch line, Sammy was glad to see a banana and an apple. He turned the two remaining sandwiches sideways to peer through the plastic wrap. He would either have to forego what was left— ham and cheese or roast beef—or take one and remove the meat. He chose the ham and cheese, hoping no one noticed as he flipped open the top slice of bread and delicately pulled out the thin pink and white slabs.

"Hey you're picking out the best part, Sammy" shouted Wolf from across the table. "Pork is trayf,[1] but I can't get enough of it. One small sin. I never understood what cloven hooves or lack thereof has to do with anything. I don't eat their feet anyway. God forgives me. Can I have your ham, Sam?"

"OK, let's get this going," announced Victor Graham, smiling at Wolf and shaking his head. "We still need to conduct three more interviews today, and we've yet to decide what to do with this one. Who wants to start?"

Wolf lifted up one hand while taking the meat Sammy had placed on a napkin with the other. "OK, this guy screwed up big-time. But what else can we do to him? The university punished him to the tune of a half year's salary. We cannot remedy the insane cycle of loathing those two adult children have going. We can't force them into couples counseling, and I don't know what we would even charge Dr. Pyle with."

"You got right to the crux of our problem, Wolf," said Victor. "An earlier version of our ethics code admonished colleagues to act respectfully amongst themselves, but matters having to do with interprofessional

---

1 Yiddish for food not conforming to Jewish dietary law.

relationships now appear in a preamble and are considered aspirational rather than enforceable."

"Isn't that good enough?" asked Sammy.

"Not really," Wolf replied. "The code states psychologists should *aspire* to get along, but nothing in the preamble can form the basis of an ethics complaint."

Victor added, "The only enforceable principle coming close appears to concern itself more with harassment based on civil rights protections, such as race, ethnicity, religion, sexual orientation, and the like. The wording is sufficiently loose to invite a hungry lawyer into the arena if we try to use it."

"I wonder why a principle dealing with respectful relationships among peers was removed," mused Sammy. "Such a mandate would sure be helpful right now."

"Not necessarily, Sammy," Stella chimed in. "Before the change we were overrun with complaints. Anyone who had a quibble with a colleague would come crying to us. Then the other one would snap back and make a counter-charge, just like Vernon Pyle is threatening to do. It was like running a camp for highly educated juvenile delinquents."

"Agreed," added Victor. "I suspect Jade Lurch is using us as a sling-shot to launch one more pebble into Pyle's forehead. Remember her initial letter. She bashed him even to us. Accused him of academic dishonesty and refers to him as some mean-spirited mammal, I forget which one, among other things."

"Oh God almighty, I remember those cases," Archie chimed in. "A psychologist charged another psychologist with giving her gonorrhea. Then he counter-charged her for seducing him with absinthe. What a preposterous nightmare. We finally told them both to go deal with their infectious relationship on their own time."

"I'm thinking of another one," said Wolf. "Remember that clinic in San Diego where a social worker complained to the administrator that the psychologist was a racist? And when the psychologist heard about it he allegedly marched into her office and punched her in the stomach?"

"What did the Committee do?" asked Sammy, a bit taken back by the thought of a psychologist physically attacking anyone, especially a woman.

"What were we supposed to do?" asked Wolf, with upturned palms. "An assault should've been handled as such. We told the social worker to file charges with the proper authorities."

Sammy looked puzzled. "It seems like the psychologist should've been held ethically accountable as well. I mean, hitting a woman!"

Wolf sighed. "She only claimed he did it. No one else saw it. He denied it. There was no physical evidence. She didn't seek medical attention or call the authorities. It was a 'she said-he said' case. Sometimes, and this can be regrettable, we just can't deal with it from here."

"Back to *this* case," said Victor sternly. "We would not open an inquiry simply because these two have mercilessly carped at each other for years. If the institution can't keep them from ripping each other apart, neither can we. It's the nature of Vernon Pyle's final act, one involving inflicting verifiable harm. That's what he has been charged with. The current code flirts with a possible application to this case: to wit, 'Psychologists do not purposefully engage in behavior resulting in harm to others.'"

"Can 'others' be rats?" asked Sammy, adding "I mean, I'm asking seriously."

Wolf laughed. "If corporations can be like people according to the Supreme Court, then rats can be like 'others.'"

"Remember Professor Pyle said he brought them joy, a short period of freedom in an otherwise miserable little existence. I actually thought he had a point," said Ted.

"Those rats were likely scared out of their wits," Charlotte snapped back. "They never knew any life besides being in cozy cages with food and water they didn't have to forage for. The ones that got away probably ended up as road kill on Colorado Boulevard. Geesh, I never thought I'd be empathizing with stressed-out rats!"

"Forget the rats," said Victor. "Jade Lurch's research project was destroyed. She may be an unpleasant person, but that is not relevant here."

Stella raised her hand with fingers wiggling to speak. "I guess what bothers me is Dr. Pyle's lack of any regrets. On the contrary, he seems to be rather satisfied with himself, as if he is some martyred hero. The animal rights people loved it, despite the rats' ultimate fate of being swallowed whole by pythons. And if Pyle is to be believed, some of his peers approved of his actions."

"One way we can inform our decision is to come to our own consensus as to whether this was a premeditated act," Ted suggested. "Juries tend to go a little easier on crimes of passion, especially when the offenders were also being abused by the victims. Do any of you think Vernon Pyle would repeat anything this extreme again?"

"I think he would if aggravated," replied Charlotte. "As Stella just noted, he was reinforced for what he did, seeing himself as some sort of rodent emancipator. And I think Jade Lurch is more than capable of bringing out the worst in him again."

"OK, well what about this? Another way to inform our opinion is to ask if this is a first-time offense or if the accused has engaged in this type of behavior before," added Ted, who likes things to turn out the best for all concerned. "We almost always go easier on first offenders, just like in the courts of law."

"Well, he hasn't destroyed property before that we know of, but he's been a long-term active partner in this sordid tango. So, in a sense, he is hardly a first offender," said Wolf, popping the last morsel of ham into his mouth.

"Here's a complicating factor. We can sanction Vernon Pyle only," said Stella with a deep sigh. "As complicit as we may believe Jade Lurch to be, at least as a trigger, she has not been charged regarding her role in escalating the conflict to its breaking point. She's not even a member of LCP. We can't touch her."

"Getting back on track, here's what I propose we do," said Victor. "Vernon Pyle did cause verifiable harm to a person, animals, and probably a whole department. He needs to be censured. I fall short of suggesting we suspend his membership or expel him, partially because his psychotherapy clients weren't at issue. Keeping him in the ranks allows us to hear another complaint of misbehavior should one be filed. We are different from a court of law," Victor continued, now looking at Sammy. "Your 'ethics resume' can build up like a rap sheet of evidence. Priors can be dragged out again, and little tolerance is left for a second or third offense."

"Will such a warning have a constructive impact on him?" Sammy asked Victor.

"Well, in addition, if we keep him in we can mandate a conflict resolution course at his own expense and ask the instructor to verify his attendance and successful completion. Too bad we can't force Professor Lurch to take the course also. We can send a letter to both of them expressing our disdain at the way two intelligent behavioral scientists are cannibalizing each other."

"Victor, what if he doesn't want to take the course?" asked Sammy. "Can't he just say, 'No thank you?'"

"Good question. Yes, he can refuse, but then he risks having us kicking him out of our organization for noncompliance. I doubt he would welcome such exposure. Expulsions are made public, and his concern for rebuilding his reputation is too great for him to weather an ejection from the LCP. So, what say you?"

All heads nodded in the affirmative.

"Done!" shouted Victor, giving two big thumbs up.

Decision and Dispositions

A letter was drafted informing Dr. Vernon Pyle that he has been censured by the LCP for destroying his colleague's research project, thus causing her harm. Included was a mandate to complete a conflict resolution course within the next six months. Two upcoming workshops taught near Pasadena were recommended. He was also informed of what would happen if he did not comply with the directive.

Dr. Jade Lurch received a brief letter containing the usual message that the case was heard and action was taken, offering no further detail.

The Committee composed a jointly addressed letter expressing the Committee's considerable disappointment with the inability of these two colleagues to neutralize their destructive relationship. Privately, the Committee members held out slim hope that sharing an outside perspective would have any salutary impact.

Vernon Pyle reluctantly agreed to take the conflict resolution workshop, but not without protesting it would be for naught if Jade Lurch was not mandated to do the same. Nevertheless, the instructor forwarded a copy of Pyle's satisfactory completion certificate to the LPC two months later.

The entire affair was irrevocably resolved in a most paradoxical and unexpected way. Jade Lurch never got the chance to reconstruct her research project. She died suddenly four months after Vernon Pyle's hearing before the Ethics Committee from a massive brain hemorrhage caused by a previously undiagnosed tumor.

Case Commentary

Among the most difficult complaints to adjudicate in my experience involve long-warring colleagues who charge and then counter-charge their foes with ethics code violations (Koocher & Keith-Spiegel, 2008). In this story both parties and the institutional leadership should have heeded the red flags flapping vigorously for far too long before the matter intensified into mayhem. The impact of this multi-year battle no doubt took its toll on students as well as colleagues and the reputation of the department.

This story also illustrates why ethics committees are not in a position to mediate between those who are angry at each other, unless verifiable harm results as occurred in this story. However, remember that this case was on the extreme end of a continuum.

The common forms of incivility—rudeness, insults, gossip, and the like—tend to remain unfettered unless effective leaders step in.

It is worth noting that the original target, Vernon Pyle, returned hostilities towards his tormenter before attaining tenure. His value to the university as a rising star apparently protected him from employment termination. Numerous authors (e.g., Crews & West, 2006; Mawdsley, 1999) express concern that personal attributes apart from the formal criteria affect tenure decisions more often than we know about, despite disapproval by the American Association of University Professors (1999).

Notes on Incivility in Academia

"Organizational civility" involves treating others with dignity, mutually respecting others' ideas (even if not always agreeing with them), interacting constructively with colleagues while regarding each other as equals, and taking a productive role in the stewardship of the institution (DiLeo, 2005; Pearson, Andersson, & Porath, 2000, 2005). One would assume that highly educated, intelligent individuals working for years alongside the same people in the same academic setting would figure out how to get along, even if they do not like each other. Alas, academic incivility appears to be rampant, often with only a single person or a small group creating dysfunction in an entire department (Reeson, 2008; Trudel & Reio, 2011; Twale & De Luca, 2008).

"Incivility" is more typically defined as milder forms of negative interpersonal behaviors towards colleagues who may not always discern why they are targets (Pearson, et al., 2000). Behavioral examples include rudeness, insulting or disparaging comments, denigration of the target's work, and spreading false rumors (Sakurai & Jex, 2012). Coping mechanisms to being treated uncivilly include support seeking, detachment, minimization, and assertive conflict avoidance (Cortine & Magley, 2009). Unfortunately organizations often dismiss incivility as transient or trivial and fail to intervene, despite having knowledge of ongoing antagonisms (Lim, Cortina, & Magley, 2008; Powers & Maghroori, 2006).

Why do scholars sometimes treat each other badly? Among the reasons offered are stiff competition for meager resources, merit pay and promotions along with pressures to do research and to publish while also excelling at teaching and contributing to the institution (Rakes & Rakes, 1997; Reeson, 2008). Combative colleagues battling for higher status or resources are actually playing a zero-sum game by delegitimizing the accomplishments of both (Powers and Mahjroori, 2006). If those in academic leadership positions fail to take action, incivility can devolve into more intense behaviors, such as outright aggression and open conflict (Basu, 2012; Johnson & Indvik, 2001; Powers & Maghroori, 2006; Taylor & Kluemper, 2012; Trudel & Reio, 2011).

Discussion Questions

1. Is it acceptable to dismiss one employee if it will resolve a problem caused by another employee? That is, should Professor Pyle have been denied tenure given the unrelenting disturbances the (already tenured) Professor Lurch's intense dislike for him caused the department?

2. On a 1-to-10 scale (1 being "no sympathy" and 10 being "very sympathetic"), how do you feel about Professor Vernon Pyle's ultimate act of retaliation? Why did you respond as you did?

3. If you were the department chair or a university administrator, what would you have done when you realized the dispute between these two players was not going to be resolved and could possibly escalate?

4. Is "incivility" a legitimate criterion when making personnel decisions? That is, should those who are doing satisfactory work as teachers, researchers, and contributors to college affairs be denied tenure solely because:
   a. very few of their colleagues like them?
   b. they constantly criticize the scholarly work of others?
   c. are often rude or insulting to colleagues during strictly personal (nonacademic) interactions?

5. *"Academic politics is much more vicious than real politics. We think it's because the stakes are so small."* This intriguing quote

is attributed to Columbia University professor Richard Neustadt (with very similar wording attributed to several others, including Wallace Stanley Sayre and Henry Kissinger). What do you think this quote means, and how might it apply to this story?

6. Barsky (2002) suggests the unique organizational structure of colleges and universities contributes to incivility. The structure has a hierarchical administration but professors view themselves as self-governing, departments seek to operate independently, and a tenure system provides job security. How does such a structure facilitate conflict?

7. Student handbooks set out behavioral expectations, but faculty handbooks rarely do the same. Do you agree with Basu (2012) that a formal policy of expectations for faculty behavior would minimize incivility?

8. "Incivility" may be only in the eyes of the beholder. That is, a remark may be taken as insulting, but was not intended to be rude or hostile. No bright line separates "academic freedom" or "scholarly criticism" from "incivility." How does this blur the possibility of dealing effectively with the problem of incivility on college and university campuses?

References

American Association of University Professors (1999). *On collegiality as a criterion for faculty evaluation*. Retrieved from http://www.aaup.org/AAUP/pubsres/policydocs/contents/collegiality.htm

Barsky, A. E. (2002). Structural sources of conflict in a university context. *Conflict Resolution Quarterly, 20*, 161–176.

Basu, K. (June 15, 2012). Bad professor. *Inside Higher Ed*. Retrieved from http://www.insidehighered.com/news/2012/06/15/how-tackle-incivility-among-faculty-members#ixzz2DpDZTSk6

Cortina, L. M., & Magley, V. J. (2009). Patterns and profiles of response to incivility in the workplace. *Journal of Occupational Health Psychology, 14*, 272–288.

Crews, G. A., & West, A. D. (2006). Professional integrity in higher education: Behind the green curtain in the Land of Oz. *American Journal of Criminal Justice, 30*, 143–161.

DiLeo, J. R. (2005). Uncollegiality, tenure, and the weasel clause. (2005). *Symploke, 13*, 99–107.

Johnson, P. R., & Indvik, J. (2001). Rudeness at work: Impulse over restraint. *Public Personnel Management, 30*, 457–465.

Koocher, G. P., & Keith-Spiegel, P. (2008). *Ethics in psychology and the mental health professions*. New York, NY: Oxford University Press.

Lim, S., Cortina, L. M., & Magley, V. J. (2008). Personal and workgroup incivility: Impact on work and health outcomes. *Journal of Applied Psychology*, *93*, 95–107.

Mawdsley, R. D. (1999). Collegiality as a factor in tenure decisions. *Journal of Personnel Evaluation in Education*, *13*, 167–177.

Pearson, C. M., Andersson, L. M., & Porath, C. L. (2000). Assessing and attacking workplace incivility. *Organizational Dynamics*, *29*, 123–137.

Pearson, C. M., Andersson, L. M., & Porath, C. L. (2005). Workplace incivility. In Fox, S., & Spector, P. E. (Eds.). *Counterproductive work behavior: Investigations of actors and targets.* (pp. 177–200). Washington, DC: American Psychological Association.

Powers, C., & Maghroori, R. (2006). How to avoid having dysfunctional departments on your campus. *Academic Leader, 22*, 4–6.

Rakes, G. C., & Rakes, T. A. (1997). Encouraging faculty collegiality: A paradigm for higher education. *National Forum of Educational Administration and Supervision Journal, 14*, 3–12.

Reeson, N. (Dec. 4, 2008). The function of dysfunction. *Chronicle of Higher Education.* Retrieved from http://chronicle.com/article/The-function-of-dysfunction/45866

Sakurai, K., & Jex, S. M. (2012). Coworker incivility and incivility targets' work effort and counterproductive work behaviors: The moderating role of supervisor social support. *Journal of Occupational Health Psychology*, *17*, 150–161.

Taylor, S. G., & Kluemper, D. H. (2012). Linking perceptions of role stress and incivility to workplace aggression: The moderating role of personality. *Journal of Occupational Health Psychology*, *17*, 316–329.

Trudel, J., & Reio, T. G. (Washington, DC, 2011). Workplace incivility and conflict management styles: Their impact on job performance, organizational commitments, and turnover intent. Paper delivered at the annual meeting of the American Psychological Association.

Twale, D. J., & De Luca, B. M. (2008). *Faculty incivility: The rise of the academic bully culture and what to do about it.* San Francisco, CA: Jossey-Bass.

Additional Reading

Braxton, J. M., & Bayer, A. E. (1999). *Faculty misconduct in collegiate teaching.* Baltimore, MD: Johns Hopkins University Press.

Braxton, J. M., Proper, E., & Bayer, A. E. (2011). *Professors behaving badly.* Baltimore, MD: Johns Hopkins University Press.

Gajda, A. (2009). *The trials of academe.* Cambridge, MA: Harvard University Press.

Gunsalus, C. K. (2006). *The college administrator's survival guide.* Cambridge, MA: Harvard University Press.

Smith, P., Phillips, T. L., & King, R. D. (2010). *Incivility.* Cambridge, MA: Cambridge University Press.

Sutton, R. I. (2010). *The no asshole rule: Building a civilized workplace and surviving one that isn't.* New York, NY: Business Plus.

five
THE JOHN

Sexual activity between psychotherapists and their clients is a serious ethical violation. In this story, a psychologist appears to justify his predatory behavior by viewing the offering of himself as a therapeutic intervention for "certain women." Although the particulars of this case are unusual, rationalizing that no harm will result from sexual liaisons with clients is far more common.

Megan Mahoney attracted attention for doing absolutely nothing. Daisy Mahoney basked in her daughter's remarkable appearance from the minute she set eyes on her newborn baby girl. "This one will break hearts," the neonatal nurse whispered as she placed the bundled infant into Daisy's outstretched arms.

By age two, strangers stopped to tousle Megan's loose locks of strawberry blonde hair and peered approvingly into her wide-set green eyes. The fawning reactions from people Daisy did not even know sustained her reason for existence. "She is the most beautiful child I have ever seen," was so frequent a comment, leaving Daisy to resent anyone who didn't take notice. Megan became a portable objet d'art, and Daisy was its creator.

Megan would become Daisy's obsession. She took complete control of the girl's every waking move. Upon leaving the house for any reason, even for a trip to the post office, Daisy dressed Megan to perfection in pastel ruffles, lace, and taffeta. A matching satin ribbon in her perfectly formed curls and shiny white patent leather shoes with tiny flowers embroidered on pink socks completed the image of a flawless living doll.

Megan's submissive demeanor became enduringly lodged during her formative years when following Daisy's orders was the sole path to receiving motherly attention and approval. Her accommodating manner also defused envy among her peers. Academically Megan excelled at nothing. Yet because she complied as best she could with any request, her teachers viewed her with fondness and passed her through one school year to the next. Daisy remained unconcerned with Megan's negligible educational achievements. As she put it, "Megan will never need brains to get to wherever *we* want to go." A life-long team with Daisy as the puppeteer.

Megan's body matured tall, slender, and stunningly curved. She prevailed in any competition requiring physical beauty rather than cultivated talent or mental prowess. Miss Valentine. School Sweetheart. Homecoming Queen. She graduated from high school at the bottom of her class, never questioning if she could have done better. No one seemed concerned with Megan's lack of academic accomplishments or any other potential talent. Her internal attributes were, by now, unexplored and undeveloped.

The symbiotic mother–daughter attachment began to splinter shortly after Megan graduated from high school. She finally grasped that her physical appearance belonged to her and her alone and began to see her mother as a tag-along, sopping up whatever adoration spilt over. Megan wanted to shake loose and knew only one way out. Get away from Daisy.

Megan met Joe Minetta at the convenience store down the street from the apartment she had shared with her mother ever since her father left when she was three for destinations unknown. Twelve years Megan's senior, Joe appeared to be markedly different from the boys she knew from school. This tall, lanky, and roughly handsome masonry supplies salesman seemed to see beyond her external appearance. Within two weeks Joe loaded up his pickup truck to head for Las Vegas with a mattress, small couch, card table, four folding chairs, a 32-inch television set, six cartons of personal items, a cat named Dillinger, and Megan. Megan left only a brief note informing Daisy of her decision to go off on her own, adding she would call when she got settled. She would never make that call.

Joe and Megan married in the Las Vegas Ice Chapel, a small mirrored room draped with gauze sprayed with silver glitter. A white altar table topped with a slab of thick transparent plastic, presumably to resemble an iceberg, and two silver candelabras in need of polishing completed the garish décor. An affable, plump woman with cropped salt-and-pepper hair wearing a white cotton peasant blouse and full white skirt processed the paperwork before conducting the brief ceremony. A podgy, bald man dressed in work clothes and heavy rubber boots served as the witness. Megan had long dreamed of a huge wedding and walking down the aisle in a Vera Wang gown. But freedom had its price.

It soon became apparent to Megan that Joe had an agenda extending beyond marital bliss. He convinced her that Las Vegas showgirls earn lots of money, enough for them to have whatever they wanted. A house in the suburbs. A Jaguar XK.

Megan never learned to dance. Indeed, she had never learned how to do much of anything. Nevertheless she agreed to take lessons. At the end of the third hour her instructor took her aside to whisper gently, "You are a gorgeous woman, but rhythm is not in your genes." Joe, not to be dissuaded from how he might profit from his young bride, had another idea he thought would bring in ten times a showgirl's evening take.

"Prostitution is legal in Nevada, you know," Joe announced one night over dinner, "which means doing guys is a respectable gig." He purposely neglected to inform her that legal prostitution existed only in heavily regulated brothels, and none were in Clark County. Furthermore, Joe had no intention of splitting her earnings with anyone. Megan objected to this crude proposition, but taking orders was the one thing she was good at. She finally relented and took to the streets almost every night, easily attracting men who left their wives at home to attend business conventions by day and transition to gambling, liquor, and purchased sex by night.

***

Now, ten years later and alone in San Francisco, Megan was tired. She had dumped Joe five years earlier just as she did with Daisy, catching a bus while Joe was out running a con or drinking, taking only what would fit into a large canvas suitcase and the seven thousand dollars she had accumulated on the sly and kept hidden in a boot in the rear of the closet. "I'm on my way back to Arkansas" was all she scrawled on a paper napkin, even though she had no intention of ever going home. Working solo with a few regular Johns and using the name Megan LaFleur, she made enough to buy the right clothes and to rent a small downtown apartment. She was proficient in the world's oldest profession, but remained unable to shake the discontent with what her life had become.

The mirror was becoming a constant reminder of how time marched forward. The slight hollows in her cheeks and barely visible lines around her eyes and mouth needed careful camouflaging. The skin on her still-well-shaped body was just beginning to show traces of slippage, sags-in-waiting. She stayed in bed, alone, more often. When she ventured out from her apartment on Hayes Street for her daily morning walk, she observed the women on Van Ness Avenue walking briskly in their stylish business attire. Briefcases swung to the rhythm of their confident strides on their way to their jobs in San Francisco's civic center. These women, many now younger than she and some almost as pretty, were going somewhere in life with assurance and pride. She longed to know how that felt.

Yolanda Houser, Megan's only close friend and another escort, had both street and book smarts. Yolanda almost completed college before cocaine abuse permanently stalled her academic career.

"Sweetie, you're depressed and in need of some serious psychotherapy," Yolanda pronounced one afternoon when Megan seemed especially worn down. Megan found herself unexpectedly attracted to Yolanda's suggestion to seek professional counseling, someone to talk to who would help her find a different way to live. Maybe she would find something fresh inside herself, a better part than she could imagine now. Thumbing through the phone book they found a listing for a licensed psychologist only five blocks from Megan's apartment. Dr. Karl Timmuck, Ph.D.

Megan took immediately to Dr. Timmuck, though not in any physical way. He appeared as a sturdily built man of 50 or so with wavy dark grey hair lying flat on his elongated head with large square-shaped ears and eyes so small that she couldn't tell what color they were. She thought he looked a little like a Mr. Potato Head, but was enchanted with the way he focused on her concerns, an experience with which she was totally unfamiliar. He listened and watched intently as she spoke, nodding with a sympathetic slightly furrowed brow, and reaching out to tenderly touch her hand with his fingertips whenever she seemed distressed or started to weep. Although she struggled to speak about herself at first, by the middle of the second session the words poured out as effortlessly as her tears. Sometimes she thought she was drowning in her own flood of articulated thoughts and emotions. Yet afterwards she always felt both lighter and steadier.

Megan started looking forward to the next session with Dr. Timmuck as soon as the one in progress ended. No one had ever cared about what she had to say. A glimmering kernel of something new was beginning to flicker inside her consciousness. It felt strong, clean, and almost large enough for her to see what it was. This nascent emergence from a robotic, reactionary existence was nothing less than exhilarating. Dr. Timmuck became increasingly adamant in his attempts to convince Megan to love herself no matter what her life had become, that she was an outstanding human being exactly as she was. This felt good. She was beginning to heal. If only she could shed the remaining weight of self-loathing, she could fly.

Megan had finally found a haven, a place to be just about her, a space to be accepted without being judged. At the conclusion of their 22nd session she sprang up to give Dr. Timmuck an extra-tight hug to express her gratitude. Appreciation turned rapidly to confusion when Dr. Timmuck gently placed his hands on her shoulders and moved her backwards as he announced how remarkable her progress had been, so admirable that she no longer required psychotherapy. She would not need to return to his office.

Puzzled, unsteady, and almost nauseated, Megan started to leave, turning around once to make sure he had not changed his mind. He smiled while giving a dismissive wave. She walked back to her apartment in a daze. After cancelling her evening appointment with one of her regular consorts, she went to her bathroom to vomit. Afterwards, as she fixed herself some cream of chicken soup to calm her ravaged stomach, she heard a knock at the door.

***

When Yolanda Houser came to visit the next afternoon, she found Megan looking miserable and lost. Still dressed in her robe with a face swollen and tear-stained, Yolanda almost didn't recognize her.

"I'll never be more than what I am now. I will only be less soon enough," Megan wailed before spilling out what happened the evening before and how she saw herself as no more than a hunk of aging meat. Even two hot showers couldn't eliminate the sensation of being awash in slime.

"Here's what we're going to do, honey," Yolanda said in her take-charge voice. "A class I took in college covered some ethics stuff. If he belongs to a professional organization we may be able to make sure this motherfucker gets what's coming to him!"

Yolanda called the LCP office to confirm Karl Timmuck's membership status. She wrote down to whom and where to send an ethics complaint. Megan awkwardly penned out the first formal letter she had ever written.

Dear Sirs,

I am not sure if you can help me. I had a very upsetting experience with a psicologist. He cost me a lot of money and he made me worse. Very much worse. I want to know if this is what psicologists do.

I am not proud of what I do. It makes me tired and sad. I am with men. I want to do more with my life. I like to talk to people. I could be a psicologist but I think you need more than just high school. Anyways I wanted to find my way out of my life I have now. I told Dr. Timmuck about this. He said nice things about me and paid me a lot of attention. I also like being the one paying to see a man and there was no sex. I saw him 22 times for $2,200 cash. I was starting to feel much better. But then Dr. Timmuck told me I was fine and did not have to come back. I said I still did not feel good about myself. But he said I had done really good in a short time. This did not feel right.

That same night he showed up at my door with a bottle and a proposition. I told him I was ill and closed the door. Then I got sick all over my bathroom.

I did not return his calls. He left messages saying he would pay me the same as I had paid him. He also said me having sex with him would make me feel much better because he was a psicologist and that was a compliment to me.

What I want to know is why I am so much worse now. Was this OK for him to do? My friend Yolanda says no and she made me write this letter.

Thank you,

Megan LaFleur

***

Karl Timmuck, Ph.D., accepted the certified letter without the slightest inkling as to why the League of California Psychologists would communicate with him in such a formal manner. His jaw dropped and his heart raced as he read the opening paragraph.

"That messed-up common whore! After everything I did to make her more comfortable with her lot in life, and at less than my usual fee," he grumbled.

Dear Dr. Timmuck,

We received a letter from Megan LaFleur, one of your previous clients, who claims you terminated your services prematurely and abruptly and then presented yourself as wanting to partake of her services as an escort. If true, this would constitute several violations of the LCP Ethics Code, including improper termination and a subsequent inappropriate act that may have worsened Miss LaFleur's emotional condition.

You must make an appointment with the LCP administrator, Mrs. Peggy Aldridge, to appear before the LCP Ethics Committee at its March meeting unless there is a compelling reason to request a postponement. We expect you will be able to respond in detail to Ms. LaFleur's allegations. Ms. LaFleur has signed a release allowing you to discuss the matter with us. Failure to contact us within 10 days of the receipt of this letter will constitute an act of noncompliance, which is itself an ethics violation.
Sincerely,

Victor Graham, Ph.D.
Chair, Ethics Committee
League of California Psychologists

"I tried to tell her she was doing everything possible given the poverty of her intellect and how she needed to understand how making the best of it would be her only salvation. And she betrays me like this!" he stammered out loud, crumpling the certified letter into a tight wad and smashing it on his desk. He recalled how he encouraged his female clients who felt empty to take some classes or at least find a distraction from their emotionally impoverished existences. Sometimes he suggested they have another baby if they were otherwise stuck at home. But Megan was unsuited to his remedies for women's unfulfilled lives.

Now she tattled about his visit to her apartment to those who could actually do him harm. He had been so careful in the past. It had been over six months since he bedded a client, a young woman he evaluated as part of her workers compensation claim. Celina Lopez, a housekeeper at a deteriorating hotel who fell down an unlit back stairway, depended on Timmuck's mental disability evaluation to qualify for some monetary relief while her injuries healed. During the last of three sessions she acquiesced to his hand running slowly down her back, slipping around her waist to the front of her blouse while leading her to the 8-foot Italian leather couch spanning the back wall of his office. He let her down gently and removed only her skirt and panties. She seemed tense, frightened maybe, but her uneasiness amplified his arousal. Only he released. He would have preferred a reciprocal climax, but it was sufficiently satisfying to elevate him to a triumphant plane he experienced all too infrequently.

Emily Timmuck, Karl's wife of 22 years, had long since let it be known that she found him unattractive, both as a man and as a human being. Too stubborn to divorce, and neither willing to leave their upscale Victoria townhouse, they stayed together as semi-functional roommates passing each other in the hallways and speaking rarely. He ate most meals out at the small ethnic eateries within walking distance from his office and would take on as many clients as hours in a day, even those unable to pay full fee or whose insurance was paltry compared to what he charged his wealthier clients. He needed to absorb their energy, laden with anguish as it often was, to feel more substantial and less wretched.

With female clients he found to be at least somewhat attractive and minimally powerful—women with self-confidence or quick to anger were excluded from consideration no matter how good they looked—he began ripening them for the taking with a three-stage process he called "The Plan." First he would gain their confidence, then become their admirer, and ultimately their redeemer, their ultimate salvation. By the third stage, he perceived them as mere putty ready to be molded anew. But California law had become strict about such liaisons, even making sexual relationships with psychotherapy clients an offense possibly punishable by jail time, thus diminishing the frequency of his sexual "treatment." Now he targeted only an occasional exceptionally fragile woman to "help," one unlikely to have either the resources or gumption to complain to anyone about his special therapeutic technique.

At first Megan LaFleur appeared a perfect fit for "The Plan." Beautiful, sad, meek, vacuous, and compliant. When he learned what she did to earn his fee, however, he made a cerebral decision to forego the opportunity as too reckless. "She may already be eaten up inside by some venereal virus," he thought to himself while shuddering. It was safer to classify Megan as a cash cow and string her out for as long as possible.

He knew Megan liked being with him, and $100 an hour was a decent enough fee for feigning active listening to her drone on, spilling out her unachievable ambitious and inaccessible dreams. At least for a while. Her unending verbal and tear streams became tiresome after the second month, especially when she began to look at him inquisitively whenever he made tentative attempts to suggest accepting her current situation as it is.

"How could such a person ever rise above her circumstances?" he often pondered after her sessions. He wanted to tell her outright there was nowhere else for her to go. Maintaining her health and appearance might work for another ten years, but she needed to start saving for beyond age 40. Yet by the twelfth session he found her soft voice and amazing green eyes gazing at him with such enormous respect seductive. Now he also looked forward to his time with Megan, and began to revise his therapeutic strategy to include himself as a more active player in her deliverance.

On those days when Megan took more care with her appearance, he felt virile again. She entered the office on the 13th session wearing a flowing white silky top with a deep scoop neck, zebra print tights, and black lace-up boots. Her pale auburn hair flowed over her shoulders and cascaded to her breasts. She smelled of lilacs. Her makeup was impeccable, not too much, just right. This day she presented herself at stark variance with her more usual attire: jeans and a sweater, hair back in a messy knot, and no makeup. Even though he surmised she had come from servicing one of her paying customers, he became aroused.

After that day, Karl Timmuck began to craft an alternative treatment plan for Megan LaFleur. He could best help her by proving how an educated man of his stature found her to be acceptable just the way she was. He would even be willing to make a substantial financial sacrifice to do it, not only by saving her the cost of his services but by paying her for hers. She would then experience an astounding breakthrough, like lightening slicing through dense fog, alleviating her insecurities and liberating her from shame. Protection would placate the fear of contracting a disease.

Now he thought of little else than his time with Megan LaFleur. Sometimes he lost track during sessions with his other clients, once having to apologize when a school teacher struggling with how to come out to her family as a lesbian asked the question three times before shaking him out of his reverie.

Fantasies of Megan's body thrashing in rhythm with his now consumed him. But not in his office. The Italian leather couch was for more ordinary female clients suited for his special treatment. He imagined himself and Megan as naked as Adam and Eve before The Fall, perhaps on a deserted grassy spot in John Muir Park among the giant redwoods and ferns, or maybe on a soft blanket on Stinson Beach as dawn broke. He would lay her down with care before thrusting himself into her. She would let out a sharp squeal from a mixture of surprise and delight. In his fantasies they never spoke, thus eliminating the distraction of Megan's banal chatter. Now he thought his groin would rupture if he had to sit with a heavy mahogany desk between them for even one more session.

Strike day arrived on the twenty-second visit. "The Plan" was ripe for implementation. As she left his office that last week she expressed with fervor how much he meant to her. She put her arms around him so tightly that her breasts and pubic bone practically indented his body, a sure sign she was obtainable, that he had succeeded in moving this liaison to its inevitable finale.

"Megan, my dear, you are doing so well. Psychotherapy is no longer required. You will not have to come back next week."

Her expression turned to shock. "What...what do you mean? I need to keep coming here. I am getting better, but I'm not done."

"I'm the professional, dear Megan. Trust me. Therapy is no longer necessary. I'll see you around I am sure." As he spoke he mentally visualized what she did not yet know. Her upset would be temporary. Only a few hours. Then she would burst into delirious delight.

Dr. Timmuck went home and fixed himself an early dinner of kielbasa and leftover tabouli, took a shower, dressed in a pale blue silk shirt, gray slacks and grey lizard loafers, yelled at Emily who was probably around somewhere that he was leaving to meet with his evening clients, and stuck a bottle of *Dom Perignon Rosé 2002* he had stowed in the back of the bar refrigerator into his briefcase. He parked his car across from Megan's apartment and waited to make reasonably sure she was alone. Various scenarios of what would happen next danced through his imagination. She would be overjoyed when she opened the door. They would toast with champagne while excitedly mulling the advantages of this new phase in their relationship before retreating into her bed to make passionate love. Or, she would fling her arms around him and joyfully declare her wildest dreams had finally come true and practically take him right there in the hallway, sipping champagne afterwards in the afterglow of exhilarating lovemaking.

It seemed safe when, after 45 minutes, no man left though the main entrance. He went up the stairs and knocked on her door, setting his jaw in a cheery smile while displaying the champagne bottle in his uplifted arms. Megan opened the door.

"Here I am. You didn't think I would really let you go, did you? Let's do it your way and I'll pay you from now on," he said, expecting her lovely mouth to break into the full smile he had longed to see.

Instead Megan gasped. "I'm ill," she mumbled as she slammed the door shut.

He stood in the hallway, bewildered. "What just happened?" he asked himself in disbelief. His right eye began to involuntarily twitch as it did when he was distressed. Yet Megan had always been forthright, so he reluctantly accepted her excuse for not inviting him in. He would wait a week and try again. Maybe she would contact him when she was better, but conceded that isn't the way call girls work. You call them.

He left two more messages, pleading the need to get together at her place and why she would be very pleased with how he was willing to help her in this new way. His calls went unreturned.

Now he had a certified letter from the LCP Ethics Committee accusing him of wrongdoing. "She screwed me alright, just not in the way I planned," he thought. At least he was confident he had a sure-fire defense, and Megan LaFleur would have to go it alone from now on, despondent and pathetic.

"That's what you get for biting the hand that feeds you, slut!" he repeated to himself many times over while plotting his vindication of all charges of wrongdoing.

The Ethics Committee:
Karl Timmuck, Ph.D. March 16, 1:05 p.m.

"Here's one for the books," Victor Graham roared with uncommon enthusiasm. Balancing cups of coffee and what was left of the cookies, the members scurried back to the conference table. "I'll read the letter from Miss LaFleur to you, and I don't want to hear a single peep until I am finished." Victor now sounded serious.

After the reading Stella Sarkosky crossed her arms over her chest and sucked in enough air to ignite a coughing spell. Wolf Levin threw up his hands, shouting "What the hell was this Bozo thinking?" Archie Wittig swung his head back and forth while rising up to get Stella a glass of water.

Sammy Halsey tried to take it in. He chose to be a clinical psychologist to help unhappy and vulnerable people, as hokey as that sounded even to him. He would have made more money as an attorney like his father. He had the grades in college to get into a good law school. But financial gain did not drive the choice for his life's work. He treated many clients at a greatly reduced fee and donated a half day a week at a walk-in free clinic in downtown Santa Cruz. Megan is the kind of client he could help, he thought to himself. She wanted to change, to emerge, to explore possibilities, and was apparently horribly betrayed.

Sammy was prepared to dislike Karl Timmuck. He pictured him as a huge pig, plump, pink and bald with pointy ears, a flat roundish nose and beady eyes. When Victor Graham went to fetch Dr. Timmuck, he returned with a middle-aged man still in pretty good shape, but with greasy hair slicked back, a long face and large ears. Only his small eyes almost touching the bridge of his nose matched Sammy's preconceived image. He wore a green sports coat with a plaid shirt and no tie, jeans, and red sneakers with white gym socks. "That's California," Sammy said to himself.

Despite his unimposing and mismatched appearance, Dr. Timmuck's stride was brusque and his expression indignant. Victor ushered him to the chair to his right. As he sat down he removed a folder from his brief-case and flung it down on the table.

"So, Dr. Timmuck," Victor drawled after announcing the names of the other members while pointing them out, "as you know you have been accused by a previous client of abruptly discontinuing therapy and engaging in inappropriate post-termination behavior. Please tell us your side of the story."

"Of course. And, as you will soon come to understand, this meeting is a waste of your time and certainly a waste of mine. I had to fly almost 400 miles, consuming my whole day for such an absurd escapade."

Karl Timmuck acted as though this matter was a wicked joke being played on him. He seemed unaware of the silent reactions of the Committee members. Ted Bates' whole face crinkled, looking like someone took at it with a Sharpie. Charlotte Burroughs wrinkled her nose, and Stella Sarkosky sucked in both lips as she always did when she knew what she would say would be unacceptable. Wolf's eyes closed into slits of disdain while Archie Wittig flared his nostrils. Sammy's face expressed disbelief at how anyone could be so crass in front of an ethics committee. It didn't strike him as getting off on a good footing. Only Victor Graham maintained a steady, sober expression.

"Let's please just hear your side of things," Victor said flatly.

"Fine. First, you know what Miss LaFleur does for a living, right? She gets paid for sex, and you know what that makes her," Timmuck said with a snide smile. "Second, Miss LaFleur would not process a word I said as I attempted to help her accept herself and her circumstances. I think she mistook it for flattery. She drew some bad relationship cards in her life, a narcissistic and controlling mother and a jerk of a husband who got her into this business, but that's not my fault. The truth is her goals were simply, well, ridiculous. She wanted to be a nurse, then a fashion designer, then of all things, a psychologist."

"You did not consider any other alternatives for her besides the life she was living? She came to therapy for that reason, did she not?" asked Ted, trying to sound business-like.

"Look. She barely graduated high school," Timmuck answered, laying out his arms with fingers splayed wide on the table. "If I thought of anything else she could do to support herself, I would have encouraged her. But she was—and I must be blunt here—dumb as road gravel. She never even read a book all the way through. She told me she started on a novel once, but lost interest. Said she read too slowly. Too many words she did not know. Where can you go from there?"

"So, you never presented other alternatives and resources?" Ted asked to make sure he understood what Timmuck just said.

"No. I told you why. What would you have done with someone like that?"

Ted appeared ready to spring with an answer, but Victor Graham interrupted. "With all due respect, Dr. Timmuck, we will ask the questions. Why did you terminate her so abruptly? She contends she had no warning."

"Well she had plenty of warning. For at least two months I had encouraged her to accept herself, and if she took my advice as mere adulation, that again is her error. She would not budge, wanting to become this or that instead of making the best of what she was. Nothing else I could do for her. In fact, I apparently need to point out to you people that I did the ethical thing by terminating her. To continue seeing her as a client would have violated your own rules. Look, look right here," he whisked a copy of the LCP Ethics Code from his briefcase and pointed to the relevant principle he had circled in red. "It says you have to terminate when a client is no longer benefitting from your services. Should I read it out loud to you?" he asked with a triumphant smirk.

"That won't be necessary," Victor answered stiffly. "Notice the code requires termination to be done sensitively. You might have considered referring her to someone else who may be more capable of treating her."

"Are you criticizing my ability to do therapy now?" Timmuck growled. "Look, I was as sensitive as I could possibly muster about letting her go as my client, but I wasn't going to just dump her. We will get to that part I am sure. But what you need to understand is if I couldn't help her with traditional psychotherapy, then no one could."

The Committee members seemed to agree silently that Dr. Timmuck had said all he had to say on this particular aspect of the complaint and continued questioning would yield unproductive vexation but no new information. It was important he remain composed enough to discuss the visit to her apartment.

"Please tell us now about why you went to her home," said Charlotte in a hushed voice, hoping to elicit a calmer response.

"Well it isn't a home *per se,*" Timmuck replied derisively. "She does sleep in her apartment, but not necessarily alone." He let out another disparaging chortle. "I went to her place of business," folding his hands on the table as if he needed to say nothing else.

"Did you go to be one of her, uh, paying patrons yourself?" asked Wolf, eyes still squinting.

"I wouldn't put it that way. I went there to continue our relationship, although I would no longer be her therapist. How better to help her accept herself? She liked and trusted me. And this would be the perfect way to help her, to prove I was willing to give myself intimately to her. So the termination was hardly abrupt because I decided to continue to be a part of her life and even forgo my financial advantage."

"So, you saw your actions as an appropriate way to help Megan LaFleur? Would that be an accurate summary of your defense?" asked Stella, in a voice barely disguising antipathy.

"Look, if you must be so succinct, although it leaves out all the detail of the rationale, you have it about right. And, even though she turned against me, I would point out we never consummated a sexual relationship. So, I am guilty of nothing, and I have a 5 p.m. plane to catch and want to leave now to miss the worst traffic. A taxi should already be waiting. I asked your girl to call one after 20 minutes." Karl Timmuck started gathering up his papers and stuffing them in a briefcase.

Ted leaned forward on the table, sporting the most serious expression the others could recall. "Dr. Timmuck, you appear to be aware of the provisions of the ethics code. Sexual relations with clients are best to avoid in perpetuity, but if a psychologist can justify that exploitation was not involved, a two year moratorium is in place. The timeframe between terminating Megan and showing up to have sex with her was what? About five hours?"

"Ah, there is where you have erred in interpreting the meaning of your own code, my good man. I planned to enter into a business arrangement with her. She's a businesswoman. The ethics code does not say anything about any waiting period to purchase an ex-client's merchandise." Timmuck sat back down looking smug, confident he had not only prevailed in the argument but also made a fool of Ted.

Stella again sucked both lips into her mouth. The others glanced at each other in disbelief.

"Have you told us all you want to say? We need to make sure you had a chance to be thorough," queried Victor.

"Yes, yes. I will let myself out. Have a good day!" Karl Timmuck said in a tone exuding condescension, and strode upright as a yardstick before bursting through the door.

***

"Can you believe that fucking pervert?" Wolf bellowed as the door slammed behind Dr. Timmuck.

"OK, let's all calm down and deal with this," said Victor, scowling at Wolf. "Karl Timmuck may not be a loveable guy, but we need to stick strictly to his professional behavior, or lack thereof. Let's start with the termination."

"I say it was inappropriate because Megan didn't accept it," said Wolf. "Termination can be tricky, as we all know. But it's something to work through between client and therapist. This creep just made up his own mind because his gratification needs weren't being met. Poor woman didn't see the bullet coming."

"I bet he's had sex with a lot of his clients if the truth were to be known," surmised Stella. "His view of women is simply appalling."

"He shouldn't be allowed to treat anyone with two X chromosomes," chimed in Charlotte.

Victor tapped on the table. "We can't know what else he has done and we can't go on what we imagine he might have done. We have to stay with what we can discern based solely on what evidence we have. Do we all agree the termination was executed sufficiently inappropriately to warrant an ethical violation?"

All hands quickly rose in agreement.

"Now, as to showing up at her doorstep. He has one point. They never actually engaged in anything qualifying as sexual behavior," said Victor.

"She didn't let him in the door!" Stella shrieked. "That's like the vile degenerate on the news last night charged with attempted murder only because the woman he sliced up with a hunting knife didn't bleed all the way out before she was accidentally discovered unconscious in a ditch by a passerby."

"Are we saying Megan herself saved him from the punishment he deserves?" Sammy proposed. "How sadly ironic."

"Not necessarily," Victor answered. "Some less specific sections of the code can be considered. He did not treat Megan with respect. He violated acceptable professional boundaries. He clearly planned to exploit her. He even admitted it. In essence, and speaking of irony, his arrogant defense was an excellent witness on behalf of Megan LaFleur."

"Well if they never had sex, isn't there something else besides a wrongful termination?" wailed Sammy "I mean, this guy is a pig."

"Sammy, don't insult pigs," quipped Wolf.

"Well, we do have something else," said Victor. "Sometimes the more general principles are handy, as they are is in this case. 'Psychologists avoid conflicts-of-interest and acts that could reasonably lead to exploitation of clients.' Timmuck all but confessed to setting out to exploit her. I think we can go with that."

"Sounds good to me," Wolf responded. The others all shook their heads in enthusiastic agreement.

Decision and Dispositions

After laying out Dr. Karl Timmuck's violations involving an improper termination and exploitation and the rationale for their decision accompanied by a statement strongly doubting any potential for rehabilitation, the Committee recommended expulsion to the LCP Board of Directors. Dr. Timmuck was informed of the Committee's decision, noting he would be hearing from the LCP Board of Directors within 60 days. Forty days later, Dr. Timmuck received a letter informing him of his expulsion from the LPC for unprofessional conduct and its pending notification to the licensing board.

Megan La Fleur received the standard follow-up letter informing her that the charge against Dr. Timmuck had been thoroughly reviewed and appropriate action taken. The LPC offered to contact a psychologist in the San Francisco Bay area who could help her find a psychotherapist who would have only her interests and welfare at heart.

Megan accepted the offer of assistance to locate a new therapist. Six months later she sent a note to the LCP office to report satisfaction with her new psychologist, had stopped seeing men for money, and enjoyed her day job on the sales staff of an upscale fashion boutique near the Embarcadero.

Karl Timmuck was outraged. He addressed a letter to "The Clowns Who Run the League of California Psychologists" vowing to appeal the Ethics Committee decision all the way to the United States Supreme Court. Several weeks later his lawyer contacted the LCP requesting reconsideration of Karl Timmuck's penalty as politely as legal language allows. Before the LCP had a chance to reject the proposition, it became known that a woman who had seen Dr. Timmuck briefly for a Workman's Compensation evaluation based on injuries during a fall at her place of work, and with the support of her new psychotherapist, had already contacted the California Board of Psychology accusing Karl Timmuck of sexual misconduct. After an investigation he lost his license to practice psychology.

Case Commentary

The committee members had no foreknowledge of Dr. Timmuck's previous exploits and decided, largely based on his demeanor and self-incriminating disclosures, he was not a suitable candidate for remaining in the ranks, even with mandated supervision, continuing education, and psychotherapy. Were they aware of all the facts, Dr. Timmuck's unsuitability for rehabilitation would have been more apparent. Some have asserted the recidivism rate for sexually exploitative psychotherapists is high (e.g., Pope, 1989) although others contend these data were improperly analyzed (see Sonne, 2012). Irregardless, the debate remains as to whether previous offenders should ever be returned to practice (Pope & Vasquez, 2011).

The Committee discussed the issue of premature termination. The timing of termination is a serious issue and must be done with thoughtfulness and care to avoid deep pain and confusion (Graybar & Leonard, 2009). Psychotherapists are at risk for ethical and legal consequences if termination is abrupt (Rappleyea, Harris, White, & Kimberly, 2009), as we saw in this story. Furthermore, abruptly dismissing a client is inappropriate termination and therefore qualifies as abandonment (Behnke, 2009). This act alone was a serious ethical violation on Dr. Timmuck's part.

The committee also did not know the full extent of this client's vulnerability, although such knowledge would not have altered their decision. All her life Megan was emotionally and sexually misused by controlling adults, only to find yet another individual seeking to manipulate her in the guise of a helper. It is sobering to note that sexually and otherwise abused clients are at the highest risk for being victimized again by their psychotherapists (Broden & Agristi, 1998; Feldman-Summers & Jones, 1984; Pope & Vetter, 1991).

Notes on Sex with Clients

Among the oldest prohibitions for health care professionals is sexual exploitation. The Hippocratic Oath states:

> Whatever houses I may visit, I will come for the benefit of the sick, remaining free of all intentional injustice, of all mischief, and in particular of sexual relations with both female and male persons, be they free or slaves.
>
> (ca. 400 B.C., see Edelstein, 1943)

Explicit language in ethics codes prohibiting sexual contact with psychotherapy clients did not emerge until the 1970s and 1980s, likely resulting from the research during that period indicating that sexual activity with clients was both prevalent and harmful (Koocher & Keith-Spiegel, 2008; Pope & Vasquez, 2011). Even earlier on, clinicians compared engaging in sex with clients to rape and incest (Kardener, 1974; Masters & Johnson, 1976). Some of the specific harms befalling sexually exploited clients include impaired ability to trust, guilt, emotional instability, feelings of isolation and emptiness, suppressed rage, sexual confusion, and increased risk of self-destructive behavior including suicide (Bouhoutsos, Holyroyd, Lerman, Forer & Greenberg, 1983; Pope, 1994).

It is difficult to estimate the rate of sexual exploitation among mental health professionals. Earlier research, based on self-reports on anonymous surveys, suggested 5–10 percent of the psychologists who responded admitted to having sex with at least one client (e.g., Housman & Stake 1999; Pope, 1993) with similar offending rates for psychiatrists and social workers (Pope & Vetter, 1991). According to later work the incidence may be declining, perhaps because of increased awareness through public education, the rise of feminism, and the harsh sanctions for offenders leading to publicized expulsion from one's professional association, suspension or loss of licensure, malpractices claims, civil suits, and criminal penalties in some states (Haspel, Jorgenson, Wincze, & Parsons, 1997). Or, due to increased exposure and heightened concern by the professions, offenders may be more hesitant to disclose sexual contact with clients, even on anonymous surveys (Williams, 1992).

The psychotherapist in this story can be described as a "predator clinician" (Gabbard & Lester, 1995). Pope and Vasquez (2011) would classify him as a "Svengali," a name from a character in a nineteenth-century novel by du Maurier that emerged to describe an individual who attempts to manipulate others and create an emotional dependence. However, this psychologist convinced himself that his willingness to have sex with clients is a compliment to them. Fortunately, this genre of ethics violator appears to be relatively rare (Celenza, 2005).[1]

---

1 See Chapter 9, Baby Steps Off a Cliff, for the more common pattern of sexual exploiters.

Discussion Questions

1. Do you believe sexual relationships between a psychotherapist and a client should be a criminal offense leading to possible jail time? Why or why not? Do you think criminalization of sex with clients would lead to fewer or more complaints?
2. The Committee viewed Dr. Timmuck as ill-suited for rehabilitation. Do you agree? If you think he was amenable to altering his practices, what program would you suggest?
3. What about middle age can make some psychotherapists vulnerable to exploiting their clients sexually?
4. Why do you think victims of incest are at such high risk for subsequent sexual abuse by their psychotherapists?
5. Plaut (2001) asserts that some practitioners who engage in sexual activity with clients can be safely returned to practice by imposing specific rehabilitative measures. A customized program for each offender may include psychotherapy, containing education, supervision, exclusion of certain types of clients. Others present the arguments against restoring exploitative psychotherapists to practice (Layman & McNamara, 1997; Pope & Vasquez, 2011; Strasburger, Jorgenson, & Randles, 1991). Where do you stand on this debate and why?

References

Behnke, S. (Sept., 2009). Termination and abandonment: A key ethical distinction. *Monitor on Psychology, 40,* 70–71.

Bouhoutsos, J., Holroyd, J., Lerman, H., Forer, B. R., & Greenberg, M. (1983). Sexual intimacy between psychotherapists and patients. *Professional Psychology, 14,* 185–196.

Broden, M. S., & Agristi, A. A. (1998). Responding to therapists' sexual abuse of adult incest survivors: Ethics and legal considerations. *Psychotherapy, 35,* 96–104.

Celenza, A. (2005). Sexual boundary violations: How do they happen? *Directions in Psychiatry, 25,* 141–149.

Edelstein, L. (1943). *The Hippocratic Oath: Text, translation and interpretation.* Baltimore, MD: Johns Hopkins Press.

Feldman-Summers, S., & Jones, G. (1984). Psychological impacts of sexual contact between therapists or other healthcare practitioners and their clients. *Journal of Consulting and Clinical Psychology, 52,* 1054–1061.

Gabbard, G. O., & Lester, E. P. (1995). *Boundaries and boundary violations in psychoanalysis.* New York, NY: Basic Books.

Graybar, S., & Leonard, L. (2009). Terminating psychotherapy therapeutically. In W. O'Donohue & S. R. Graybar (Eds.). *Handbook of contemporary psychotherapy: Toward an improved understanding of effective psychotherapy.* Thousand Oaks, CA: Sage.

Haspel, K. C., Jorgenson, L. M., Wincze, J. P., & Parsons, J. P. (1997). Legislative intervention regarding therapist sexual misconduct: An overview. *Professional Psychology, 28*, 63–72.

Housman L. M., & Stake, J. E. (1999). The current state of sexual ethics training in clinical psychology: Issues of quantity, quality, and effectiveness. *Professional Psychology, 30*, 302–311.

Kardener, S. H. (1974). Sex and the physician-patient relationship. *American Journal of Psychiatry, 131*, 1134–1136.

Koocher, G. P., & Keith-Spiegel. P. (2008). *Ethics in psychology and the mental health professions.* New York, NY: Oxford University Press.

Layman, M. J., & McNamara, J. R. (1997). Remediation for ethics violations: Focus on psychotherapists' sexual; contact with clients. *Professional Psychology, 28*, 281–292.

Masters W. H., & Johnson V. E. (1976). Principles of the new sex therapy. *American Journal of Psychiatry, 133*, 548–554.

Plaut, M. S. (2001). Sexual misconduct by health professionals: Rehabilitation for offenders. *Sexual and Relationship Therapy, 16*, 7–13.

Pope, K. S. (1989). Therapists who become sexually intimate with a patient: Classification dynamics, recidivism, and rehabilitation. *The Independent Practitioner, 9*, 28–34.

Pope, K. S. (1993). Licensing disciplinary actions for psychologists who have been sexually involved with a client: Some information about offenders. *Professional Psychology, 24*, 374–377.

Pope, K. S (1994). Sexual involvement with therapists: Patient assessment, subsequent therapy, forensics. Washington DC: American Psychological Association.

Pope, K. S., & Vasquez, M J. T. (2011). *Ethics in psychotherapy and counseling: A practical guide.* Hoboken, NJ: Wiley.

Pope, K. S., & Vetter, V. A. (1991). Prior therapist-patient sexual involvement among patients seen by psychologists. *Psychotherapy, 28*, 429–438.

Rappleyea, D. L., Harris, S. M., White, M., & Kimberly, S. (2009). Termination: Legal and ethical considerations for marriage and family therapists. *American Journal of Family Therapy, 37*, 12–27.

Sonne, J. L. (2012). Sexualized relationships. In S. J. Knapp (Ed.). *APA handbook of ethics in psychology. Vol. I.* (pp. 295–310). Washington, DC: American Psychological Association.

Strasburger, L. H., Jorgenson, L., & Randles, R. (1991). Criminalization of psychotherapy-patient sex. *American Journal of Psychiatry, 148*, 859–863.

Williams, M. H. (1992). Exploitation and inference: Mapping the damage from therapist-patient sexual involvement. *American Psychologist, 47*, 412–421.

Additional Reading

Gabriel, L. (2005). *Speaking the unspeakable: The ethics of dual relationships in counseling and psychotherapy.* New York, NY: Routledge.

Gutheil, T. G., & Brodsky, A. (2008). *Preventing boundary violations in clinical practice.* New York, NY: Guilford.

Reamer, F. G. (2012). *Boundary issues and dual relationships in the human services.* New York, NY: Columbia University Press.

six
THE RAID ON
HOLLYWOOD
BOULEVARD

Are psychotherapists allowed a private life beyond the scrutiny of ethics committees and licensing boards? The answer is not an easy "yes" or "no." This story reveals a psychologist's long-held secret in a most open and embarrassing way, opening up a discussion of the right to be left alone v. the public trust and client welfare. Should this psychologist, who always understood the risks of exposure, have better controlled the expression of a clandestine feature of his life?

Dr. Broderick Kingsley readily surmised the contents of the certified letter the instant he spotted the postal carrier poised with pad and pen at his office door. Never before had he considered what would happen if his private and professional lives collided, especially in such an outrageous way. He had been so careful, foregoing establishing deep, intimate relationships to conceal that part of himself.

Broderick waited until after his last psychotherapy appointment before reaching for the envelope from the League of California Psychologists. As he opened the letter he felt thankful to still have clients. After the story broke three weeks ago, two longer-term clients failed to show for their last two appointments or return his calls, and his newest client left a message declining to receive further counseling from, as she put it, "someone sicker than I am."

Dear Dr. Kingsley,

A colleague in Century City forwarded to the LCP Ethics Committee a news-paper article appearing in the Hollywood Post *(copy enclosed). As you know, it contains references to your lifestyle and activities. A concern was expressed about how this publicity impacts the reputation of mental health professionals in the community.*

We invite you to discuss the article with us as well as your competence to deliver psychotherapeutic services. We do realize that news accounts may contain embellishments and inaccuracies.

Please make an appointment with the LCP administrator, Mrs. Peggy Aldridge, to appear before the Ethics Committee at its March meeting, unless a compelling reason requires a postponement. Failure to contact us within 10 days of the receipt of this letter will constitute an act of noncompliance, which is itself an ethics violation.

Sincerely,

Victor Graham, Ph.D.
Chair, Ethics Committee
League of California Psychologists

Nothing in the letter surprised him. He was exposed, and someone would inform the League of California Psychologists sooner or later. He had anxiously anticipated the other shoe to drop, and now it had. The secret he had kept for over 15 years would now become the center ring of a dark circus performed before the LPC Ethics Committee.

Broderick tried again to make sense of it all. He thought about what he heard a hundred times: *The main reason students choose to major in psychology is to find out what's wrong with them.* He also thought it to be largely inaccurate. He believed most individuals who enter a helping profession to be mentally fit and genuinely motivated to mend psyches in pain. Getting paid to help people is a win-win. But Broderick Kingsley also knew for him the old adage had a ring of truth to it.

Even as a kid he felt different, set far apart from everyone else. It was a pervasive and diffuse awareness running like a well-saturated aquifer: water mixed with fractured rock just underfoot that no one could see. Even he didn't understand this urgency sweeping over him, as if he would burst apart.

He couldn't blame his parents for "messing with his head," a complaint lodged by many of his clients. His stay-at-home mom was like a Mother's Day Hallmark card. He couldn't recall an instance when she was cruel or distant. He loved her completely and grieved for months after her death two years ago. Father and son never became close, but not because they didn't get along. His father was on the road as a textbook sales representative, calling on colleges across the western half of the country for most of the academic year. The two still exchanged occasional emails after his father moved to Oregon, but they hadn't seen each other since his mother's funeral.

Broderick could not pinpoint his exact age, maybe 11 or maybe 12, when putting on makeup and women's clothing released the pressure building up over a period of days, sometimes weeks, and replaced the intense compression with a sweet rush of serenity. A twang of shame always surfaced afterwards, but the more urgent sensation squeezing everything else out of his mind abated, at least for a while.

He was tall for his age, so his mother's clothes were almost his size. When she left him alone to run errands he often took the opportunity to co-opt her makeup and whatever else would make do in her dresser drawers and closet. He dreaded her unexpected return before he could put back things as he found them and scrub off the lipstick and eye pencil. He knew his mother would be upset with him for disturbing her belongings, but he also believed her reaction would extend beyond simple annoyance. Even though he did not understand why he felt compelled to engage in this clandestine practice, he sensed she would also be disgusted, a far more disgraceful response than enduring disapproval for invading her space.

When Broderick moved away to college, the first two years of dorm living presented a formidable challenge. Other students were always around, and locked doors in occupied rooms signaled something was going on that shouldn't be. He didn't dare purchase items to keep in his room. His roommate, an ultra-conservative Republican from Orange County, would likely blow Broderick's cover far and wide if any clues were left lying around. He considered keeping at least a bra and panties in his car explaining, should he be discovered, the girl had forgotten to take them after a heavy date. But he rejected such a fib as too risky, too absurd, and, despite his covert ritual, he was not taken to outright lying.

Broderick chose instead to drive the 75 miles most weekends to the family home, hoping his mother would leave the house for at least an hour during his brief stay. She felt free to enter his old digs to collect dirty laundry or dust, so he had not yet acquired anything to hide at home. Summers were challenging, what with his father around much of the time. He hated summers.

Everything changed after his sophomore year. He convinced his parents he would do better in school if he could rent his own place near campus away from the constant dormitory clamor and disruptions. Then an economics major, the hefty assigned reading required quiet solitude. He believed this pitch, even though prospects for his hidden agenda would open up.

The tiny studio apartment seemed like a free range to Broderick. The closet housed his props and its sliding mirror doors became a stage. He used almost all of the funds in his personal savings account to "buy things for his sister's upcoming birthday," or "for Mom for Christmas," or "for my girlfriend." The sales staff were usually friendly and accommodating, inquiring about sizes and tastes and exclaiming how thoughtful he was to try so hard to please the women in his life. Broderick sensed a few had their suspicions. The wily look in their eyes seemed to say, "OK kid, we'll play along." Broderick never returned to those shops.

Having his own place was not the only feature setting Broderick free to liberate the tension, or "The Volcano" as he had come to name it, any time the pressure built up. Now he could select attire and related accessories, as his likes deviated substantially from his mother's modest wardrobe. His new stash contained a vibrantly colored wrap-around dress, two skin-tight mini-skirts and a close-fitting jersey top, long silk scarves, elbow-length gloves, thigh-high black leather boots, and stiletto shoes with 4 inch heels. His undergarments included fishnet stockings and front closure bustiers in black and red satin along with lacy panties, a heavily padded bra, and silky lingerie. He loved the way these clothes felt against his skin. He felt pretty, even though he knew others would not likely agree.

During his rituals whenever "The Volcano" was building he would first apply makeup, heavily now because he could purchase far more exciting cosmetics than were available in his mother's dresser. Thick ivory foundation, bright lipsticks and blushes, false eyelashes and sparkly shadows. Next came the undergarments, then the outfit sometimes taking ten minutes of mental foreplay to decide what it would be, then footwear, usually boots as they hid his prominent calf muscles. He crowned himself with a flowing blonde wig that had set him back $799.95, plus tax. He often selected a silk scarf to drape around his neck, adding long stretch gloves as the final touch. He would then stand and admire his own recreation, posing this way and that in front of the closet door mirror, until, like a rush of melting butter, the crest subsided.

Only one complication invaded Broderick's oasis. Now he was free to act on his inclinations but was also convinced he was a freak and no one else in the world had a desperate need to purge in this particular way. No longer was this just a high-risk pleasurable game. That's when he decided to drop his major in economics in favor of psychology. Maybe he would learn why he had to do what he did. Maybe someone wrote about it somewhere. Maybe there was a way out, a cure, although he felt ambivalent when he imagined his life without women's regalia. Some of who he is would be missing if his dress-up sessions were no longer part of his life. That part of him would have to die.

Broderick proved to be an excellent student and was accepted into a top clinical psychology graduate program. Others responded well to his amiable disposition. He eschewed close friendships, however, which also meant he had plenty of time to study. Although always scoring at the top of his class he sought out the less popular internships in hospitals and agencies, those placements with a seriously disturbed or atypical clientele. He was not sure if being with people who were more peculiar than himself made him feel more normal or if he actually excelled at working with challenging clients. Regardless, he was good at his craft and earned kudos from patients and supervisors alike.

Yet after all this education and experience Broderick still could not alter himself, let alone discover a reason that seemed correct as to why he did what he did. He had read books and learned the terms—cross-dresser, fetish, transvestite, drag queen, female impersonator—each with its own definitional and causation twists depending on what resource he consulted. But they provided little insight beyond assigning labels to his obsession. He knew all the theories; a schizophrenogenic mother and absent father, an innate proclivity, a confused sexual orientation, a need to be submissive, and so on. Still, he couldn't find one to fit him. He took some measure of comfort in learning he was hardly unique, and many others like him seemed content, even happy.

Broderick knew he wasn't gay. He had no interest in becoming a transsexual. Sometimes he would fantasize about finding the perfect woman, one who could gleefully participate in a celebration of The Volcano. He wasn't even sure if his secret was about sex. He did not masturbate during his fashion posing sessions, but the sequence had a similar anticipation and deliverance, though more like a heroin addict's hit than an orgasm.

Only after his mother passed away could he break from the aloneness of his existence and display himself beyond his own mirror image. He would need to be very careful, disguise himself flawlessly so even his clients could not recognize him. The cover of darkness would be essential, but he also needed to consider personal safety. He drove around at night for weeks looking for places where street people gathered peacefully, the locations that would become his new stage.

Now Dr. Broderick Kingsley would be facing his adjudicators, those who can rule on whether he was a sinner beyond redemption or just an odd but harmless duck caught up in an inconvenient web of events. He decided to speak truthfully to the LCP Ethics Committee. No excuses. They would see him as he was, warts and all.

The Ethics Committee:
Broderick Kingsley, Ph.D. March 16, 2:15 p.m.

Dr. Victor Graham stood up straight as a nail at the head of the conference table, chest stuck out as if he were about to perform an operatic solo or salute the President. "Our next case is a monumental challenge," he bellowed followed by a devious smile, "and it's a bit kinky." He cleared his throat, perhaps considering his last remark to be misplaced and out of character.

"You may experience some distress. Paradoxically, you may find ourself stifling an urge to make wisecracks." Victor was all business now, and glaring straight at Wolf Levin. "This one comes to us from an old friend of mine, Jerry McCreadie, who manages a clinic with eight other mental health professionals on the 9th floor of a spectacular glass and marble office building in Century City. Jerry sent along this newspaper clipping from the *Hollywood Post*. Please circulate it while I read his letter to you."

Victor passed the cut-out article to Sammy Halsey. "Oh good Lord," Sammy uttered, drawing a deep breath. "Local Psychologist Nabbed for Turning Tricks on Hollywood Boulevard." The other members looked at Sammy with expressions ranging from puzzled to disbelief.

"Hey, Sammy. You're too new here to start making bad jokes," said Wolf in a light-hearted tone.

"I'm not kidding," wailed Sammy, distressed because one of his colleagues might think he spoke tastelessly.

"Hurry up, Sammy," said Ted Bates. "This I have to see with my own eyes. Just when you're sure you've heard it all."

Victor pounded lightly on the table. "What did I tell you? Shush!"

A large photograph of police officers loading a group of a dozen peculiarly dressed and unhappy looking people into a patrol van dominated the front page. Leading the line-up was a much taller, thinner, blonde woman in exceptionally heavy makeup, a revealing lacy tube dress, and platform stilettos, being led off in handcuffs with a facial expression so drawn and painful, it caused Sammy to wince. The caption identified this figure as "Psychologist Dr. Broderick Kingsley in his alternative lifestyle as 'Honey Bucket.'"

Victor read the charge letter aloud, oblivious to the muffled reactions exhibited by each committee member as the newspaper clipping snaked around the table.

Dear Victor,

I am sending this piece from a local paper to you as the Chair of the League of California Psychologists Ethics Committee. Dr. Broderick Kingsley lives, how to say it best, a complicated life. He is well regarded as a compassionate and competent therapist. Hence we were stunned to read an article in the Hollywood Post *describing a roundup of Hollywood Boulevard prostitutes. Included in the queue was, of all people, Broderick sporting a blonde wig, female regalia, and makeup thick as cement.*

We are concerned about what impact this revelation might have on the reputation of mental health professionals in our community. We seek counsel from the LCP Ethics Committee as to whether an ethics violation is involved and how to help us allay any concerns the public may harbor about the ethics and emotional stability of psychotherapists who set up practices here.

Thank you for your consideration. A copy of the newspaper article is enclosed.

Sincerely,

Jerrod L. McCreadie, Ph.D.
Century City Mental Health Clinic

Victor sighed and asked if everyone had gotten a chance to read the article. The group nodded in unison, but no one spoke. No use punching Victor's buttons again.

"Ted, please go out and ask Dr. Kingsley to join us," ordered Victor. All eyes focused on Ted as he opened the door and called out, "Come in, please," wondering which persona would enter the room.

Dr. Broderick Kingsley, slender and about 5 feet 10 inches tall, walked in cautiously and slightly bent, looking like a student trying to creep unnoticed into the classroom long after the bell had rung. Behind wire-rimmed glasses were watery gray eyes. His shoulder-length brown hair was wispy and thin despite his mere 29 years. A skinny blue tie dribbled down the front of a white dress shirt. His navy wool sports jacket and rumpled gray polyester slacks created the image of a casual guy. This thin young man bore little physical resemblance to the almost glamorous newspaper photo bringing him to this table today. Sammy was chagrined upon finding himself appreciating what makeup, a wig, some stuffing, and a scanty dress can do for a guy.

Victor introduced the Committee members, pointing at them by name, while ushering Dr. Kingsley to the seat on his right. Broderick sat himself down carefully, deliberately, folding his slender hands on the table. Now he looked almost frightened, as if he were about to be hit across the face by disapproving tormenters.

"Thank you for coming here today, Dr. Kingsley," said Victor. "You know, of course, why we invited you. Before we discuss the matter amongst ourselves, we wanted to give you the opportunity to tell us anything you think would be helpful to us so we can better understand the incident described in the newspaper article."

Broderick paused for almost half a minute, but it seemed longer. "I know I've offended you," speaking in a voice so soft that no one dare even shift in their seats lest they create overriding noise.

"I have no excuse except to say I have urges, callings, to do what I do. I am not saying I am psychotic. I hear no voices telling me, 'go dress up like a woman and hit the streets.' I am not gay, and I don't want to be a woman. I do not have a dissociative disorder. I am aware of myself; there's just the one me. I do this because it's part of who I am, who I have always been." Broderick's gaze shifted back to his hands.

"I do have a defense of sorts," he continued a bit louder and looking up again. "I go out at night two or three times a month when I need to satisfy an impulse because it gets so…well when I have trouble concentrating. But I don't turn tricks!" his voice rising now. "You will never find anyone who paid to have sex with me. You will never find anyone I approached asking to buy sex. It never happened. I just like to dress up and stroll around where those of us who are different congregate at night. I sometimes talk to the others who live lives most people don't want to know about. They accept me for who I am in my alternative appearance, and I am at ease around them. I know I've actually helped some who felt hopeless and cast out by listening and giving casual advice. I refer them to colleagues when I think they need professional help. A streetwalker who *only* walks and talks. That's it."

"Let me be blunt," said Wolf, though in a kind voice. "How do you rate your emotional stability?"

"Fair question. I do have this issue. I don't think I hurt anyone except, well, maybe myself. I dreaded being discovered. But I've become more accepting of my situation and isolate it from who I am 98 percent of the time. I take good care of myself, constantly monitoring my health and stress levels. I can count numerous friendly acquaintances, many of them colleagues with whom I interact often. And I have my clients. I remain fully aware of appropriate boundaries with them. They are not stand-ins for family and friends. If I thought for one minute I was doing any harm by exploiting them emotionally, that I was less of a psychotherapist because of my...uh....issue, I would quit this profession today." Broderick Kingsley took a handkerchief from his inside pocket and blew his nose, appearing to be on the verge of tears. "Excuse me," he whispered.

"It's OK. It's a tough question," said Charlotte Burroughs. "So let me ask this. Did you get charged with anything? Do you have a record now?"

"No, they were satisfied that I wasn't drunk or on drugs. The police sergeant who interviewed me was quite considerate. I didn't even get a ticket for loitering, which is the penalty had they believed I was soliciting."

"Do you think you've tarnished how the public views your colleagues in the community?" asked Ted.

"That's the hardest question of all, and I deeply regret any distress caused by who I am. I may be guilty, and I only hope this whole incident is just my 15 minutes of fame—or infamy in my case—and pray such an impact has already dissolved. I did lose three clients because of this, but I also got a new one this last week."

"As a follow-up, do you think you violated our ethics code?" continued Ted.

"I want to say 'no.' My clients were never involved. But, of course, that's not my call." For the first time, Broderick Kingsley emitted a faint smile.

Victor looked around the table and said, "If we've asked you all of the relevant questions or unless you want to add anything, I think we are through here."

Everyone glanced at everyone else, but no one spoke.

"Thank you for your candor, Dr. Kingsley. We will be in touch with you soon." Victor stood to usher Broderick out.

Broderick caught the eye of each committee member as he slowly rose from his chair and headed for the exit. "Thank you for hearing me out." He closed the door softly behind him.

***

Sammy sat back, feeling mixed emotions. Broderick's actions were those he associated with porn films and fetish magazines, neither of which had any part in his adult life. He thought about a high school caper when he and three friends drove to the south side of Indianapolis using a friend's mother's car without her permission. Based on a tip from an older boy, they located the adults-only store with a proprietor who didn't care how old his customers actually were. They took their magazines to a deserted wooded area close to their homes in Yorktown and pored over the pages, laughing uneasily while experiencing the rush of both fascination and repulsion. Sammy had tucked this memory away as a youthful indiscretion, grateful he escaped being implicated in the escapade. Dale, the boy who took his mother's car, wasn't so lucky. He hid the illicit booty in the trunk and forgot to retrieve it. The next day his mother opened up the trunk to put in groceries. Sammy and the others didn't see Dale for the rest of the summer, and the incident was never again discussed among them.

"OK people," said Victor, slapping the table with the palm of his hand. "Let's settle down." Sammy's mind snapped back to the present. While recalling his adolescent caper he hadn't noticed his colleagues whispering, their heads bobbing.

"Here's what makes this a tough one for us," said Victor. "Regardless of what else you think, we must follow the ethics code. Broderick Kingsley was not performing psychotherapy while engaging in his…uh…other lifestyle. The people he talked to out there at night cannot be designated as clients, even if he gave them casual advice. The ethics code and licensing law are clear about protecting the right to a private life. Except in extraordinary circumstances, one's actions can be judged only while functioning in the role of a psychologist."

Sammy looked confused and asked, "What would extraordinary circumstances be? Leaving the door open for what?"

"Conviction of a felony is the main one used as a standard exception," answered Victor. "To be dropped from the LCP, that's all it has to be. After that it's a judgment call."

"Let me share an example, Sammy," said Stella. "One psychologist had two DUIs. His name appeared in the arrest record of a local paper. A citizen sent the article to us. So we wrote this fellow and expressed our concerns about his drinking and his ability to deliver competent psychotherapy. We struck a deal by putting him under supervision and getting him into a program. Sometimes we can do that sort of thing."

"Remember the psychologist who killed her housekeeper? Or the guy who also ran guns for an unfriendly nation? Libya I think" added Ted. "We dropped them quick."

"Those two were serious legal matters. They are the exceptions," said Victor. "But Broderick Kingsley was not charged with anything at all, and quickly released once they took him to the Los Angeles Police Department over on Wilcox Avenue. We checked it out."

Stella was ready to move on. "Even if we say Dr. Kingsley cannot be held ethically accountable because he was functioning as a private citizen at the time, we need to hash out the original concern posed by Dr. McCreadie, the one who sent the newspaper article to us. Is it a violation to cause other psychotherapists embarrassment, even if the therapist did not seek the attention?"

"Well, yes, of course it's embarrassing," said Ted. "But the story is also false. Kingsley was never charged with soliciting. He can't be held responsible for what the journalist claimed he was doing."

Wolf chimed in. "And just how do you get *that* story out? That bell can't be un-rung. You think the reporter will write a retraction? Nothing juicy there. And even if a correction came out, whole incident gets stirred up again—'Psychologist a.k.a. Honey Bucket doesn't put out after all.' This fahrblunget mess would get a second life."

"We may find what he does peculiar, even disturbing, but he's on his own time and not committing any crimes," said Stella, "He got snared. Wrong place, wrong time. However, he should've known about risks attached to his midnight consorts with prostitutes and other street people who may be into illegal activities. I'm not sure he thought this one all the way through."

"I think we should ask Dr. Kingsley and Dr. McCreadie if they would like to meet and discuss what really happened. Set the record straight. Such an encounter could work out, and the risk/benefit ratio is favorable," suggested Charlotte.

All heads nodded in agreement. Sammy smiled. He was beginning to feel a part of a compassionate process far more complex and fascinating than he ever expected. The image of his role as a relentless avenger was fading and being replaced with something nuanced, satisfying, and even more significant.

"We can wrap this up after quickly considering one additional issue," said Victor. "Is Kingsley emotionally stable enough to conduct competent psychotherapy? We cannot do a definitive diagnosis here, but how does he strike you?"

"I have a position," said Wolf. "This leads to a whole can of worms about our society and how we perceive behavior outside the norm. In other cultures, no one would give a rat's ass about something like this. Hell, if he lived in San Francisco, no one would even take notice. But, if he lived in Iran he'd be stoned, or his junk lopped off at the very least."

"But we have to go with the society we have," said Stella. "I agree. Even our profession's diagnostic criteria are sexist. Men dressing as women are slapped with a label, as if it's weak or worse to be feminine. Women dressing as men is almost the norm. How often do you see women wearing skirts anymore?" Stella waved her hands in the air.

"He seems like a nice enough fellow—straight talker—and I believe him when he says he isn't taking money for sex," added Ted.

"Victor, isn't it true no client ever complained before?" asked Archie.

"Yes. Correct. Apparently he lost a few clients after the story hit, but none has contacted us."

Wolf changed the subject. "Well I always get a little concerned when people tell me they experience urges telling them what they *have* to do, *or else*. Addicts. Cutters. Serial killers, for chrissake."

"He just dresses up!" snapped Ted. "It's not like he physically harms anyone or even himself, except for walking around in four inch heels. Bunions. Ankle sprains." Ted's face broke into a wide grin, self-assured that he just contributed something clever to the conversation.

"It's not unethical to be odd," Archie added, "although there may be a time and place for displaying it."

Sammy tentatively jumped in again. "I watched a story on TV. I can't remember who the therapist was, a psychiatrist I think, and he's great with autistic kids. He can communicate with them as no others are able to, not even their parents. He is schizophrenic. He couldn't cure himself, of course, but he could put his mental illness to good purpose. Dr. Kingsley may be similar, working largely with clientele living on the fringe or who also have something hidden in their closets. He must have a lot of empathy."

"Interesting, Sammy," said Charlotte. "And not all diagnoses are equal in at least three ways," holding up a new finger with each point. "First, what it is. Second, its severity. Third, how it is viewed in a given culture, like Wolf already said. Take my friend Chet. He is a fanatic list maker, rigid enough to be diagnosed with an obsessive compulsive disorder. And everyone knows about the lists because he carries them around on a clipboard at all times. But, no one thinks Chet requires therapy. On the contrary, he gets more done than anyone. He's actually rewarded for his compulsive behavior. Compare Chet to my OCD client who has to point his pinky finger high above his head every time he takes a step. He's appears to be psychotic."

"I always get a twinge of guilt when we're in a position to punish someone because they have emotional issues," said Ted. "I mean, we are supposed to be the broadminded ones who are tolerant of people who are different or strange. If any of our colleagues are gravely compromised they need to back away until their minds are firm again. But when I look at this guy, I don't sense any diagnosis precluding him from practicing competently."

Victor interrupted the discussion. "Does everyone agree that, to the best we can ascertain, Dr. Kingsley is not impaired sufficiently to be censured or mandated to receive more therapy?"

Stella spoke up. "Personally, I would like to send him into psycho-therapy, not to eliminate his paraphilia because the prognosis is poor and he doesn't appear to be interested in changing anyway, but to support him through the transition into the public arena. Being exposed will carry some impact, and no one yet knows its extent. His colleagues know his secret, but they remain uninformed of the errors in the newspaper story. Interactions may be awkward as he'll no doubt intersect with them in the future. His practice might be affected. His current clients who know about the article will see him differently. He needs to accommodate the awareness inflicted on his clients from the outside, to figure out how to disclose the true story while avoiding overwhelming them."

"I worry about depression," added Ted. "He's already ashamed because of this article."

"Good, Ted," said Victor. "I would like to suggest recommending a minimum of ten therapy sessions. I'm thinking Ken Anton over on Pico near the 405. Ken is a compassionate guy with a stellar reputation. We wouldn't need to know anything about what they talk about, only the number completed."

"What about an ethics violation?" Sammy asked.

"Well, I was thinking we could see if he would agree to entering psycho-therapy despite not finding him guilty of anything," answered Victor. "Does everyone like this, even though he has the right to refuse?"

All hands went up, eventually. Wolf needed a few seconds to think about it.

Decision and Dispositions

The LCP Ethics Committee passed on pursuing any charges against Dr. Broderick Kingsley, but did strongly recommend that he enroll, at his own expense, in ten therapy sessions with Dr. Anton or another qualified practitioner subject to the Committee's approval. Dr. Kingsley was also asked if he would be interested in meeting with the colleague who sent the *Hollywood Post* article to the Ethics Committee to discuss the incident informally and correct the errors appearing in the published story.

Dr. McCreadie received a note of thanks from the Committee for forwarding the newspaper article. He was also informed that Dr. Kingsley cooperated fully with the Committee's suggestions. The two did get together over coffee several weeks later. During a phone conversation with Victor Graham, Dr. McCreadie described an agreeable and constructive discussion.

Broderick Kingsley did enter therapy and continued by his own choice as Dr. Anton's client for over a year.

Case Commentary

Whereas even unusual private behavior is tolerated as a right not easily breached by ethics committees, emotional problems can serve as the basis for a complaint if competence may be compromised. In this case the psychologist appears to match the diagnosis of transvestic fetishism (American Psychiatric Association, 2000). The key diagnostic criteria, described only for heterosexual men, include intense urges to cross-dress accompanied by significant distress or impairment socially, at work, or elsewhere. Such men are usually satisfied with their gender (Friedman, 2006).

Dr. Kingsley's brand of sexual diversity is one that makes many people uncomfortable (Lance, 2002). Whereas the particulars of this story are unusual, the underlying issues bear careful attention due to their relevance to *all* mental health professionals. Technological advances—from social media, Twitter, and Google to smart phones with video capabilities—make it increasingly difficult to limit access to one's private speech and behavior. This psychologist learned that lesson the hard way.

Based on the information available to the Committee, and despite the stigma attached to Dr. Kingsley's urges and public outings resulting in an inaccurate news account, he was seen as managing his stress reasonably well by being self-aware, active socially, and maintaining a healthy physical life style—all important regimes for remaining emotionally competent (Barnett & Cooper, 2009). So, whereas

Dr. Kingsley was unwilling to disclose his urges and suffered embarrassment over the raid incident, he appeared to function well professionally, even garnering a solid reputation among his peers.

This story also raises the sometimes complicated issue of drawing a distinction between behavior displayed in one's private life and behavior while in a professional role (Pipes, Holstein, & Aguirre, 2005). Character, good and bad, can be revealed in both realms.

Notes on Psychotherapists' Right to Privacy

The United States Constitution does not confer specific privacy rights. However, some amendments (e.g., freedom of speech and to peaceably assemble, protection from unwarranted search and seizure, and to be "secure in their persons, houses, papers, and effects") provides safeguards against unbridled government intrusion, as expanded in Justice Brandies' oft-cited dissent in *Olmstead et al. v. U.S.* (1928).

> The makers of our Constitution undertook to secure conditions favorable to the pursuit of happiness. They recognized the significance of man's spiritual nature, of his feelings, and of his intellect. They knew that only a part of the pain, pleasure and satisfactions of life are to be found in material things. They sought to protect Americans in their beliefs, their thoughts, their emotions and their sensations. They conferred, as against the Government, the right to be let alone—the most comprehensive of rights, and the right most valued by civilized men.

The American Psychological Association (APA) and American Association of Marriage and Family Therapists (AAMFT) are among those professional organizations with ethics codes specifying the right to a private life separate from one's role as a practitioner.

Earlier versions of the APA ethics code, however, contained an exception: "Psychologists' moral and ethical standards of behavior are a personal matter to the same degree as they are for any other citizen, except as these may compromise the fulfillment of their professional responsibilities or reduce the public trust in psychology and psychologists" (p. 41, American Psychological Associsation, 1987). This exception has since been deleted, probably because the disputed act must be knowable by the public, leaving the underlying and certainly unintended message, "just don't get caught." Furthermore, what one person could do to violate the trust in an entire profession entails a highly subjective judgment.[1] Action can be taken when APA member psychologists are convicted of a felony committed in any context. The California State Licensing Board, however, requires the disputed act to be committed while in the role of a psychologist.

---

1   The American Psychiatric Association allows that any illegal act, regardless of context, could be the basis for an ethics violation.

Discussion Questions

1. What do you think of the Committee's decision? Are you comfortable with it? Why or why not?
2. What if Dr. Kingsley had been soliciting for sexual clientele? How might your opinion of him change? Would you then declare him unfit to practice? (Remember that solicitation is a misdemeanor in most jurisdictions, not a felony.)
3. Even though he got along well with people, do you think Dr. Kingsley's intentional avoidance of close intimate relationships could affect his ability to conduct competent psychotherapy?
4. Do mental health professionals who embarrass other professionals by their speech or behavior as private citizens reveal

prima facie evidence of professional incompetence? Consider these examples:

a. A psychotherapist is known around town as an obnoxious bully because of his loud and insulting outbursts in restaurants and other public places.

b. A psychotherapist authors a newspaper article espousing inferior intellects and problem solving ability among women and Blacks. He argues they should never be placed in positions of authority.

c. A marriage and family counselor appears naked in a men's magazine along with the article about her titled, "Shrink in the Nude."

d. A male counselor appears frontally nude in a photo calendar titled, "Twelve Beefcakes."

e. A psychiatrist is featured in a popular tell-all newspaper showing photos of him embracing and kissing the wife of a high profile local politician in some dark place. The psychiatrist is also married with small children.

5. Do you think such a thing resembling privacy exists in today's world? How does your answer impact on how you do (or would) conduct yourself outside of your role as a psychotherapist?

References

American Psychiatric Association (2000). *Diagnostic and statistical manual of mental disorders* (4th ed., text revision). Washington, DC: Author.

American Psychological Association (1987). *Casebook on ethical principles of psychologists* (Rev. ed.). Washington, DC: Author.

Barnett, J. E., & Cooper, N. (2009). Creating a culture of self-care. *Clinical Psychology, 16,* 16–20.

Friedman, H. R. (2006). The drive toward completion. [a review of the film, *Transamerica*]. *PsychCritiques, 51.* Retrieved from http://psycnet.apa.org/critiques/51/46/20.html

Lance, L. M. (2002). Acceptance of diversity in human sexuality: Will the strategy reducing homophobia also reduce discomfort of cross-dressing? *College Student Journal, 36,* 598–602.

Olmstead v. United States (1928) 100 U.S. 119 F. (2d) 842, 848, 850, affirmed. Retrieved at http://www.law.cornell.edu/supct/html/historics/USSC_CR_0277_0438_ZD.html

Pipes, R. B., Holstein, J. E., & Aguirre, M. G. (2005). Examining the personal—professional distinction: Ethics codes and the difficulty of drawing the boundary. *American Psychologist, 60,* 325–334.

Additional Reading

American Civil Liberties Union. *Your right to privacy.* Retrieved from http://www.aclu.org/technology-and-liberty/your-right-privacy

Barnett, J. (2008). *Impaired professionals: Distress, professional impairments, self-care, and psychological wellness.* In M. Hersen & A. M. Gross. *Handbook of clinical psychology,* Vol. 1. (pp. 857–884) Hoboken, NJ: Wiley.

Warren, S. D. & Brandeis, L. D. (December, 1890). The right to privacy. *Harvard Law Review, 4.* Retrieved from http://faculty.uml.edu/sgallagher/Brandeisprivacy.htm

seven
KILL THE BOSS

Psychotherapy sessions are safe havens for clients to say what they are thinking and feeling, including what's bothering them. Up to a point, that is. This story traces a psychologist's wild race against time when her client utters what may be a serious threat to harm an identifiable victim. With heightened sensitivity and pre-planning the crisis may not have been averted, but she might have better managed the therapy along the way with less risk to both herself and her client.

The challenge every mental health professional dreads just collided like a runaway train into Dr. Paula Zinni. She sat in her desk chair, hands covering her eyes and shaking. She looked at the clock. Already after 8:00 p.m. The sky was ominously dark, and the predicted storm was imminent. Hard to reach anyone who might be able to help. "Oh God," she thought, "What am I going to do? What am I *supposed* to do?"

***

Of her eighteen regularly scheduled clients, William Barge was the most exasperating and ultimately the most frightening. She likened his verbal outbursts to a sawed-off shotgun spraying words like shrapnel in wide circles, inflicting psychic injury on anyone unfortunate enough to wander into his sights.

"I hate all Democrats for bailing out those rich crooks on Wall Street," Billy, as he wanted to be called, blurted out during a recent session. He had little use for the President and the members of his administration whom he referred to as "thugs in suits." Another time Billy got more personal when he grunted, "My next door neighbor voted for those Democrat bamboozlers who are flattening our US of A and needs to be slapped upside his head."

Billy didn't have much use for Republicans either. During an early session with Paula Zinni he admitted to knocking over a life-sized cardboard stand-up of George W. Bush propped in front of the Santa Barbara Republican Campaign Headquarters 11 years ago. He took another swing at the volunteer staffer who rushed out to protest, just missing bopping him square in the face. A night in jail and a $500 fine for causing a public disturbance failed to mute Billy's fury at the then-President for not trying hard enough to find and kill Osama bin Laden.

Dr. Paula Zinni excused much of Billy's ranting as chronic emotional spillage from whence he came. He grew up in a wildly dysfunctional family with parents who failed utterly to model gentleness or patience to their seven children, three of whom remain perpetually incarcerated and another two dead—one from a heroin overdose and a second who bled out after a gunshot to the throat. The other, the only female, left home as a teenager and has not surfaced since. Paula was intent on saving Billy from a past in which he remained trapped as a blameless casualty.

Yet, until tonight, Billy never threatened anyone with harm in a way Paula took seriously. Once, when his father refused Billy's request to borrow his car for a week after he smashed his own on the 101 freeway divider, he told Paula he wanted to "stick him in the clothes washer set to 'heavy dirt.'" During another session he recounted flashing his middle finger and yelling, "Next time I will chase you down, you SOB!" to a stranger in a passing car who cut him off. Recently he hissed, "I could strangle my wife for always taking too long to get herself ready to go out," causing Paula's eyelashes to flicker. But despite her follow-up questions to evaluate actual intent, no convincing signs emerged to suggest that Billy would act on any of his threats. He was a chronic blowhard. All bark and no bite, except for the pop at the cardboard standup and a misfired swing at the hapless volunteer over a decade ago.

Paula knew no bright line separates impulsive hostile threats from acting them out, a dilemma standing ever-poised to strike all mental health professionals. And Billy came to her for help. He said he needed "lots of calming," as he labeled his therapeutic goal, and was determined to succeed.

Tonight was different. Billy burst into his 8 p.m. appointment with a face turned purple with fury and fists clenched tight against his body. He squatted hard into the client chair and breathed so furiously that his throat rattled.

"Has something happened, Billy? You seem upset and out of breath."

Billy only glowered at first and said nothing. A minute later he looked up at her and spoke with flattened emotion, a voice quite incongruous with his exterior tough expression and demeanor.

"I'm going to kill my boss. It'll be tonight. Tomorrow at the latest."

Billy shot up from his chair and stomped out the door.

"Billy, get back in here, please! Let's talk more about this," Paula shrieked as she ran out into the narrow office hallway and peered both ways. But Billy had evaporated into the stormy night.

***

Billy Barge had never been this direct before, nor had he ever left before his full 50 minutes were up. He always insisted on draining every second out of his sessions, often complaining about insufficient time to spill out everything on his mind.

Now he was gone. Paula prayed Nelson Cawley, the psychologist from the office across the hall, hadn't left. But his door was locked tight. "Why didn't I create some sort of folder labeled 'What to Do When Your Client Threatens to Murder Someone'? Dammit," she said to herself, slapping her own cheek.

She returned to her office, feeling dizzy yet trying to focus on her predicament. "Was Billy just blowing off more steam?" she asked herself. "No, this feels like something else. He never looked this angry. He was never specific about timing. He always answered my follow-up questions after his improbable threats. He never left a single minute before the session was over."

Paula tried to come up with reasons not to be concerned. After all, Billy always ranted about something but he never went through with any of his stated intentions.

"Where are those notes I took on violence assessment at a conference a few years back?" she asked herself. "The H2O[1] or something like that, a list

---

1 Dr. Zinni is no doubt referring to the *Historical, Clinical, Risk Management-20* (HCR-20), a tool to help professionals assess the risk of violent behavior. It contains 20 risk factors spread across three subscales.

coming out after I graduated. I remember being male is a risk. Something also about a dysfunctional family, Billy fits that one, too. He speaks impulsively, but he doesn't act out. And, he's not seriously mentally ill. He's been married for 15 years and he's gainfully employed. He's always on time for his sessions and wants to work with his anger issues. A mixed bag."

Paula tried to remember more. She ascertained long ago that Billy drinks a beer or two when he watches sports games on TV but does not use drugs. He told her he did not hunt, and she had no reason to believe he owned a gun. She also recalled that a previous violent act is a major risk factor, but Paula always believed that Billy's swing at the volunteer happened too far back to reflect his current mental status.

Now that she thought about it, however, Billy complained a lot about his work lately. He didn't like his new assigned hours because they interfered with a television show he liked to watch in the morning. Last month his boss refused to give him a raise despite adding on extra duties. He also mentioned being upset with a saleswoman for ordering the wrong parts, and his boss admonished him harshly for his outburst. Paula thought, "That's just Billy" at the time, but ominous clues were now accumulating. "The last session he mentioned he needed to work harder in therapy because of his wife's complaints about his verbal outbursts. He feared she might leave."

Putting her head in her trembling hands, Paula made her decision. She shouted out loud, as if to convince herself once and for all, "THIS TIME BILLY MEANS BUSINESS!"

***

First she would see if Billy was home. She hoped he was now grumbling and winding down, while swigging a beer and watching his Wednesday night wrestling match. She would ask him to come back now or tomorrow to talk.

A woman answered the phone. Paula knew Billy's wife's name was Lil, but she wasn't sure if Lil was aware of Billy's therapy. Billy wanted to focus on becoming a "calmer man," and viewed psychotherapy as his road to what he called "an emotional upgrade." They never discussed what his wife knew about his quest to soften, and he was adamant about not including her in any sessions. But this was a possible emergency.

"Hello, is this Lil Barge?"

"Yes. Who is this?"

"Uh, my name is Dr. Paula Zinni. Is Billy home?"

"No, and who are you?"

"I'm your husband's psychologist."

"His *what?*"

"He comes once a week to my office, and I am worried about him."

"Is this some kind of joke?"

"No, Mrs. Barge, I assure you this is no joke. He seemed very angry at his boss. I need to find him. Do you know where he is?"

There was a click and a dial tone.

"Dammit," Paula yelled, "she hung up on me." Even though she wished her wording had been less direct, calling again would be an unproductive use of precious time. Billy wasn't home. That's all she needed to know for now.

Besides attempting to warn Billy's boss, other options were closed. She couldn't lure him back into the office or implement any of the alternatives she vaguely recalled, such as committing Billy involuntarily for an evaluation. She needed to try to warn the intended victim. She didn't know Billy's boss's name. Opening her desk drawer, she scrambled though her files looking for the one marked "William 'Billy' Barge." She recalled at least scrawling down his place of employment on his intake form.

"Ah, here we go," she said, hoping this would be a good lead. "It looks like Weirdwood or maybe Wildwood Plumbing and Electrical Supplies. Now what? It's almost 9:00 p.m. and the shop won't be open."

Paula turned on her laptop to search the Internet for Wildwood Plumbing and Electrical Supplies, the more likely interpretation of her scribbled notation. "Maybe he has a Website," she thought. "Maybe the owner's name is listed." She found only the name of the company with an address and a phone number in a business directory under "Plumbing Supplies Near Santa Barbara."

Adrenalin surged through Paula's body like a torpedo, leaving her feeling simultaneously anxious and yet tightly focused. Her hand shook as she punched the number into the telephone. No answer, but a possible jackpot on the message machine. "Hello, this is Max Bellows, owner of Wildwood Electrical and Plumbing Supplies. No one is available to take your call…"

"Max Bellows. How many can there be in Santa Barbara?" she asked herself. She grabbed the white pages directory from her desk drawer and shuffled to the Bs, praying his home number would be listed. "Ah, there he is. Maximilian Bellows, 555–0076."

After three tries with shaky fingers she got the number right. One ring. Two rings. Three rings. On the fourth ring a woman answered.

"Hello, Bellows residence."

"Is this Mrs. Bellows?"

"No, I'm his sister. Who's this?"

"My name is Dr. Zinni. May I speak to Max, please?"

"Is something wrong with my brother?"

"No, I only need to talk to him. Is he home?"

"Just a minute."

To Paula, time stood still. Finally a man's voice spoke.

"What's this about?" he asked, sounding suspicious.

"Uh, are you the owner of Wildwood Plumbing and Electrical Supplies?"

"Sorry, I don't take business calls at home. Call me tomorrow at the office." Max sounded like he was going to hang up.

"No, no, this isn't a business call. Please, it's very important. Your employee, Billy Barge, is very angry at you. I am his psychologist and I have a legal duty to warn anyone I think may be a potential victim. I think Billy means to do you harm."

There was a long pause.

"How do I know you're who you say you are?" Max responded in a distressed and still mistrustful voice.

Paula didn't prepare for any follow-up questions. She stammered, "You can look me up in the phone directory."

"What would that mean? You could just be saying you are...what did you say your name was again?"

"Dr. Zinni. Dr. Paula Zinni. Call me back at the office number. I will tell you what it is, but you can check a directory to see it's a match. I am both very serious and completely legitimate." She heard herself almost yelling now.

"I'm not calling you back, but I am calling the cops." Max Bellows hung up.

✳✳✳

Still in the office building parking lot, Paula sat in her car not sure where she should go. The rain was heavy now, and she dreaded driving in a downpour. Max Bellows' address also appeared in the phone directly, so maybe going to his home was the next best step. If Billy showed up, she would try to talk him out of doing anything stupid. Or, she could be putting herself in danger.

"Well, I did warn Max," Paula thought to herself. "He didn't seem interested in talking to me. Am I not at least off any legal hook? And was Max calling the police about Billy or me, thinking I'm some sort of crank? Maybe I should call the police myself."

She had another idea to try first. Although it seemed whacky, she could at least find out more. She and Dr. Cawley arranged to cover for each other if one fell ill. Still in the office parking lot, she called from her mobile phone and managed to reach Nelson Cawley at home.

"Hey, Nelson. It's Paula. I'm in a bit of a jam here…well, a big jam." She tried to sound relaxed, but her voice cracked. "Would you call 555–0112 and ask for Billy? If anyone other than a man's voice answers say you're a friend from work. If a man answers make some excuse about getting a wrong number or something. Call me right back and let me know what happened. Right now? OK? I'll explain."

Dr. Cawley called Paula almost immediately. "A woman answered. She said Billy wasn't home and she didn't know where he was or when to expect him."

Paula spilled out her dilemma to Dr. Cawley. He agreed with her contemplated move to involve the police. Reluctantly, Paula got hold of a lieutenant in the Patrol Division of the Santa Barbara Police Department. They agreed to issue a BOLO for Billy Barge.

***

Paula decided to drive home. She was out of options and ideas, but still agonized over how this would play out. She tried unsuccessfully to think about something else. Where was Billy, and was he implementing his deadly plan? Would the police stop him in time? Billy was more agitated than usual, but could it have been just another empty threat? Would Billy be coming after her for ratting on him? Did she do enough? After two glasses of wine and checking her doors and windows for the fourth time, she fell into a fitful sleep on her living room couch.

***

Early the next morning Paula Zinni called the police department for any news. Billy had been located around 11:30 p.m. sitting in his car in front of a municipal park less than a mile from the Bellow's residence. He was unarmed, and nothing qualifying as a deadly weapon was found in his car, save for the usual paraphernalia in the trunk for fixing a flat tire. Billy vigorously denied any intent to do anyone harm. The officers released him after 20 minutes when he convinced them he often parked in a quiet place to unwind rather than take out the frustrations of his day by yelling at his wife or the dog. He was also about a mile from his own home in another direction.

Paula felt simultaneously relieved and unnerved. Max and Billy were safe. She fulfilled her legal duty to warn someone, who, in her clinical judgment, was an intended victim of serious bodily harm. She worried about her sloppy execution with Billy's wife and with Max Bellows. Neither one took it well. They didn't even seem to take her seriously. "How did others in the same predicament make this bizarre call to a complete stranger?" she wondered. "And is this the end of it?"

***

"Can you believe that friggin' broad?" Billy yelled as he burst into his home just before midnight. Lil was still awake, shaken by the strange calls from earlier in the evening.

"Where have you been?" Lil shrieked. "Some woman called here and said you were going to hurt Max. She said she's your psychologist. Then some guy called looking for you. Billy, are you seeing another woman? I want the truth!"

"No, no. OK. I didn't want to tell you but I've been seeing a head doctor for a while now. When you almost left me a while back I realized I don't treat you right. I want to try to control my temper better. My mouth runs foul too much, Lil. It gets away from me sometimes."

Lil was taken aback. How strange. Billy had never done anything so loving for her before.

"So why did she call me and say those things about you being dangerous?" Lil asked.

"Beats me, but she called the cops on me. I always tell her what's pissing me off. That's what you're supposed to do with a head doctor."

At 7 a.m. the next day the phone rang at the Barge home. Max Bellows had only three words to say.

"Billy, you're fired."

***

Billy didn't show up for his next appointment with Paula Zinni. Or the next. She got mixed messages from colleagues as to whether she should try to contact him. She did leave one message inviting him to discuss what happened and why, but he never responded.

Perhaps Paula had heard the end of Billy Barge, even though things felt unfinished. "I probably wouldn't go back to a psychotherapist who called in the police on me," she thought. But the lack of closure was maddening.

Then, six weeks after the incident, a certified letter from the League of California Psychologists arrived.

Dear Dr. Zinni,

William and Lillian Barge are asserting that you violated Mr. Barge's rights to confidentiality by calling his boss and the police after his last therapy session. He claims he was simply disclosing problems he was having at work.

We advised him that he cannot seek monetary damages from us for the resulting loss of his job, but we need to discuss with you the circumstances under which you decided to alert his employer and the authorities.

You must make an appointment with the LCP administrator, Mrs. Peggy Aldridge, to appear before the Ethics Committee at its March meeting unless a compelling reason requires a postponement. Mr. Barge has signed a release allowing you to discuss the matter with us. We expect you to respond in detail to Mr. Barge's allegations. Failure to contact us within 10 days of the receipt of this letter will constitute an act of noncompliance, which is itself an ethics violation.

Sincerely,
Victor Graham, Ph.D.
Chair, Ethics Committee
League of California Psychologists

"Oh God, he got fired." A wave of thick guilt followed quickly with the realization that she would now be required to answer for everything she did and didn't do that stormy night. "First thing," Paula thought, "is to write it all down in chronological order." She admonished herself for not documenting the incident at the time, but the memory was still vivid. She left a message at the LCP Office saying she would appear as requested.

The Ethics Committee:
Paula Zinni, Ph.D. March 16, 3:50 p.m.

"Come to order, please," said Victor Graham sharply. "This one is about the thorniest dilemma the majority of mental health professionals must grapple with at least once in their career. Making the decision to break a client's confidence."

The others nodded their heads in agreement, except for Stella Sarkosky who just frowned.

"We know the law and ethics principle mandating a duty to protect, including allowing for the disclosure of confidential information with appropriate others under a specific set of circumstances. But too few know what to do when faced with this dilemma," Victor continued. "You hit it right and you may save a life. You make the same decision and even if nothing comes of the client's threat, things can still get complicated for everyone. Let me read the brief complaint letter from the client."

To the Ethics Committee

My husband and I found out about your committee from my cousin who is a paralegal. We want to press charges against Dr. Paula Zinni. For no reason she called my husband's ex-boss and the police and told them Billy was dangerous. Billy got fired from the job he had for over five years. She must be held responsible. We also seek restitution from your organization for lost wages and pain and suffering.

Sincerely,
Lillian and William Barge

"This kind of thing happened to me once," said Charlotte Burroughs. "My client threatened to kill herself and was depressed enough to follow through in my professional opinion. I couldn't talk her into voluntary hospitalization and she wouldn't promise to not do it. I asked her what she had planned, and she said she had saved up a bunch of 'bad pills.' She didn't know what they were called."

"What did you do?" Sammy Halsey asked.

"She was an adult but still living at home. I got off easy I guess. I talked to her mother who searched her stuff and found an old mustard bottle with a collection of over-the-counter tablets, mostly acetaminophen. The head of the clinic where I work, a psychiatrist, got her on depression meds right away, and I kept seeing her. Thank God she wasn't mad at me for calling her mother. I think her true motive behind the suicidal gesture was to make sure her mom understood how unhappy she was."

"I've always had problems with the way the laws are written in most states" said Stella, sounding exasperated. "Some legislators seem to think we all hover over crystal balls hidden in our desk drawers and predict exactly who will blow wide open. If you get others involved, you lose clients' trust when they need psychotherapy the most." Stella tossed her head back and made a grunting sound.

"That's why you need to warn your clients when you might have to disclose what they say before they say anything first," said Ted meekly.

"So what does that do?" snorted Stella. "They just keep their mouths shut. And that can make the menacing ones even more dangerous."

"Let's talk about Dr. Zinni's experience, shall we?" said Victor in his back-to-business voice. "Sammy, would you show her in? I stuck my head out a few minutes ago, and I assume she is the young woman with the long black hair and wearing a shiny purple blouse."

***

Victor Graham introduced Paula Zinni to the others and pulled out a chair for her next to his.

"Let me start by saying we all recognize and appreciate your difficult judgment call. We need to find out more about the circumstances under which you made it," said Victor.

"Yes, thank you. These are my notes." Paula paused to put on her glasses and glanced down at the papers she had spread out. "Billy Barge expressed anger frequently, right from our first session over six months ago. He was determined to work on his temper, to become a gentler person. Oh, he did take a swing at someone once, a long time ago. He missed. Now he would say threatening things, but they seemed improbable to me. I got used to his irritability."

"Like what would he say?" Wolf Levin asked.

"Well, for example, he told me he was thinking about terrifying his wife by sneaking into the house wearing a werewolf costume to teach her to stop complaining whenever he forgot to shave. Or another time he wanted to get a dumpster filled with cow dung to put on a neighbor's roof because their dog pooped on his front lawn. Stuff like that. Never did any of it. We would explore why he was upset with whoever he wanted to intimidate and come up with more constructive alternatives. He always quieted down after a few minutes."

"What was so different about this time?" asked Wolf.

"He had been complaining about work for a while. His boss sounded to me like a disagreeable individual, and Billy's quick temper didn't help matters. This one night, it was December 12th, he showed up on time looking uncommonly irate. He announced a general plan to kill his employer, Mr. Bellows, that very night or the next morning. Didn't say how he was going to do it. He got up and left. I chased after him, but he disappeared. Totally unlike him."

"Then what?" Wolf continued.

"Well, this was a stressful time for me. His boss could've been in imminent danger. So I called Billy's house to see if I could talk to him first.

He wasn't home and his wife hung up on me. I found his bosses' number in a round-about way, and he hung up on me, saying he was calling the police. I wasn't sure if he meant to call them about me or if my warning came across. I then talked to another psychologist in my building, and he agreed I should call the police.

"Just to make clear. You didn't get a chance to try to talk him down? Correct?" asked Stella Sarkosky.

"Right, he ran away."

"Does he own a cell phone?"

"I don't think so. I never saw one."

"Dr. Zinni, did your client understand the concept of ethical and legal disclosures and what the parameters are?" Stella continued.

"Yes. My clients take home a three-page document informing them about what psychotherapy is and the importance of arriving at their appointments on time and the like. The conditions under which I would be mandated by law to disclose any threats of harm to others or to themselves to proper authorities or appropriate others as well as to an intended victim are spelled out in lay terms. Here. I brought the copy Billy signed during his second session indicating he read it. I asked if he had any questions. He said 'no.'" She passed the papers to Victor.

"You haven't heard from Billy since that night in your office?" asked Charlotte Burroughs.

"No. I left a message asking him to contact me so we could talk, but he has not returned my call. No threats or anything unexplained happened to me since. I confess I watch my own back more than ever before. Quite an unsettling way to live."

"I can imagine," Victor said in a sympathetic tone. "Does anyone else want to ask a question?" No one responded.

"Anything else you think we should know, Dr. Zinni?"

"No, thank you. I think I covered everything I could. I feel so bad for Billy. I liked him, I really did. I wish I could've done more for him. When will I hear what you decide about me?"

"We won't keep you waiting long. Within two weeks. Thank you for your cooperation." Victor escorted her out.

***

"What else could she have done instead?" Ted blurted out almost before Victor closed the door behind Dr. Zinni.

"In my professional opinion, she should have pressed for Billy to invite his wife to get involved with his psychotherapy early on," said Stella. "Not taken 'no' for an answer."

"I'm one of those few lucky ones. This never happened to me...yet," said Archie. "What *do* you say when you warn an intended victim?"

"Sometimes it's easier to send in an agency like law enforcement to do the tough job if no other way to make contact with the client or an intended victim is possible," answered Victor. "But Dr. Zinni did some fast thinking, and I believe she did better than many of our colleagues would've done. The police don't necessarily act fast on mere threats, especially if they're tied up with other emergencies involving situations in progress."

"True," said Charlotte. "One of my marriage counselor friends called the police when a client's husband left a message with the clinic receptionist threatening to beat up my colleague unless he made his estranged wife take him back. You know what the police told him? 'Call 911 when you see the guy coming at you.'"

"Threats are a dime a dozen," added Wolf.

Archie Wittig looked apprehensive. "So, again, how *do* you make those calls to a complete stranger? Do you say, 'Hi, you don't know me, but your daughter wants you dead by dinnertime?' I mean, that would freak anyone out."

"It's a tough one," said Victor. "No cut-and-dried technique and no guarantees about the outcome. But lives have been saved, and children and the elderly have been rescued from sordid circumstances, thanks to mandated duty to protect laws."

"I think the critical part of Dr. Zinni's response rested on her evidence proving Billy was informed about the duty to warn, even though he might've forgotten in the meantime," said Ted. "I do feel bad about the consequences for Billy and his family though."

"Hey, that's what happens when you do or say something you shouldn't. Can't blame the boss, even though I suspect he might be a putz," added Wolf.

"I get the sense we do not judge Dr. Zinni to be guilty of violating the ethics code," said Victor. "She would benefit from getting up to speed on the latest in risk assessment and management though."

All heads shook in the affirmative.

"OK, let's get our letters drafted for Peggy to send out. Those who are available will meet here to drive to dinner at 6:15 p.m. sharp," said Victor. "I made reservations at Jedi's Bistro on Ventura Boulevard. We can all fit into my SUV."

Decision and Dispositions

The Committee decided that Dr. Zinni acted as appropriately as might be expected under difficult circumstances. She was advised, however, to create an accessible file containing all contact and other useful information, such as the latest risk assessment information, as well as a list of emergency community resources. She was also strongly encouraged to seek continuing education in the management and treatment of clients who might become violent.

The letter to Billy Barge and his wife sympathized with the unfortunate consequences resulting from Dr. Zinni's disclosure. Mr. Barge was gently reminded that he was apprised of the conditions under which information shared in confidence can be divulged to others and signed a form indicating he understood what it meant. Also enclosed was a copy of California law regarding psychotherapists' duty of care.

The Barges or their lawyer never contacted Paula Zinni. Nevertheless, Paula remained hyper-vigilant. Her front and back doors were always locked. She kept the windows in her home closed and secured, even when hot outside. She moved her office to a building with a security guard and monitored parking. She quit seeing any clients after dark or on weekends when the other offices were almost all empty.

Five months after the incident, a headline in the local Santa Barbara newspaper caught Paula Zinni's eye. "Owner of Wildwood Plumbing and Electrical Supplies Survives Attack." The story described Max Bellows closing up his shop for the day when he was struck from behind with a brick by an unknown assailant. A full recovery was expected. An unidentified person of interest was being sought for questioning.

Case Commentary

The duty to protect—to do something proactive when clients seem poised to endanger others—poses dilemmas for mental health professions beyond an inability to accurately predict violent acts. Clients' threats to inflict physical harm to others or to themselves are among the most formidable situations psychotherapists encounter (Shapiro & Smith, 2011). Psychotherapists are not expected to predict exactly what will happen in the future, but they are required to carefully assess the risks and create a plan of treatment accordingly (Berman, 2006). This story puts human faces on the intense challenges involved in implementing a duty of care.

Dr. Zinni did almost everything as well as could be expected when faced with possible imminent danger to a third party, given the information she had to work with. Without access to her client, attempting alternatives to warning the intended victim and the authorities were impossible. Although she was not current with the risk assessment literature, she did recall a few items appearing on the lists as well as some protective factors (e.g., married, employed) worth taking into consideration (Robbé, de Vogel, & Stam, 2012).

Dr. Zinni was not found guilty of any ethical violation. However, had she been doing careful risk assessment and management along the way with a client who clearly had anger issues, the course of therapy might have gone differently. As absurd as most of Billy's threats seemed at the time, she may have been too quick to conclude that he was "all bark and no bite."

The last entry in the story opens the possibility that Dr. Zinni missed many red flags. The Committee rightly encouraged her to update her knowledge and understanding of and preparation for managing potentially violent clients. However, if Billy Barge did, in fact, perpetrate the attack on Max Bellows, we must consider whether the critics of duty to protect statutes have a point when they suggest that mandatory reporting laws may actually cause *more* violence. Had Billy not been fired because his boss was never informed of the threat made against him, might Max have been spared a brick to the head?

Notes on Dangerousness

A fatal stabbing in 1969 changed the practice of psychotherapy forever. Prosenjit Poddar, distraught because a young woman rebuffed his interest in a serious relationship, expressed an intent to kill her to his psychologist at the health care center of the University of California, Berkeley. Two months later Tatiana Tarasoff was dead.

Sufficiently concerned at the time of the threats, the psychologist consulted with colleagues and called the campus police. Poddar was picked up, held briefly before being released and never returned to psychotherapy. No further action was taken by the University. Tatiana's parents sued the psychologist, the UC Berkeley Health Service, and the University for failing to protect their daughter once the threats became known.

Most states now expect mental health professionals to take protective action when clients make specific threats as alluded to in the final opinion of the California Supreme Court.

> We shall explain that defendant therapists cannot escape liability merely because Tatiana herself was not their patient. When a therapist determines, or pursuant to the standards of his profession should determine, that his patient presents a serious danger of violence to another, he incurs an obligation to use reasonable care to protect the intended victim against such danger. The discharge of this duty may require the therapist to take one or more of various steps, depending upon the nature of the case. Thus it may call for him to warn the intended victim or others likely to apprise the victim of the danger, to notify the police, or to take whatever other steps are reasonably necessary under the circumstances
> (*Tarasoff v. Regents of University of California*, 1976).

Similar tragic incidents since Tarasoff include the shooting resulting in multiple serious injuries and deaths in a packed movie theater in July 20, 2012. The gunman, University of Colorado graduate student James Holmes, was being seen by a University psychiatrist. She indicated that she treated Holmes more than a month before the shootings but had no contact with him after June 11 when she reported concerns about his mental status to campus police. Remaining to be seen as of this writing is whether Holmes' process of withdrawing from the University at the time constituted sufficient reason for the university to take no further action (Goode, Kovaleski, Healy, & Frosch, 2012). In the meantime as a result of another horrific incident in Sandy Hook, New Jersey, New York hastily legislated the NY SAFE Act, requiring mental health professionals and other health care workers to report clients believed to be dangerous to themselves or others to officials who may then search and remove guns from their homes (Ritter & Tanner, 2013).

State laws vary as to how or whether a duty of care to third parties pertains (Benjamin, Kent & Sirikantraporn, 2009), and unless clinicians remain abreast of the law, they function with a double burden of ignorance and anxiety (Beck, 1990). Unfortunately, many psychotherapists are apparently unaware of the laws in their jurisdictions, often misinterpreting a duty to warn possible victims as the only recourse (Pabian, Welfel, & Beebe, 2009). Alternative protective options in many states include increasing the frequency of sessions and communications, minimizing environmental enablers or other elements that may encourage violent behavior, changing medication, voluntary hospitalization or commitment, involving family members or other support systems, "do-no-harm" contracts, and consultation (Shapiro & Smith, 2011).

Of course, the ultimate goal of such laws is to save lives. However, some mental health professionals argue lives could be lost as a result of overzealous reporting mandates (Shapiro & Smith, 2011). Clients who need therapy the most may not return to therapy, perhaps placing others or themselves at increased risk. Aggressive or angry persons may avoid engaging the services of mental health professionals if they suspect their confidences could be disclosed to law enforcement or others. Or, even those who do enter therapy may not express what they actually feel or intend to do (Ritter & Tanner, 2013). More recently California courts have ruled that mental health professionals must heed warnings from third parties (e.g., a concerned parent of a client), putting them in the difficult position of assessing the credibility of individuals they do not know (*Ewing v. Goldstein*, 2004; Eisner, 2006; Greer, 2005).

Given that many clients are depressed or angry, deciding whether a client's threats to harm themselves or others are serious, as opposed to venting, is almost inevitable at some point in every psychotherapist's career. Taking action to warn or protect an intended victim is not an easy decision. Compilations of risk factors exist to help assess violence potential (Berman, 2006; Douglas, Ogloff, & Nicholls et al., 1999; Harris, Rice, & Camilleri, 2004; Scott & Resnick, 2006), but violent fantasies alone are not likely to predict violent criminal behavior (Gellerman & Suddath, 2005). Forecasting imminent violent behavior remains largely in the realm of clinical judgment rather than manual-driven assessments (Shapiro, 2011), and the best predictor remains past behavior (Shapiro & Smith, 2011).

Discussion Questions

1. Would you be more prepared than Dr. Zinni if a client made a serious threat of bodily harm? If not, what would you have to do now to become better prepared?
2. Did Dr. Zinni's decision match the usual criteria—a direct communication of a credible threat against an individual who can be identified—to elicit a duty to protect the intended victim? If not, in what way was her decision deficient?
3. Should Dr. Zinni have been more concerned about Billy Barge's potential for violence? That is, should she have been doing serious risk assessments earlier on, given his difficult upbringing and verbal outbursts? Or was she justified in focusing on his positive signs (married, steady employment, showing up for sessions on time, motivated to improve)?
4. If Billy Barge had killed Max Bellows that stormy night, do you think the Committee (or a licensing board) would have rendered the same decision regarding Dr. Zinni's actions? If not, why not?
5. A depressed client says, "I am so tired, I just wish it was all over." How would you respond?
6. An angry client says, "I hate gays. I think I will go out now and get rid of one or two of them." You know she carries a knife in her car "for protection." Now what?
7. Your client calls at 3 a.m. threatening to kill herself. She demands that you to come right over to her apartment or else she will take 100 pills. This client is attention-seeking and manipulative. Do you get up and go over?
8. Let's say you called a psychiatric emergency team instead of going to the clients' apartment (see above question). She had

taken no pills and was subsequently evicted from her apartment for causing another disturbance (not her first) and blames you. She writes to an ethics committee claiming incompetence and emotional damages. How would you defend yourself?

9. You receive an email from an angry adult client threatening to confront an abusive father who molested her when she was 10. You are not sure what she plans to do, but her parting words are, "Revenge is best served up cold." You see that as an ominous clue. You do not know where she is. She does not answer her cell phone. Now what?

10. Do you think the "duty to protect" (which may include warning intended victims) is the most formidable challenge facing psychotherapists? Why or why not?

References

Benjamin, G. A., Kent, L., & Sirikantraporn, S. (2009). A review of duty-to-protect statutes, cases, and procedures for positive practice. In Werth, J. L., Welfel, E. R., & Benjamin, G. A. H. (Eds.). (pp. 9–28). *The duty to protect: Ethical, legal, and professional considerations for mental health professionals.* Washington, DC: American Psychological Association.

Beck, J. C. (Ed.). (1990). *Confidentiality versus the duty to protect: Foreseeable harm in the practice of psychiatry.* Washington, DC: American Psychiatric Association.

Berman, A. L. (2006). Risk management with suicidal patients. *Journal of Clinical Psychology, 62,* 171–184.

Douglas, K. S., Ogloff, J. R. P., Nicholls, T. L., & Grant, I. (1999). Assessing risk for violence among psychiatric patients: The HCR-20 risk assessment scheme and the Psychopathy Checklist: Screening Version. *Journal of Consulting and Clinical Psychology, 67,* 917–930.

Eisner, D. A. (2006). From Tarasoff to Ewing: Expansion of the duty to warn. *American Journal of Forensic Psychology, 24,* 45–55.

Ewing v. Goldstein (2004). 15 Cal. Rptr.3d 864 120 Cal.App.4th 807. Retrieved from http://scholar.google.com/scholar_case?case=8624239105913702855&q=ewing+v.+goldstein&hl = en&as_sdt = 2,5&as_vis = 1

Gellerman, D. M., & Suddath, R. (2005). Violent fantasy, dangerousness, and the duty to warn and protect. *Journal of the American Academy of Psychiatry and the Law, 33,* 484–495.

Goode, E., Kovaleski, S. F., Healy, J., & Frosch, D. (August 26, 2012). Before gunfire, hints of bad news. Retrieved from http://www.nytimes.com/2012/08/27/us/before-gunfire-in-colorado-theater-hints-of-bad-news-about-james-holmes.html?pagewanted=all&_r=0

Greer, M. (February, 2005). Expansion of duty to warn in California. *APA Monitor on Psychology, 36,* 45.

Harris, G. T., Rice, M. E., & Camilleri, J. A. (2004). Applying a forensic actuarial assessment (the Violence Risk Appraisal Guide) to nonforensic patients. *Journal of Interpersonal Violence, 19,* 1063–1074.

Pabian, Y. L., Welfel, E., & Beebe, R. S. (2009). Psychologists' knowledge of their states' laws pertaining to Tarasoff-type situations. *Professional Psychology, 40,* 8–14.

Scott, C. L., & Resnick, P. J. (2006). Violence risk assessment in persons with mental illness. *Aggression and Violent Behavior, 11,* 598–611.

Shapiro, D. L. (2011). To warn or not to warn, that is the question. In W. B. Johnson, & G. P. Koocher (Eds.). *Ethical conundrums, quandaries, and predicaments in mental health practice.* (pp. 55–61). New York, NY: Oxford University Press.

Shapiro, D. L., & Smith, S. R. (2011). *Malpractice in psychology: A practical resource for clinicians.* Washington, DC: American Psychological Association.

Ritter, M., & Tanner, L. (January 15, 2013). Experts say proposed NY gun law might hinder therapy. Retrieved from http://news.yahoo.com/experts-proposed-ny-gun-law-might-hinder-therapy-164728039.html

Robbé, M., de Vogel, V., & Stam, J. (2012). Protective factors for violence risk: The value for clinical practice. *Psychology, 3,* 1259–1263.

Tarasoff v. Regents of University of California (July 1, 1976). 17 Cal.3d 425, S.F. No. 23042. Supreme Court of California. Retrieved from http://www.stanford.edu/group/psylawseminar/Tarsoff%20I.htm

Webster, C., Douglas, K., Eaves, D., & Hart, S. (1997). HCR-20: *Assessing risk for violence (Version 2).* Burnaby, British Columbia, Canada: Mental Health, Law and Policy Institute, Simon Fraser University.

Additional Reading

Kamph, A., McSherry, B., Ogloff, J., & Rothschild, A. (2009). *Confidentiality for mental health professionals.* Bowen Hills, Australia: Australian Academic Press.

Monahan, J. (1981). *The clinical prediction of violence.* Beverly Hills, CA: Sage.

Fisher, M. A. (2013). *The ethics of confidentiality: A practice model for mental health professionals.* New York, NY: Oxford University Press.

Werth, J. L., Welfel, E. R., & Benjamin, G. A. H. (Eds.). (2009). *The duty to protect: Ethical, legal, and professional considerations for mental health professionals.* Washington, DC: American Psychological Association.

It was only 5:35 p.m. on a balmy Saturday evening, and Sammy was exhausted. He almost tripped over his own feet during his trek back to the motel to freshen up for dinner. He dared not lay down, even for a minute; he would never be able to fully wake up in a half hour. Missing the first dinner with the Committee was unthinkable.

Even though Sammy and the others were sitting all day, save for bathroom and stretch breaks, their mission was emotionally draining. So many upset people to try to take care of, to understand where they were coming from and why they did what they did, to figure out how it all went wrong, to judge based on the available information while trying to separate out distortion and hyperbole, and then to make fair and just decisions.

Sammy walked back to the LPC office by 6:15 p.m. where only two others besides Victor showed up. Charlotte and Ted looked as weary as Sammy felt.

So, what's your choice for dinner?" Charlotte asked Sammy as they sat in the patio at Jedi's Bistro.

Sammy chose Ravioli Giardino, the least exotic vegetarian item on the Jedi's Bistro menu, and lubricated it with water only. A glass of wine would have sent him to the floor right then and there.

Victor offered a toast of sorts. "We need to take time out to remind ourselves that what we see is only a sliver of what our profession is about, the mistakes that are made. Don't let our work here drag you down." The rest of the dinner conversation was light and scattered.

"You should get a good night's sleep, Sammy," said Victor as he picked up the tab.

"Yes, thanks." Sammy smiled just thinking about crawling into bed, hoping the eye-opening events of the day would not interrupt his sleep.

eight
BROKEN

It comes as a most unpleasant surprise when a psychotherapist intends to do a client a favor and gets brought up on ethics charges instead. In this story the disputed act was not in and of itself unethical, although ethics codes advise caution. Rather, the story illustrates how mental health professionals are wise to evaluate before embarking on what seems like an uncomplicated deviation from standard practice to benefit a client. The clues suggesting the psychotherapy might go sideways were lined up, but missed.

Candy Bean scurried frantically from room to room, her face flushed and streaked with silvery tears. "Jerry! Where in the hell are you? My psychologist is ripping me off!"

She was bawling by the time she found her husband in the back yard watering the lemon tree. She put her arms around him and wailed, "All that therapy for nothing, and I get abused again! You can't trust anyone. I let my guard down."

"What happened, Jelly Bean? Is this about the television set?" Jerry asked, drawing her into his arms and kissing her on the forehead.

"Yes it's about the television set!" Candy replied impatiently. "He said it's broken and wants me to take it back and charge me for the last two therapy sessions and the one we were supposed to have today. My emotions are being molested!"

"It worked fine last time we watched," said Jerry. "That was a while ago though."

"Nothing was wrong with it!" Candy snapped, brushing away tears. "It was in perfect condition. I'm going to write a letter to that organization he belongs to. They need to know about this. I trusted him and he tricked me, even knowing our money problems."

***

Candy thought back to her reason for seeking psychotherapy in the first place. It was horrific enough that her father brutally raped her in her own bed when she was eight years old. Only her screams kept him from completing his brutal intent. If he feared he was hurting her or was worried her mother might hear was never quite clear, but he did sprint from her room, twisting around only to warn her to keep quiet before slowly closing the door behind him. At the time Candy didn't even know what that thing was jutting out from between his legs. The next time he put his hand over her mouth so she could not scream. She wanted to poke his eyes with a free hand, but the consequences might be worse than enduring those minutes of torment, hardly able to breathe. She remembered what happened when the cat accidentally scratched his leg while batting at a loose thread hanging from his easy chair. He picked up Muffy and tossed her across the room. So Candy endured the torture until, after the third time, she threw up all over him and her bed. He never tried to touch her again.

At 27, Candy thought she had gotten beyond the petrifying memories of her now deceased father. She was 17 when he died, and she did not shed a tear on that day or ever. Her mother admonished her for being a heartless and ungrateful child, yet her secret remained untold.

Jerry Bean's entrance into her life proved a godsend. He was the sweetest and most patient man she could hope to find. But she knew something dark kept her from being the trusting, amorous wife she wanted so much to be. Committed to fixing the part of herself her father violently impaired, she turned to Dr. Terrance Gambon, a local psychologist in downtown Sacramento who came highly recommended by her hairdresser.

When Candy called the office of the League of California Psychologists to ask how to launch a complaint. Peggy Aldridge confirmed Dr. Gambon's status as a LPC member and informed her of the procedure. Shifting around until comfortable in the chair in front of her computer, Candy pounded out a brief letter. It felt good to be big enough, strong enough, to finally fight back.

TO: The Ethics Committee
FROM: Mrs. Candy Bean
RE: GETTING RIPPED OFF BY ONE OF YOUR MEMBERS

Terrance Gambon is almost as bad as my father when it comes to abuse. I asked if he would take my very good television set in exchange for three more therapy sessions because my family is on a tight budget. He said yes. He took it and broke it. Now he wants me to pay for those sessions. This is not right
I need you to deal with this. He keeps trying to force me to give him money. He still has my TV.

Sincerely,
Mrs. Candy Bean

***

"Damn! Janice! Come down here!" Dr. Terrance Gambon called out, standing in the front hallway with a letter in one hand and an envelope marked "certified" in the other. "She can't let go of this!"

Janice Gambon ran down the stairs, alarmed by the frantic tone in her husband's voice. "What? Who is *she*?"

"Listen to this." Terrance read the letter aloud, omitting his client's name. "How could something that seemed so simple turn into such a bloody nightmare?"

Dear Dr. Gambon,

Mrs. Candy Bean, a previous client, has complained about a bartering agreement that worked to her ultimate disadvantage. Mrs. Bean claims you destroyed the property she gave you in lieu of payment for three psychotherapy sessions and then reneged on the agreement.
If Mrs. Bean's version of the incident is truthful, your client's welfare may not have been adequately protected.
Please make an appointment with the LCP administrator, Mrs. Peggy Aldridge, to appear before the LCP Ethics Committee at its meeting in March unless a compelling reason requires a postponement. We expect you will be able to respond in to Mrs. Bean's complaint. She has signed a release allowing you to discuss the matter with us. Failure to contact us within 10 days of the receipt of this letter will constitute an act of noncompliance, which is itself an ethics violation.

Sincerely,
Victor Graham, Ph.D.
Chair, Ethics Committee
League of California Psychologists

"Just tell them what happened," Janice said, as she patted Terrance gently on the back. "You had the right motives."

***

Terrance remembered welcoming Candy Bean's offer six weeks ago. It seemed to make sense on all levels. She required only a few more sessions to come to terms with the merciless actions her father forced upon her as a child.

"We're really short on cash right now," Candy had stated at the end of their fifth session. "But I have a proposition for you. We have an extra color television set, a nice one. It's in perfect condition. Thirty-two inch screen. It's in the living room and almost never watched. Would you accept it in payment for three or four more sessions? I figure it's worth at least three hundred dollars. My brother will visit with his SUV in two weeks. I can bring it with me then."

Terrance doubted a used 32 inch television could be worth that much unless it was a newer model. Nevertheless Terrance needed a set for his 16-year-old son's room to reduce the never-ending after-dinner tension between parents and child. He and Janice enjoyed programs like *Masterpiece Theater* while Kenny preferred the likes of *Pimp My Ride*.

"Sure, we can probably do that," Terrance replied. "But let me check first to make sure no rule forbids exchanging therapy sessions for goods." Upon review, the ethics code did not disallow bartering outright, but such an arrangement must not be exploitative or therapeutically contra-indicated.

"What can possibly go wrong?" Terrance thought without any reflection as he punched the Bean's number into his phone. "Hi, Candy. We're on with the TV deal."

He remembered walking into his house announcing to his wife and son, "I have a big surprise for Kenny, well for all of us. He's getting a television set for his room! One of my clients is giving us a good one in exchange for a few therapy sessions."

"GREAT! Thanks Dad," shouted Kenny, as he gave Terrance a bear hug.

Two weeks and two more sessions later Terrance drove the family van to work. When he opened the back door of Candy's brother's SUV, he felt a twinge of regret. The TV's faux oak finish had scratches and scrapes. The bulky unit looked to be a much older model than he expected, and the screen appeared to be smaller than 32 inches. But, he reasoned, if it worked it would be good enough for Kenny's room. With assistance from the office building security guard, they transferred the TV into his van.

Terrance and Kenny dragged the TV into the house on a dolly. They lugged it up one stair at a time and into Kenny's room. The screen looked small. Out of curiosity Terrance got a yardstick and, sure enough, the diagonal measurement was 28 inches. Still no real problem, he thought, even though he began to think his client may have taken advantage of him.

Cables were attached. The set was plugged in and turned on. Only the splutter of white noise. Kenny's face, aglow with anticipation seconds ago, faded to disappointment. Terrance ran next door to solicit assistance from a neighbor who used to work for an appliance repair company.

Terrance did not want to hear the news. "It'll cost you less to buy a spanking new one," the neighbor declared, pulling his head out from behind the cabinet. "Whoever pawned it off on you pulled a fast one. This heap is at least 12 years old, and the picture tube's either broken or shot."

The look of disappointment on Kenny's face made Terrance feel both sad and angry. Letting his son down was the last thing he ever wanted to do.

So, Candy Bean had misrepresented the merchandise, or, giving her every possible benefit of a doubt, was unaware of its actual dimensions and defunct condition. Now Dr. Terrance Gambon had to consider his options.

"I can handle this in one of two ways," he told his wife. "I can ignore this whole debacle as if nothing ever happened and suck up not getting paid. Or, I can reject the agreement because my client falsified her end of the deal, return the dead set to her, and tell her she will have to find some other way to pay for the two sessions we've already had and any more from now on."

"I hate to see you exploited," Janice responded. "And now we need to go out and buy Kenny a new TV. He's feeling let down."

Terrance decided he deserved to be compensated for his services. His practice was also a business after all. Candy would certainly understand and probably even apologize upon becoming aware of her malfunctioning merchandise.

***

"Best to get the bartering misfortune out of the way first thing," Terrance thought as he waited for Candy Bean to arrive for her eighth session. He knew Candy was getting a fresh outlook on what happened to her, a better understanding of why her now deceased father exploited her sexually, and a start to forgive without also making herself complicit in her father's deplorable behavior. She seemed so close to being free from what felt like a padlock on her sexuality.

She appeared at his open door.

"Hey Candy. A quick item before we start. Come take your chair. I'll explain."

Candy sat down, looking puzzled. "Does your son like the TV set?" she asked with a quizzical smile.

"Well, that's what I wanted to talk about. The TV set doesn't work, so I need to give it back to you. You need to find another way to compensate me for the last two sessions and this one."

"Well, YOU broke it then!" Candy practically shouted. "It worked fine the last time we watched it!"

Terrance was startled by her abrupt response. "You said you didn't use it anymore," he responded, trying to speak in a soothing tone. "Something happened to it in the meantime."

"No, you likely DROPPED it. Now you're re victimizing me, just like my father did!" A hot tear ran down each cheek and her body went rigid, gripping the arms of the chair as if her hands were glued down.

Terrance felt his body go tense, almost shaking. Her sharp words instantly undid all the work they accomplished over the last seven sessions. "But if I back down" he thought to himself, "it will look even worse. That would be like admitting I broke the TV myself and am trying to blame her."

"I'm sorry, Candy. I was very careful. Even brought in a professional to diagnose the problem. A bad picture tube. Really, it's as simple as that." Terrance tried to remain composed.

"Well, you had it last. It's yours!" Candy replied sharply. She snatched her purse and sweater from beside the chair, stood up and stalked towards the door. "You are a very bad man!" she shouted, without looking back.

Terrance sat motionless, trying to absorb what just happened. "How could something that seemed so right take such a sharp left turn?" he asked himself. "It was supposed to be a straightforward exchange to help out a client."

Later that day he made the first of several attempts to restore the therapeutic relationship with Candy Bean. She did not answer her phone or return his call. Over the next two weeks she did pick up on one occasion, but her stance had not softened. "I won't be paying for the sessions," she shrieked and hung up.

Terrance left messages offering other ways to restore their relationship, first a reduced fee and then to forgive the bill altogether. She remained unresponsive.

Three weeks later Terrance and Kenny hauled the TV to the local electronic waste site. Terrance then tried to put this unsettling incident behind him. He would forgive Candy Bean for stiffing him.

When the certified letter arrived from the League of California Psychologists, his perspective hardened again. He called the LCP office to confirm the appointment to tell his side of the story to the Ethics Committee.

The Ethics Committee:
Terrance Gambon, Ph.D. March 17, 8:29 a.m.

Peggy Aldridge didn't come in on Sundays, but she did leave a box of pastries in the office refrigerator and made sure the coffee supplies were sufficient to last through the morning. Ting's Café would not open until noon.

"First case for today, people," announced Victor Graham, eliciting little response from the tight circle surrounding the counter in the back of the room, pouring coffee and frowning over the assortment of cold donuts and croissants. The coffee tasted even less palatable when Stella Sarkosky made it. She vowed during the last meeting to bring a fair traded Columbian brand with her, but she forgot it.

"Except for the coffee, I hope today's cases all go smooth as silk," said Ted Bates in a too-cheery voice for so early in the morning.

"Fat chance," said Wolf Levin. "When has that ever happened besides in your dreams?"

"Wolf seemed got out on the wrong side of bed," Sammy Halsey thought to himself. Yet dealing with these cases was wearing him down, too.

Finally everyone gathered at the table as Victor announced the first case of the day. He read Candy Bean's complaint aloud, adding in a stern voice, "This one seems trivial on the surface, but it illustrates a profound dilemma. If I had my way, I would disallow trading clients' services and tangible goods in exchange for psychotherapy sessions."

"Why is that?" Sammy asked. "In such economic hard times, exchanges instead of money seem reasonable."

"Vulnerable clients could give a service or an object worth far more than psychotherapy session fees. Or clients might later claim being ripped off, even if they weren't. We use a monetary system for a reason. Everyone's on the same page."

"It's true. We aren't the *Antique Road Show*." added Ted.

Victor shook his head in agreement. "And don't forget the IRS issue. Psychotherapists who barter should claim the value of what they received in trade on their tax forms. But, mostly it's about cases like this. When things don't go as planned, real damage is done. It's not only a business transaction gone awry. The therapeutic alliance can collapse as well."

"Does this happen very often, Victor?" Sammy asked.

"Such agreements can work out. We don't hear those stories. We probably don't hear every one that goes south either. But when these arrangements unravel like a cheap sweater, things get nasty for the client, for the therapist, and for us when a complaint arrives on our doorstep."

"Remember the case with the attorney and psychologist swapping services?" asked Archie Wittig, glancing around for any glimmers of recollection on the faces of the others. "The psychologist got upset because his clinically depressed attorney-client was doing a lousy job with the psychologist's divorce. So the psychologist spent the therapy hour berating the attorney instead of treating him for his depression. The attorney pressed ethics charges claiming to be harassed mercilessly, and the psychologist's license got suspended for a year."

"I remember another outrageous one," said Stella, wiggling her fingers in the air as she liked to do whenever she was about to speak. "The psychologist traded 12 sessions of therapy for, of all things, an oil portrait of himself. His client was on the verge of being well-known in the right artists' circles. So they arranged for two-hour sessions—an hour of therapy followed by an hour of sitting while she painted. He wasn't allowed to peek until she finished. Her rule. Well, wouldn't you know, he hated it. Said it made him look cruel and monstrous, like *The Portrait of Dorian Gray*. He demanded she burn the canvass and pay for those 12 sessions. What a debacle, with both parties the put-upon victims."

"What happened next?" Sammy asked.

"Well, it's idiotic to take such an offer in the first place," Stella continued. "Her style was Picassoesque, I guess you might say. You know, body parts and facial features not necessarily lined up. Apparently he wasn't familiar with her work or he would've been forewarned. We suggested he drop his pursuit of payment. He very begrudgingly agreed. No happy ending to these cases."

Wolf sighed. "He should've taken the painting. If she's getting famous he could have sold it. No one had to know who it was supposed to be."

Sammy didn't have his own story to tell involving a barter dispute, but was familiar with the concept while living and practicing in rural Indiana.

"I see another related problem," Sammy added. "In Muncie we have a lot of farmers. They sometimes want to barter their produce for psychotherapy. One of my colleagues accepted corn. Then he waded in it. He gave away as much as friends would take, but corn piles up everywhere in Indiana, so most of it ended up rotting in his basement."

"Where's Muncie?" Wolf asked, although it wasn't clear if he cared about getting an answer.

"Forty-five minutes northeast of Indianapolis, not far from the Ohio border as the crow flies," answered Sammy.

"Back to California please," Victor said, sounding anxious to move on.

"Sorry. So what do you do when you don't want what the client has to barter?" Sammy asked.

"Good point, Sammy," said Wolf. "It doesn't match up if they don't offer something we can use. One of my clients wanted to trade a llama rug for more sessions with me. Dragged the damn thing in with him one day. It made me sneeze. Repeatedly. I politely refused and suggested how he might find a buyer. Case closed."

"Why did they relax the ethics rules against bartering anyway?" asked Sammy.

"It's probably about the economy going to hell in a hand basket. People have less to spend, but do have stuff or skills to offer. Makes sense, I guess," answered Ted.

"I think stingy insurance companies cutting clients off after a few sessions feeds into this also," added Wolf. "My friend in New York worked with a nine-year-old boy who routinely smeared himself with his own feces before banging his head against the wall. The insurance company allowed eight psychotherapy sessions. Can you imagine fixing something like that in 400 minutes? This kid's problems were serious. But if families can't pay for more sessions, they have no choice but to barter their chotskies or their furniture."

"Or if they're uninsured they face other challenges, like no job" said Charlotte Burroughs, sounding provoked. "So how are they going to get therapy? Barter their car? Then how do they find work?"

"That reminds me of the car swap," Ted exclaimed, taking a deep breath. "Remember that head-on collision, if I may wax metaphorical? The therapist accepted a classic Mercedes for a promise of 100 therapy sessions *in advance*?"

"Oh, hell yes." Wolf interrupted. "And the client didn't need 100 sessions and wanted out after about fifteen. Wanted his car back and offered to pay for the sessions he used up, but the psychologist insisted their contract was valid and held him to it. He actually told the poor schmuck he was keeping the car but the 85 sessions were always available if he ever needed them. Can you believe that tool?"

"I wanted to tell it," Ted said, looking disappointed.

"Sorry, man," said Wolf.

"Yes, these stories are pretty disheartening, but we're veering off course here again," said Victor. "Let's see if Dr. Terrance Gambon arrived. Go fetch him, Stella, if you would please," asked Victor.

***

As Dr. Gambon and Stella entered the room, Sammy noted yet again an accused colleague who didn't appear as he imagined. Instead of a callous appearance, this pleasant looking man, probably in his late-30s, was well dressed in a light tan sports coat and shirt, brown slacks, and a brown and tan striped tie. He had blonde hair cut short, blue eyes with long eyelashes some women would kill for, and a dimple in his chin. Dr. Gambon appeared apprehensive like most of the accused usually do, but managed a congenial smile while being introduced around the table.

"Well, you know why we've invited you here," said Victor. "We do take all complaints seriously and also want to ensure those accused of wrong-doing receive a fair shake. Let's not argue the condition of the disputed TV set for the moment. We're more interested in understanding your decision to enter into this swap agreement and how you handled the unfortunate outcome."

Terrance Gambon rubbed his hands together as if warming them up. "I go back over what happened often. It seemed so easy, so natural, at the time. The client was short on cash, so she made the offer to trade her television for three therapy sessions. I could use another TV for my son's room. It didn't have to be new or large, just in working condition. I didn't think beyond that point."

"Did you consider turning her down politely?" asked Charlotte.

"I do recall at the time thinking I could buy a new one for less than my regular therapy fees," Terrance answered without hesitation. "But I thought more about Mrs. Bean who is a very proud woman and embarrassed by her family's financial downturn. I guess I should've realized anything with fragile parts would pose a problem if something broke during a move from her possession into mine, but to be honest that never crossed my mind. Again, it seemed like a win-win at the time."

"Have you ever bartered your services before?" Ted asked.

"No, never. I had to look in the ethics code to be sure we were even allowed to do it."

"So you did make your best clinical judgment that Mrs. Bean was a suitable client for bartering?" Stella asked.

"I did, yes. I figured we only needed three, maybe four more sessions for her to mend her memories and the fallout from her father's sexual abuse when she was a child. We were making good headway. I thought we were anyway."

"So you now think she was more vulnerable than you imagined?" Wolf asked. "Childhood sexual abuse survivors also have fragile parts well into adulthood. Serious trust issues often hang on, especially with others of the same sex as the abuser. You were probably about the same age as the father when it all happened."

"Yes, I'm aware of the parallel," answered Terrance, furrowing his brow. "However she seemed so motivated to get beyond her history. We agreed early on that our collaboration would be limited with very specific goals. We didn't go deeply into her past, except for the issue with her father."

"Did you ever consider offering her a lower fee? Or perhaps taking her on *pro bono* for a few sessions?" asked Archie.

"I didn't at the time. She initiated the idea for a swap, and we focused our attention on the TV set. Her offer seemed like a graceful solution to her family's financial pressures, and we both were satisfied with it. After everything fell apart I did leave a message offering to forgive the bill, but she never responded."

"I'd like to know how you got the TV from her house to your house," asked Stella.

"I think we acted properly. We didn't go to each other's homes. She brought the TV to the office right before the seventh session. We got some help loading it into my van. Later when we got to my house Kenny, my son, and I took it up to his room."

"So you must believe the TV set broke *before* you loaded it into your vehicle or else you wouldn't have asked Mrs. Bean to take it back," said Stella, now sounding more like a district attorney

"Yes, I do believe the TV was kaput before it came into my possession," he answered, looking Stella squarely in the eye.

"Can you be 100 percent sure?" Stella added, her eyes slightly squinted and the vertical crease between her eyes deepening.

"I guess I can't be that sure. But we were so careful. The TV was old. I assumed the tube wore out." Terrance Gambon looked a little unsettled now, like he blew it on the witness stand.

Victor looked around the table. Sensing no one else wanted to speak or ask more questions, he said, "Thank you Dr. Gambon. Unless you want to add anything we will get back to you within two weeks." Terrance Gambon shook his head.

"Thank you," said Victor, gesturing to Sammy. "Dr. Halsey, show Dr. Gambon out please."

***

"He's not a bad guy," said Ted. "If you look at it from where he was coming from, the deal makes some sense."

"He wasn't defensive," added Sammy.

"Well, I see two problems," said Stella sternly. "First, a sexually abused client is not right for *any* boundary crossing. Period! These clients need to feel totally safe. They need to *be* totally safe."

"I agree," added Charlotte. "Bartering adds a financial proposition on top of psychotherapy. As anyone knows unless they've been living in a gopher hole, business deals have a way of going sour."

"Let me state the second problem, please," said Stella, frowning at Charlotte. "Who knew when the set ceased to function? Many opportunities for damage occurred after the TV left the client's vehicle."

"Yeah, he should've been open to the possibility of some little twist or jiggle somewhere along the TV's journey causing damage, even if he believed that possibility to be remote," Sammy added.

"What's important, Sammy," said Stella sounding even more authoritative than usual, "is even if the deal seemed simple, it wasn't therapeutically indicated. Dr. Gambon should have known better. He's been in practice long enough. My good friend Anna Freud would agree with me on this one if she were still with us. Candy Bean may have suffered a serious setback. We will never know."

Wolf winked at Sammy. The Anna Freud connection.

"I think he should've let the matter drop, even to the point of saying the TV worked if the client asked," added Charlotte. "Like any business, sometimes deals made between the therapist and the client fall apart, and we lose. Customer service. It's part of our profession, too."

"So, let's decide on what to about Dr. Gambon," said Victor.

Decision and Dispositions

The Committee agreed Dr. Terrance Gambon was not trying to exploit Candy Bean. He did fail to consider what could go wrong with both an older, delicate device and a sexually abused client. Because he attempted to correct the situation, including offering to forgive the bill altogether, the Committee decided to issue a letter of reprimand, the least punitive sanction. The Committee also imposed a directive mandating two continuing education courses at his expense; one on psychotherapy with clients who were sexually abused as minors and another on ethical decision making. He was to send a report of satisfactory completion within six months.

Dr. Gambon responded with a brief note apologizing for taking up the Committee's time and declaring he would never again trade psychotherapy for anything but traditional payment methods. He claimed to understand so clearly now how he lost sight of what he knows as a clinician, allowing a seemingly harmless diversion to override sound clinical judgment. He agreed to sign up for the courses.

The letter to Candy Bean indicated the matter had been examined, appropriate action taken, and the Committee members wished her well. The note included a willingness to assist in locating a new psychologist in her geographical area with considerable experience in treating adults who were sexually abused as children and who would work with her at a greatly reduced fee.

Candy Bean called the LCP office a few days after receiving the letter. She wanted to know more about what action was taken against Dr. Gambon, signifying continued resentment. She also refused the offer of assistance in finding a new psychotherapist. Peggy Aldridge politely reminded her of the Committee's policy to hold details confidential, but attempted to reassure her that the matter was handled appropriately.

At the meeting of the Ethics Committee the following June, as the minutes from the March meeting were reviewed the members expressed their continued concern for Candy Bean. They reflected again on how seemingly uncomplicated decisions, even those with helpful intent, can have such potentially harmful consequences if one loses sight of the big picture.

Case Commentary

Dr. Gambon believed himself to be supportive and compassionate and doing everything by the book. He took notice that the client's family was not using the object to be traded, hence minimizing a potential for exploitation. He was willing to take the item even though the value was lower that the fee for the services he would supply in return. However, his attention was diverted away from the underlying psychotherapeutic contra-indications.

The Ethics Committee took into consideration Dr. Gambon's attempt to rectify the matter, but in the end the therapeutic relationship was destroyed and an exceptionally vulnerable client endured additional harm.

Psychotherapists would do well to consider the risks of entering into bartering relationships with clients because untoward outcomes are not always easy to discern in advance. True equity is difficult to quantify when one of the "products" is a set amount of time that would earn a known fee paired with a service or tangible object with variable values depending on who is doing the appraisals in the context of an intimate therapeutic relationship.

Notes on Bartering

Trading goods, services, or other nonmonetary compensation for psychotherapy sessions was considered unethical in early versions of the American Psychological Association ethics code as well as those of related professions (Zur, 2007). Subsequently, and perhaps influenced by adverse economic times, ethics codes have softened on the acceptability of nonmonetary exchanges. Such arrangements are considered acceptable so long as they are neither therapeutically contraindicated nor exploitative (American Psychological Association, 2010).

The client is the party who usually suggests a non-traditional payment method. The psychotherapist may perceive agreement as doing the client a favor (Woody 1998). A host of additional factors should weigh in before going forward. These include the client's diagnosis and duration of therapy, the client's dependency needs, the psychotherapist's theoretical orientation, local community norms, and the nature of what is being bartered (Canter, Bennett, Jones, & Nagy, 1994; Pope & Keith-Spiegel, 2008). When an arrangement entails provision of services by the client, the psychotherapist may be dissatisfied with the outcome, a situation that could sully the therapeutic relationship (Peterson, 1996). Or if the service brings the client into close proximity with the psychotherapist's personal and family life, such as exchanging babysitting or housecleaning for psychotherapy sessions, the resulting disclosures may well have unanticipated disruptive influences on the psychotherapy (Gutheil & Brodsky, 2008). Conflicts-of-interest or charges of exploitation are heightened if clients later perceive they were short-changed, coerced, or manipulated (Gandolfo, 2005; Gutheil & Brodsky, 2008).

It is possible that bartering and other boundary crossings can result in beneficial outcomes if all contingencies are carefully considered before acting. Boundaries protect, but they also constrain (Sommers-Flanagan, Elliott, & Sommers-Flanagan, 1998.) A boundary crossing can demonstrate a psychotherapist's humanity and boost a client's self-esteem, for example by accepting a proud but destitute client's artwork for an agreed-upon number of psychotherapy sessions. Arm's-length bartering, as when a client readily agrees to volunteer for two hours a week at a local shelter, is a creative way to avoid some of the risks surrounding service exchange (Zur, 2007).

Discussion Questions

1. Did Dr. Gambon deserve the sanctions imposed by the Ethics Committee? Why or why not?
2. If a financially-strapped client offered to paint your house in exchange for psychotherapy, and you perceive no therapeutic contraindications, how would you value your client's time compared to your usual session fee? An hour for an hour? Or?
3. A client offers an item valued at $1,500 in exchange for psychotherapy. You can use the item, the other signs seem favorable,

but in your professional opinion the client requires only a few more sessions. How do you respond?

4. Generally it is not advised that the psychotherapist be the one to initiate a bartering agreement. Under what circumstances, if any, might an exception be appropriate?

5. A financially-strapped client who, in your professional judgment, needs at least 10 more sessions offers a golf cart in exchange for psychotherapy. You have absolutely no use for a golf cart. What do you say?

6. Discuss why bartering psychotherapy for tangible items is "ethically safer" than exchanging psychotherapy for a client's service.

References

American Psychological Association (2010). *The ethical principles of psychologists and code of conduct.* Washington, DC: Author.

Canter, M. B., Bennett, B. E., Jones, S. E., & Nagy, T. F. (1994). *Ethics for psychologists: A commentary on the APA ethics code,* Washington, DC: American Psychological Association.

Gandolfo, R. (2005). Bartering. In S. F., Bucky, J. E., Callan, G., & Stricker, G. (Eds.). *Ethical and legal issues for mental health professionals: A comprehensive handbook of principles and standards.* Binghamton, NY: Haworth Maltreatment and Trauma Press/ The Haworth Press.

Gutheil, T. G., & Brodsky, A. (2008). *Preventing boundary violations in clinical practice.* New York, NY: Guilford Press.

Peterson, C. (1996). Common problem areas and causes resulting in disciplinary action. In L. J. Bass, S. T. DeMers, J. R. P. Ogloff, C. Peterson, J. L. Pettifor, R. P. Reaves, T. Retfalvi, N. P. Simon, & R. M. Tipton (Eds.). *Professional conduct and discipline in psychology* (pp. 71–89). Washington, DC: American Psychological Association, and Montgomery, AL: Association of State and Provincial Psychology Boards.

Pope, K. S. & Keith-Spiegel, P. (2008). A practical approach to boundaries in psychotherapy: Making decisions, bypassing blunders, and mending fences. *Journal of Clinical Psychology, 64,* 638–652.

Sommers-Flanagan, R., Elliott, D., & Sommers-Flanagan, J. (1998). Exploring the edges: Boundaries and breaks. *Ethics & Behavior, 8,* 37–48.

Woody, R. H. (1998). Bartering for psychological services. *Professional Psychology, 35,* 255–260.

Zur, O. (2007). *Boundaries in psychotherapy: Ethical and clinical explorations.* Washington, DC: American Psychological Association.

Additional Reading

Reamer, F. G. (2012). *Boundary issues and dual relationships in human services* (2nd ed.). New York, NY: Columbia University Press.

nine
BABY STEPS OFF
A CLIFF

Tidy little moves commencing with mild attraction and ending in seduction describe how many psychotherapists fall from grace. The process plays out in this cautionary story, complete with the typical conclusion that is anything but happy. As you read, try to imagine what the client is thinking and feeling as their relationship begins to transform. Although she never resisted the psychologist's advances, and even made a few passes of her own, empathizing with where she is in her life and why she came for psychotherapy helps to understand the ultimate harms befalling sexually exploited clients.

She was tall, young, and primed to go—just embarking on a life of her own. He did not see her as a beauty in the usual sense. Although not yet overweight, he surmised her voluptuous figure would turn obese with time. Her full, almost round face was framed with light blonde hair pulled into a single braid hanging down her back. Her eyes were sparkling blue, though a little on the small side. "Good Norwegian stock," he thought. Nevertheless, his attention diverted the minute she broke out in a wide, hearty smile. "What white, straight teeth she has," he said to himself, and felt even then a faint spark registering beyond his appraisal of this young woman's dental assets.

After only two sessions with Bettina Johansson, Sebastian found himself looking forward to her 1:00 p.m. Wednesday appointments. She had a pleasing simplicity to her, an unsophisticated woman in search of a life containing more ups than downs. Such a stark contrast to Catherine Powers, his wife of 19 years. There was nothing simple about Catherine who kept her maiden name because it "worked so well," as she put it, with her successful career as a political scientist. Catherine had written two bestselling books on presidential elections, was a frequent guest on cable TV news and PBS radio, and held an endowed distinguished professorship at Los Angeles University. Currently under contract for a book about how the country would be different now had Hillary Clinton been elected President in 2008, the publisher's advance payment alone exceeded Sebastian's annual net income. He never got used to being referred to as "Mr. Powers" and cringed every time it happened. It happened often.

Catherine did not flaunt her frequent achievements at home, but Sebastian didn't look forward to the "How was your day?" exchange over dinners with their two teenage daughters. Some shiny episode always materialized during Catherine's average day. And although Sebastian struggled to retrieve a tidbit to share without violating his clients' confidences, his offerings reminded him of his failure to fulfill the many aspirations of his youth.

During the small talk at the tail end of the therapy sessions with Bettina Johansson, Sebastian realized he found uncommon pleasure in sharing his interests with her. She seemed to find his commentary on articles from the morning paper fascinating, listening intently as if she had invisible antennas arching towards him from her forehead. Bettina thanked him after each session, telling him how much better she was doing, giving him all the credit.

"You lighten my day," she would say. "I feel like I am coming alive. Oh, and call me Bet."

What he did not yet divulge, even fully to himself, was a growing sense that she also lightened *his* day. He was experiencing what was missing for so long, feeling important and appreciated. Something was coming to life inside of him.

Along with excursions into Bettina's unsatisfactory family background and her failure to find enduring adult relationships, the therapy session conversations increasingly dealt with the present and immediate future. Sebastian found material from his own life creeping into their sessions with greater frequency. He disclosed Catherine's unavailability much of the time, how she often flew off to Washington D.C. or to a convention, and the kids' annoying stage where everything was about them and every minor disappointment transformed into a major calamity. Now, nine sessions into Bettina's therapy, her appointments consisted primarily of mutual dumping, casual flirting, and giggling.

In the course of their conversations, they discovered a shared liking for sashimi. Catherine would have nothing to do with raw fish, claiming one could get a worm as long as a football field despite Sebastian's fervent argument that salt water fish were unlikely to carry parasites. Yet here was this young woman who shared a liking for a guiltless pleasure. "What would be the harm in having sashimi together" he thought.

"I just had an idea," said Sebastian at the beginning of their tenth appointment. "How about a late lunch at Mikado down the street after we're finished here? I have a yearning for sashimi, haven't had any for weeks. And Akiyo, the owner, creates the magnificent delicacies himself." Although Sebastian spoke as if the idea popped into his head that minute, he dreamed it up two days prior and had already moved his 2:00 p.m. client to 4:00 p.m. in anticipation of her positive response.

"Sure," Bettina replied. "Sounds great!"

The restaurant with its minimalist but tasteful black and white decor with a touch of red was almost empty by the time they arrived. The dining room had been darkened, presumably to save energy, yet the resulting ambience felt alluring. At a small round table near the back they feasted on Katsuo, Ika, Tako, and Unagi, enthusiastically extolling the delicate flavors of each dish. Bettina mentioned Fugu, knowing the raw puffer fish could kill with its tetrodotoxin unless prepared exactly right, and suggested it would be an especially exciting climax to this clandestine feast. They chuckled like teenagers while inventing the possible headline; *Psychologist and young blonde woman perish in tragic blow fish mishap.* Their uproarious laughter caused Akiyo to rush over to see if everything was all right. Mikado didn't have the special qualifications necessary to prepare Fugu properly, and Akiyo had no intention of ever trying it. "So, we shall live another day," Sebastian declared, as he handed Akiyo his credit card and winked at Bettina. Something new sparked just then, and they both felt it.

* * *

"Thanks for the lunch last Wednesday," Bettina said at the beginning of her next session, running her finger along the deepest scratch on the top of the old wooden desk.

"We'll do it again," he answered, with a smile that was also a promise. "By the way, we're getting a new desk. This one has seen too many better days. My officemate and I found one on Craig's list. Solid rosewood. A retiring physician is selling it for a song. We just have to figure out how to get it here since neither of us has a big enough vehicle."

"I have a big van!" Bettina chirped and clapped her hands as if she had just won a prize. "We can pick the desk up whenever you want."

The following day, Bettina arrived after Sebastian's last client. They took off to the physician's building in Studio City. The remaining items in Dr. Stanley Bakalian's offices were getting thin, but aside from the pre-purchased desk and some miscellaneous pieces of small furniture were several framed prints still available for sale.

"Oh, look," squealed Bettina. "I always loved this one with the dogs playing poker. It's only twenty dollars!" Sebastian winced at her taste in art, but quickly exclaimed, "It's yours as thanks for picking up the desk." He realized he would have bought the poster for her in any event. Giving Bettina joy, taking in her extra wide smile, was a reward in itself.

During subsequent sessions, Sebastian mined their conversations for excuses to spend time with Bettina out of the office. They exchanged frequent emails and phone messages, his always starting with "Wanna Bet?" as code for letting her know he wanted to see her, even if for a cup of coffee at the Denny's across the street or tea at Mikado. Although they had not yet touched, he found himself wanting desperately to hold her hand. When she mentioned she had never been to Griffith Park, Sebastian made another move.

"Well, let's try that for our next session. It's very pretty in places, a perfect setting for talking about life."

Bettina smiled with a mischievous glint in her eye, as if she already had that idea in mind. "Shall we meet here?"

Sebastian moved his later Wednesday afternoon clients to different days. Now he would always be free after Bettina's sessions until he was expected home for dinner at 6:30 p.m.

The nature trail off Fern Dell Road offered the optimum ambience for a romantic walk in Griffith Park. Dozens of varieties of lush ferns and tropical flowers edged the sparkling stream shaded by a canopy of sycamore trees. Wood benches spaced along the way provided the ultimate props for an idyllic interlude. Sebastian gently curved his hand into Bettina's as they strolled slowly on the meandering trail to follow the stream before settling down on a bench dappled in sunlight and just right for two. He put his arm around her, and she snuggled in. They sat in silence, neither knowing quite what to say, yet both knowing their relationship just shifted into something quite apart from psychotherapy.

The ride back to Sebastian's office parking lot took only a few minutes, and the sparse conversation avoided mention of what had happened in Fern Dell Park.

"See you next Wednesday," chirped Bettina as she slipped out of his car.

"If not before," he replied, not sure about what he meant by his spontaneous response.

By Friday morning it was taking every bit of control Sebastian could muster to refrain from calling her. By the afternoon he no longer had to restrain himself. Bettina left a message at the office asking him to call her as soon as possible.

"Hey," she said. "A carnival is coming to Glendale tomorrow evening. Interested?"

Sebastian was eager to agree, but was also taken somewhat aback. Saturdays were always reserved for a special family dinner. Afterwards he and Catherine would take the girls to a movie or stay home and play *Scrabble*, *Rummy Tile*, or *Ticket to Ride*. It was a tradition they vowed to preserve for as long as possible. The girls would soon enough go off with their own friends on weekend evenings. His judicious internal voice—the one questioning why Bettina would think a married man with a family would be available to attend a Saturday night event close to home with another woman in front of thousands of other people—failed to fully register.

"Sure, OK. Meet me at the office at 6:30 p.m.," he replied. After hanging up he felt a wave of guilt fused with anxiety. He could tell the family he had an emergency, a client's suicide attempt perhaps. Catherine would not question him. After all, she had occasionally been out of town on Saturdays. "But, was this a good idea?" The question flashed through his mind, but he did not want to pause long enough to hear his own answer.

***

Bettina wore a strapless summer dress showcasing her ample cleavage. Her pale blonde hair cascaded down her back, almost reaching her waist. They stayed at the carnival long enough to enjoy corndogs and chocolate sodas, listen to a couple of bands, and huddle in a photo booth before deciding the time had come to be alone, together. They drove along Ventura Boulevard looking for the first motel with no expectations that clientele brought luggage or would stay for more than a couple of hours.

The walls and ceiling in their dark room at the Paradise Inn were painted a purplish red. A leopard-pattern spread on a king-sized bed, a cheap mirror tacked onto the ceiling, and a tawdry plaster statuary of a nude couple embracing completed the ugliest décor Sebastian had ever seen. Now, standing in this gaudy place alone with her, he felt painfully awkward, like a school boy about to get his first real kiss.

"I think we're in the stomach of a whale that also swallowed a wild animal," he blurted, pointing to the bed spread and trying to ease the clumsiness of the moment.

Bettina grinned and rolled her eyes, as she slowly removed her dress and sandals, undid her lacy bra, and pulled down and stepped out of her panties, letting them fall into a small heap on the floor.

"You like?" she said, with arms outstretched and palms upturned.

"She is a little chunky," was the first thought popping into his mind. "Yes, of course," he replied aloud, without entirely meaning it.

Bettina pulled back the leopard spread and lay down on her side, propping her head up with an elbow.

"Well?" she said, patting the mattress where he should now join her.

Sebastian undressed himself methodically, folding each garment and placing it neatly on a small bed stand, utterly aware of his own body being scrutinized and judged.

"You're quite the slow poke," she said with a hint of impatience in her voice.

Sebastian found Bettina a vigorous sexual partner, wondering if she was especially experienced or had watched too many pornographic movies. She directed position changes frequently. She was limber as a boiled noodle, making him feel old and out of shape by comparison.

After that evening, most Wednesdays after confirming a rendezvous by email they met for lunch at smaller out of the way places where Catherine or her friends would not likely frequent. Sebastian convinced Bettina he chose them expressly for their romantic appeal, and she never questioned his motives. Then off to the Paradise Inn. The proprietor always saved what they named "The Shamu Room" for them. Sebastian had begun working out in the early mornings, hoping to keep up with Bettina's progressively more complicated sexual antics. Now each week she brought along new massage products and fetish paraphernalia in a plain tote bag. He enjoyed some of it, the mutual feather tickling and the backrubs with fragrant lotions, but the leather masks and sadomasochistic toys required him mostly to act as though he was having fun. Handcuffing her felt more like rustling cattle than making love. Sebastian refused to be restrained himself, despite her obvious disappointment. He could not give up this last vestige of control.

Now Bettina wanted to see him more than just one day each week. Sebastian somewhat reluctantly agreed, with the stipulation of at least a three-hour break in his schedule. He sensed he was losing command of the affair, and a creeping apprehension started to eclipse the anticipation. Bettina was becoming less interesting, not because her oft-stated appreciation of him lessened, but because the praise had become wholly predictable. The sense of adventure waned, and the Shamu Room was feeling more like a cage.

One Saturday evening, three months into their liaison, the phone rang at the Lark home. Sebastian and his family were watching a movie. Catherine answered.

"It's for you. A Bettina something," Catherine said with an inquisitive look as she handed Sebastian the phone.

Sebastian's heart lurched forward a beat. What could she possibly want?

"Hello," he said, trying for a composed voice, although it cracked anyway.

"Hi. Your office machine must be broken. Couldn't leave you a message. Was that your wife who answered?"

"What can I do for you Miss Johansson?"

"Miss Johansson?" Bettina let out a bellowing laugh. "Oh, OK, you don't want the little political woman to get it. Understood. Look, would you like to take a drive to Newport Beach tomorrow? The weather is supposed to be great. And I know a place…"

"No," Sebastian interrupted. "No, thank you. You may call me at the office on Monday." He hung up the phone, taking a deep breath before turning around to face Catherine.

"What's that about?" Catherine asked, with one eyebrow raised.

"Nothing. A sales call. Apparently my office message machine is on the fritz."

"She sounded like she knew you."

"Nope, just a friendly saleswoman."

"On a Saturday night?"

"Don't worry about it, Catherine." He kissed her softly on the cheek. "How about I get us a glass of chardonnay?"

First thing Sunday morning while Catherine and the girls were still asleep, Sebastian went to the garage and called Bettina from his mobile phone.

"What the hell do you think you're doing?" he yelled. "And how did you get my home telephone number?"

"I have my ways. And how in the hell could you brush me off like that? 'Miss Johansson.' You made me feel like your on-call piece of ass."

"You called my home. My wife answered. My kids were right there. Since when did you think it was acceptable to call me at home?"

"Hey. Sorry. I'll see you Wednesday at the Inn." Bettina hung up.

***

Sebastian arrived at the Paradise Inn a half hour early to make sure Bettina would not already be on the bed, naked and surrounded by various sexual enhancement paraphernalia.

"You're here already!" she exclaimed with a wide smile, arriving at the usual time. "Why are you still dressed?"

"I can't do this anymore, Bettina. It's not right. This is not good for either of us."

Bettina dropped her tote bag and clasped a hand to her chest. "What are you saying, exactly" she wailed. "What we have is special. You said so yourself. Soul mates, remember?" She began to shake.

"Look, this got out of hand. You're a wonderful girl. I like you. But I have a family. I can't keep doing this." Sebastian felt sad in that moment, not because he was extracting himself from what had become an overly intrusive and demanding sex partner, but because he was losing a client he could have helped find herself, a therapeutic alliance that would have been successful had he kept the boundaries firm.

"Are you sure about this?" she shrieked. "You aren't just playing some sort of new erotic game? If that's what it is, I don't like it."

"No, I want us to stop. I'm leaving now. I'm sorry, really. This was a mistake."

"That's it? You're sorry? You haven't heard the end of this. I'll tell you that much, Mister. You can't play with people like this. That's what's not right." Bettina was screaming now.

Sebastian walked out the door without looking back. He prayed he would never have to look back.

***

Bettina sat alone on the bed in the Shamu Room, mumbling to herself. "I've been with men before. Too many of them. He's not great looking, and he's old enough to be my father. He's not even that good in bed. So why did I fall hard for this one?"

But, of course, she knew why Dr. Sebastian Lark was different from all the others. She had spilled out the contents of her soul to him, and he had actually paid close attention. That she had to pay for his company in the beginning soon became irrelevant. No amount of money could buy her emerging self-confidence, a renewed capacity for having fun, and the thrill of falling in love. He had given her all that. Or, so it seemed.

As the middle child sandwiched between a gorgeous older sister and a baby boy, the family's attention was sucked up before anyone even noticed Bettina was in the room. Now 23 and trying to make it on her own, she realized she wouldn't know how to respond if someone initiated a conversation about her. She had survived socially by being reactive to what others were saying about themselves, asking questions, and feigning fascination regardless of how tedious the conversation was for her to endure. Most people are so caught up with their own lives, never noticing she was little more than a talking mirror. Even when she was having sex with a man she picked up at a club, as she did frequently, the questions were rarely about her save for the likes of, "What's your sign," and "Have you been tested for HIV?"

Dr. Lark had given Bettina a compliment within 20 minutes of their first meeting.

"I like working with clients like you, clients who want to grow. And that smile of yours will make it even more enjoyable." He probably had no idea how special that made her feel.

Just as unexpected and extraordinary was how in the beginning he listened to her talk about her family and her hopes and dreams without once interrupting to change the subject.

"That's about the best hour I have spent for as long as I can remember," she said as the first session wound down.

"I enjoyed getting to know you also, Miss Johansson," he replied. "I can see you again next Wednesday afternoon, same time if you like."

"Yes, I like."

She recalled the gentle evolution of what she thought was their special friendship. It seemed so clear to her, after reciprocating by listening to his complaints about his marriage and children, that in just a matter of time he would leave them behind to be with her instead. She anticipated an announcement and a special gift, jewelry perhaps, after their friendship turned decidedly romantic. But except for some lunches and paying in advance for the motel room, he always arrived empty-handed. She tried to keep it exciting by spending most of her own discretionary income on merchandise from Sexxx Heaven on Melrose Avenue, but he was never as receptive as she expected him to be.

Then, just now, he dumped her. He walked right out of the room. "UNACCEPTABLE!" she barked out loud, more furious than she could ever recall being. Yet only now would she admit it to herself; Sex with Sebastian Lark was mostly a chore.

She sat on the side of the bed, grabbed the mobile phone from her purse, and entered his home number. Catherine answered.

***

When Sebastian arrived home, Catherine was waiting at the door, her face reddened and her expression grim as an executioner.

"I got a call from that girl. She told me everything."

"What are you talking about," he asked, trying to sound innocent.

"You lying bastard! I haven't said anything because I hoped my friend Marcy had it wrong when she told me she saw you with a large blonde woman half your age at a carnival a while back. I even let the strange scent you sometimes reeked of go unquestioned, preferring to think you had sprayed your office with cheap air freshener."

"Let me try to explain," Sebastian said softly, not knowing quite what he could say to defuse the ambush.

"Let me tell you to get your things, and then get out, you cheating piece of shit. I don't want you here when the girls come home."

***

After Sebastian Lark's wife ousted him from their home using language he didn't realize she had in her, he took up residence in the Iron Gate Motel on Van Nuys Boulevard, only a half block from the Paradise Inn he rented by the hour before his life plunged off a cliff. He left a stern message for Bettina Johansson, telling her in no uncertain terms to stay away from him and his family.

He continued to see clients every day. How long he could keep it up remained unknown, given the certified letter from the League of California Psychologists that arrived at his office three weeks after his abrupt departure from his family. As early as spring, if the LCP found him guilty and passed their findings onto the state licensing board, he could be without a license to practice, a hefty fine, or possibly denied his freedom as well. Spending six months in the County lock-up was an abhorrent prospect in its own right, but it also crossed his mind that his jail mates—rough guys who disturbed the peace by getting into barroom brawls or breaking into houses at night or selling heroin in back alleys—would ask him what he was in for. Screwing a psychotherapy client not only sounded ridiculous, but would reveal even to toughened lawbreakers that he was an imbecile. "If you're going to do time," he thought, "it might as well be for something sounding more macho than the equivalent of shooting a fish in a barrel."

To keep his license and avoid an even worse living condition than the Iron Gate Motel—a name he now found chillingly ironic—he would have to deny everything. His word against hers. She came on to him, after all, with that seductive smile. His profession was all he had left. If Bettina had to take the fall, so be it.

Dear Dr. Lark,

We received a complaint from Ms. Bettina Johansson alleging you engaged in improper sexual activity with her while she was your client. We will need to hear your response at the March meeting of the Ethics Committee.

You must make an appointment with the LCP administrator, Mrs. Peggy Aldridge, to appear before the Ethics Committee at its meeting in March unless a compelling reason requires a postponement. Ms. Johansson has signed a release allowing you to discuss the matter with us. We expect you will be able to respond in detail to her allegations. Failure to contact us within 10 days of the receipt of this letter will constitute an act of noncompliance, which is itself an ethics violation.

Sincerely,
Victor Graham, Ph.D.
Chair, Ethics Committee
League of California Psychologists

Sebastian read the letter so many times that it was almost memorized. He finally called Peggy Aldridge to inform her he was ready to tell the Ethics Committee the truth about an affair that never happened. He only needed to know where and when.

The Ethics Committee:
Sebastian Lark, Ph.D. March 17, 10:05 a.m.

"Sadly, here's one we still get more often than we should," announced Victor Graham holding a large padded envelope up over his head. "Amazing how they almost all go the same way. Baby steps leading to an ethical violation that can even get you tossed into a county jail for a spell in California, let alone lose your license to practice. I'll read it out loud."

Dear Ethics Committee of the League of California Psychologists,

My name is Bettina Johansson. I was Dr. Sebastian Lark's client for four months and we started having sex while I was still client. Then I became his lover for three more months. We started exchanging mild flirting from the first session. I admit I was flattered by the attention he paid to me. We started having some innocent fun outside of the office. But within a few months we were meeting in an X-rated motel for just sex. I confess I fell in love with him. He gave every indication he loved me. He once said we were soul mates. To me that meant we would always be together.

Then last week at the motel where we always met he said he didn't want to see me anymore. I was devastated and warned his wife about the kind of person she married.

I kept a diary. I have photographs I took with my mobile phone of us and of the motel room. I kept copies of emails we exchanged. I made tapes of phone messages he left for me, some very loving but in the last one after I spoke with his wife he called me horrible names. Some of this material is included with this letter, but I have much more if you need it.

Dr. Lark told me I would be made the fool if I told anyone about us and he would tell everyone I belonged in a mental hospital.

I read your ethics code and the California State licensing section about sex with clients, and both are clear. I'm not proud of my part in this, but Dr. Lark needs to be dealt with. I trusted him. I don't want any other woman to go through this. Let me know if I should also contact the licensing people.

Sincerely,
Bettina Johansson

"Sounds like another colleague who was smart enough to earn a Ph.D. degree, but when it comes to sex he thinks with his putz," said Wolf Levin, shaking his head.

"What else is in the big puffy envelope, Victor?" asked Charlotte Burroughs with anticipation.

"Some pretty damning evidence. Copies of a few emails, a phone tape confirming their weekly rendezvous, some with sexual references, and, finally, an ugly one where he admonishes her to keep her mouth shut."

Ted Bates looked perturbed. "Those could be faked."

"Doubtful," answered Victor, still rummaging around in the envelope. "Here are two photos of Dr. Lark who appears to be naked and asleep on a big bed covered with a cloth with leopard spots," passing them to Archie Wittig.

"Yikes. I hope we recognize him with his clothes on," exclaimed Archie, looking shocked and amused at the same time.

"Don't pass them my way," said Charlotte, nose wrinkled.

"What else, Victor?" said Stella Sarkosky, sounding irritated as she always did whenever therapists are accused of betraying their singular allegiance to the well-being of their clients.

"Well, here's a postcard from the Paradise Inn on Ventura Boulevard with 'You can check with Jake about Wednesdays in the Shamu Room,' whatever that means, in what looks like her handwriting. And here's a photograph of what appears to be the two of them on one of those paper strips—you know, the kind where you sit in a little kiosk while it automatically takes four shots? They do look cozy. And here are copies of pages from a diary she kept. Very detailed. Quite kinky in places."

"Give me that," said Stella, reaching for the diary pages. "I need to thumb through these before Dr. Lark comes into the room."

The others knew then and there. Dr. Lark was in for a bumpy ride. Stella was gearing up for a showdown.

"And she has even more?" asked Sammy.

"That's what she says," said Victor. "Let's give Stella a few more minutes with the diary and then see what Dr. Lark has to say for himself. Our discussion will be more informed once we see if he can offer an explanation for the allegation and this cache of material. Then, Charlotte, I'll send you out to show him in, if you will."

***

Sebastian Lark appeared haggard. His gray linen suit looked as though it was in need of a good pressing. He was an average looking guy, Sammy thought. Short brown hair with a little silver at the temples, big and slightly bulged brown eyes, brown plastic-framed glasses, thin lips, medium build. He looked like a stereotypical accountant, not the type that would get himself into this kind of predicament.

Sebastian took his seat, looking restless as Victor introduced him around the table. He barely made any eye contact, and before Victor had a chance to invite him to tell his side of the story, he spoke.

"I must say something right off. Miss Johansson is a very disturbed young lady who became obsessed with me from the start," Sebastian declared sounding determined but rehearsed. "I tried to set the appropriate tone while remaining empathic with her disappointing life. But she kept pushing the envelope. She called me at home, telling lies to my wife. I had to terminate her to try to save my marriage."

"Are you saying you had no romantic involvement with Miss Johansson at all? She just made it all up?" asked Ted.

"That's exactly what I'm saying. I don't know what she told you, but it was psychotherapy only between us. Nothing more. She has a wild imagination. Tells all kinds of stories. I never knew whether anything she told me actually occurred or not. I'm not even sure she knew what was real."

"Why do you think she would make these accusations?" asked Charlotte. "Even disturbed clients almost never invent a sexual affair with their psychotherapists."

"As I just said, she was obsessed. She's a pathetic case, really. No one ever paid much attention to her. She's been with a lot of men, but they didn't care about her. It was just the sex. She's not much to look at. Nordic peasant stock. She had so many needs, and she actually believed I was the one who was going to fulfill them. I couldn't convince her otherwise. I tried to terminate her, telling her she needed to find someone else who might be better suited to treat her."

"Did all of your interactions with Miss Johansson take place in your office?" asked Stella in her stern voice with squinty eyes.

"Of course! I'm a professional. This terrible mistake is bringing me all sorts of grief."

Then Stella pulled the plug. "What if we informed you that Miss Johansson supplied us with photographs, emails, and tapes of telephone messages suggesting you were her…how should I put it…therapist with benefits? Would your declarations remain the same?"

The others froze like statutes, and the color drained from Sebastian's already tense face.

"If you aren't trying to trick me by making up this so-called evidence, they're all fakes," Sebastian mumbled and cleared his throat. His previous bravado vanished. "Photoshop, forgery, someone imitating me, whatever. She is manipulative enough to do that sort of thing."

"Well, Miss Johansson may have been obsessed with you as you allege," Stella continued, "and I say that because she documented every social interaction with you in a diary she kept along with some hard evidence. Her diary reads like a woman desperately in love with her reciprocating therapist, until she put on the pressure."

"We're through here," snapped Sebastian Lark. He stood straight up, almost knocking over his chair, his face now flushed and glistening. Pausing only to grab his briefcase, he sprinted out the door.

Victor chased after him, stopping him in the foyer. "We have no authority, of course, to keep you here, Dr. Lark. But you do need to understand something. We will have to forward our decision based on the information available to us to our Board of Directors. They will likely want to involve the licensing board. You can come back and explain more now if you wish."

"You'll be hearing from my attorney," Sebastian muttered and bolted through the swinging glass doors leading to the street.

***

"I bet my Rolex the California Board of Psychology will pull his license," said Wolf. "All for a few romps in the hay. What a schlemiel."

"Never underestimate a woman scorned," added Stella.

"I don't get it," said Sammy. "If someone wants to have an affair, all sorts of opportunities are out there without a high level of risk. Even in Muncie, that town in Indiana near where I grew up and eventually set up my practice, everyone knew where sex was for sale on South Madison Avenue. I never went there, of course." Sammy felt a little embarrassed wondering what the others might think of an admission of knowing where prostitutes hang out. "When you live in small towns you know everything," he quietly added.

"It's far more complicated than just sex," said Victor. "The ethics code focuses on sexual acts, but it's often more about the wrong mix of two needy people finding themselves alone together in an environment characterized by trust and a special kind of intimacy. It can become quite enticing when the needy one is the mental health professional who fails to maintain enough control to honor professional responsibilities."

"Agreed," said Stella. "For a while these two appeared to water each other's dried up lives until one of them, our colleague, started to sink."

"Good analogy," added Victor. "Miss Johansson has created quite a flood!"

"Enough with the wet talk," said Wolf, grinning. "What are we going to do about this guy?"

"This one is decidedly different from our "he said, she said" cases that create such a dilemma for us," said Archie, looking at Sammy. "In these cases, we know someone is lying, but it can be difficult to be sure who it is. This time we have external evidence that tips the scale on its side."

"I gather it's rare to have this kind of confirmation?" asked Sammy.

"It happens," said Archie. "Especially when everything can now be recorded so easily. One psychologist fell so hard for a female client who complained to us because he was the one getting overly demanding.

He wouldn't leave her alone after she told him the affair was over. Nevertheless, he wrote scores of emails professing his love, even *after* receiving the complaint letter from us!"

"Dumb fuck," grumbled Wolf under his breath.

"We're skirting around the primary issue," Said Stella. This isn't only about two people satisfying each other's needs. If therapy is going well, that's what happens. The client gets better and the therapist benefits both financially and from the satisfaction of helping to restore a client's well-being. The ethical focus is on sex for a reason. 'Sexual intimacies with clients are unethical.' It doesn't get much clearer."

"How is sex more damaging than all the moves leading up to it?" asked Sammy. "I mean, I doubt any therapist just jumps a client out of nowhere."

"It's happened. Well, one case. That was rape," answered Wolf.

Stella continued as if she had not been interrupted. "Sexualizing psycho-therapy has been referred to as a form of incest, a position with which I fully agree. No matter how evolved and tolerant we humans think we are, sex is not an insignificant act. It carries special meaning to most people, especially women. Clients come to us for a protected space to work on whatever brings them to us. We have a duty to shelter them from any extraneous experience that could violate that trust or lead them to believe the relationship is other than for the sole purpose of working on the issues they bring to us."

Despite Stella's often aloof lecturing style, the others knew she nailed it.

"So, since he stalked out, did we get enough information to make our decision?" asked Sammy.

"He was denying everything, blaming the client he characterized as seriously mentally impaired," said Charlotte, looking disgusted. "He wasn't about to change his story, and he will probably be consulting an attorney."

"I don't like his willingness to gut his client," said Archie. "Even if he were innocent, and I don't believe he is, at the very least he mismanaged this client's therapy."

"The problem is he never admitted anything, and we do not have the resources to verify the authenticity of what the woman sent to us, although I do believe it meets the preponderance of evidence" said Victor.

"Are we ready to proceed?" asked Charlotte?

Decision and Dispositions

Because Dr. Sebastian Lark made no admission of guilt, instead attempting to offer the client's mental status as a defense, the members of the Ethics Committee agreed to recommend transferring the case to a venue with the resources to conduct a thorough investigation. They also agreed they had sufficient information to recommend to the LCP Board of Directors that Dr. Lark's membership be suspended until the California Board of Psychology completed its review. Should Dr. Lark be found guilty by the licensing board, he would be expelled from the LCP. In the meantime, his name would be removed immediately from the referral roster.

Bettina Johansson received a letter informing her of the Committee's thorough review of her complaint and, because of the seriousness of the charge, the recommendation would be to refer the case to the licensing board. Peggy Aldridge would be communicating with her about how the process works. An offer for help with a referral to another psychologist was also extended.

Miss Johansson declined the offer of receiving assistance in locating a new psychotherapist. She added she no longer trusted "any type of mental doctor" and reported being severely depressed. She would, however, actively participate in any California Psychology Board procedure.

The licensing board investigated the charges against Dr. Sebastian Lark and found him guilty of sexual misconduct with a client. His license to practice psychotherapy was revoked. The criminal matter remains pending.

Case Commentary

Client-said/Therapist-said cases are difficult for ethics committees to decide, even with more investigatory resources than portrayed in this story. False complaints are assumed to occur (Williams, 2000; Wright, 1985). In the absence of disconfirming information, however, an innocent psychotherapist could conceivably be found guilty if the evidence bar is set too low. So, one might ask, can a guilty psychotherapist wriggle out of trouble by denying the charges, even blaming the victim as occurred in this story? It appears to be true that a guilty psychotherapist may dodge the bullet once because an ethics committee cannot decide who is credible and who is lying. But, that case stays on the books. The decision is "no finding," not "innocent," leaving the case in doubt. Any subsequent charge by another client will be taken very seriously (Koocher & Keith-Spiegel, 2008).

In this day of extraordinary technological advances, gathering incriminating data at reasonable costs is easy. Miss Johansson displayed an array of damaging email, text messages, and smart device photos that ultimately prevailed in her complaint against Dr. Lark, even though her original motivation was to document the romance.

Loss of belief in the benefits of psychotherapy is yet an additional harm befalling sexually exploited clients along with mistrust, guilt, and depression. Research conducted by Bouhoutsos, Holroyd, Lerman, Forer, and Greenberg in 1983 found that clients became suspicious of psychotherapists and relationships in general. This is most unfortunate, as this story also illustrates, because the client now harbors additional emotional burdens besides those bringing her into therapy in the first place.

The psychologist's life in this story ends badly and similarly to other cases I've reviewed. If he is ever allowed to return to practice, it will be under a cloud. His loss of family appears to be permanent. Should the client choose to press the matter in civil court, his malpractice insurance will pay for his defense but not for any monetary damages awarded to her. He will always have to report his offense when requested by insurance companies or professional or employment review boards.

Notes on Attraction and Sexual Relationships with Clients

Feelings of sexual attraction towards clients are common, especially those the psychotherapists find physically good-looking (Landany, Friedlander, & Nelson, 2005; Pope, Keith-Spiegel, & Tabachnick,

1986; Pope & Tabachnick, 1993; Rodolfa et al., 1994). Such feelings are not unethical *per se*, but they require careful self-examination.

The pattern wherein small erosions of appropriate boundaries are rationalized as acceptable practice over a period of weeks or months without the psychotherapist taking heed of the possible pitfalls that lay just ahead is a common one (Gutheil & Gabbard, 1993; Simon, 1989; Somer & Saadon, 1999). Telling oneself *"Just this once," "No one will be hurt," "It will be therapeutic"* are among the red flags that warrant an immediate assessment.

It is not unusual for psychotherapists who are accused of sexual misconduct to eventually want to call it off for any number of reasons. Aggrieved clients with sufficient resources to complain proceed to do so (Koocher & Keith-Spiegel, 2008). Lamb, Catanzaro, and Moorman (2003), sampled psychologists admitting to sexual affairs with their clients, supervisees, or students. They found such liaisons tend to be short lived, and half of their sample reported retrospectively that the affairs weren't worth having.

The most common profile of a sexually exploitative psychotherapist is a middle-aged male who takes advantage of a female client, usually one who is younger or vulnerable (American Psychological Association, 1996; Bouhoutsos et al., 1983; Celenza, 2005; Sonne, 2012). Such psychotherapists typically have their own conflicts and relationship problems, including sexual anxiety and guilt, allowing their unresolved needs to take precedence over those who consulted them for counseling (Haspel, Jorgensen, Wincze, & Parsons, 1997; Herman, Gartrell, Olarte, Feldstein, & Localio, 1987; Hetherington, 2000). Female psychotherapists have also been accused of sexual misconduct with clients, though at a lower rate (Gartrell, Herman, Olarte, Feldstein, & Localio, 1986).

A red flag should be recognized whenever male or female psychotherapists are unhappy or unfulfilled in their personal lives and most certainly if they also find themselves sexually attracted to a client. Self-care is not only important in its own right, but can minimize poor decision-making and ethical misconduct (Norcross & Guy, 2007; Weiss, 2004).

Discussion Questions

1. The client in this story played an active and reciprocal role during the seductive process. Do you believe clients bear some responsibility for the ultimate consequences? Why or why not?
2. Might the Committee have considered another penalty—perhaps a stipulated resignation or some form of monitoring—had the psychologist admitted his ethical failure instead of claiming the client made the whole affair up? Given that this psychologist apparently had no previous sexual encounters or other ethical issues with clients, might he have been viewed as a reasonable candidate for rehabilitation had he been forthright?
3. Sexually exploitative psychotherapists are far more likely to be men than women. What factors do you think account for the disparity?
4. Have you felt sexual attraction towards a client? (If so, you are in the majority.) How did you handle these feelings? Did you consult with anyone? How were these feelings managed?
5. What would you do if you suspected an office mate was having an affair with a client? Would you intervene? If so, what would you do?

References

American Psychological Association (1996). Report of the ethics committee. *American Psychologist, 50,* 706–713.

Bouhoutsos, J., Holroyd, J., Lerman, H., Forer, B. R., & Greenberg, M. (1983). Sexual intimacy between psychotherapists and patients. *Professional Psychology, 14,* 185–196.

Celenza, A. (2005). Sexual boundary violations: How do they happen? *Directions in Psychiatry, 25,* 141–149.

Gartrell, N., Herman, J., Olarte, S., Feldstein, M., & Localio, R. (1986). Psychiatrist-patient sexual contact: Results of a national survey: I. Prevalence. *American Journal of Psychiatry, 143,* 1126–1131.

Gutheil, T. G., & Gabbard, G. O. (1993). The concept of boundaries in clinical practice: Theoretical and risk-management dimensions. *American Journal of Psychiatry, 150,* 188–196.

Haspel, K. C., Jorgensen, L. M., Wincze, J. P., & Parsons, J. P. (1997). Legislative intervention regarding therapist sexual misconduct: An overview. *Professional Psychology, 28,* 63–72.

Hetherington, A. (2000). A psychodynamic profile of therapists who sexually exploit their clients. *British Journal of Psychotherapy, 16,* 274–286.

Herman, J. L., Gartrell, N., Olarte, S., Feldstein, M., & Localio, R. (1987). Psychiatrist–patient sexual contact: Results of a national survey, II: Psychiatrists' attitudes. *American Journal of Psychiatry, 144,* 164–169.

Koocher, G. P., & Keith-Spiegel, P. (2008). *Ethics in psychology and the mental health professions.* New York, NY: Oxford University Press.

Lamb, D. H., Catanzaro, S. J., & Moorman, A. S. (2003). Psychologists reflect on their sexual relationships with clients, supervisees, and students: Occurrence, impact, rationales, and collegial intervention. *Professional Psychology, 34,* 102–107.

Landany, N., Friedlander, M., & Nelson, M. L. (2005). Managing sexual attraction: Talking about sex in supervision. In N. Landany, M. Friedlander, & M. L. Nelson (Eds.). *Critical events in psychotherapy supervision: An interpersonal approach* (pp. 127–153). Washington, DC: American Psychological Association.

Norcross, J. C., & Guy, J. D. (2007). *Leaving it at the office: A guide to psychotherapist self-care.* New York: Guilford.

Pope, K. S., Keith-Spiegel, P., & Tabachnick, B. G. (1986). Sexual attraction to clients: The human therapist and the (sometimes) inhuman training system. *American Psychologist, 41,* 147–158.

Pope, K. S., & Tabachnick, B. G. (1993). Therapists' anger, hate, fear, and sexual feelings: National survey of therapist responses, client characteristics, critical events, formal complaints, and training. *Professional Psychology, 24,* 142–152.

Rodolfa, E., Hall, T., Holms, V., Davena, A., Komatz, D., Antunez, M., Hall, A. (1994). The management of sexual feelings in psychotherapy. *Professional Psychology, 25,* 168–172.

Simon, S. I. (1989). Sexual exploitation of patients: How it begins before it happens. *Psychiatric Annals, 19,* 104–112.

Somer, E., & Saadon, M. (1999). Therapist-client sex: Client's retrospective reports. *Professional Psychology, 30,* 504–509.

Sonne, J. L. (2012). Sexualized relationships. In S. J. Knapp (Ed.). *APA Handbook of Ethics in Psychology.* Vol. I. (pp. 295–310). Washington, DC: American Psychological Association.

Weiss, L. (2004). *Therapist's guide to self care.* New York, NY: Routledge.

Williams, M. H. (2000). Victimized by "victims": A taxonomy of antecedents of false complaints against psychotherapists. *Professional Psychology, 31,* 75–81.

Wright, R. H. (1985). Who needs enemies. *Psychotherapy in Private Practice, 3,* 111–118.

Additional Reading

Bates, C. M., & Brodsky, A. M. (1989). *Sex in the therapy hour: A case of professional incest.* New York, NY: Guilford.

Pope, K. S. (1994). *Sexual involvement with therapists.* Washington, DC: American Psychological Association.

Pope, K. S., Sonne, J. L., & Holroyd, J. (1993). *Sexual feelings in psychotherapy.* Washington, DC: American Psychological Association.

Robertiello, R. C., & Schoenewolf, G. (1987). *101 common therapeutic blunders.* Northvale, NY: Jason Aronson.

Schoener, G. R., Milgrom, J. H., Gonsiorek, J. C., Luepker, E. T., & Conroe, R. M. (1990). *Psychotherapists' sexual involvement with clients: Intervention and prevention.* Minneapolis, MN: Walk-in Counseling Center.

ten
CAR CRASH

A well-meaning psychologist's disclosure of personal information was perhaps justified when it was uttered. Unfortunately it ignited an unexpected downward spiral that failed to be checked in time. Early corrective action might have salvaged the therapeutic relationship and saved this psychologist from an ethics inquiry.

"I own one," Dr. Paul Greenspan said in a soft voice, almost a whisper.

"You're shittin' me!" Jackson Spire shouted gleefully. "Wow, I had no idea. Can we go look at it? Our session is will be over in a few minutes."

"Sure, I guess so," Dr. Greenspan replied after a slight hesitation. After all, this client had extolled the positive features of the BMW 6-Series convertible during small talk upon greeting or departure. Paul had even considered mentioning several sessions ago that he bought that particular car last year, figuring Jackson could conceivably see over the three foot wall separating the staff parking area from the visitors' lot. Jackson might observe him driving in or out. He might even be puzzled, perhaps disappointed or even miffed, that something of unmistakable interest to this passionate automobile aficionado was left unmentioned.

As they got off the elevator Jackson spotted the BMW instantly. The bright sun's rays reflecting off the metallic black finish made it appear to be sprinkled with stars.

"What a beauty!" Jackson cried out as he ran to the car, gently patting the hood as if it were a friendly dog. "Can we take a quick spin around the block?"

Paul Greenspan paused briefly again, but seeing Jackson so uncharacteristically cheerful took him off guard. Surely once around the block wouldn't cause any harm. In fact, Jackson had serious trust issues, viewing most people as dissimilar to himself and to be approached with considerable caution. Having this diversion in common might enhance the strength of the therapeutic alliance which, in turn, might facilitate their progress into deeper territory. Paul's next client wasn't for another half hour, and Jackson's mood was the most cheery he had yet seen. "Extending him this brief pleasure couldn't possibly do any harm," Paul reasoned.

Paul reached in his pocket and pulled out his keys. "Get in, Jackson. Let's do this."

Jackson rocked back and forth, as if he was making the car go faster. They headed up Centinela to Woodbine, down Colonial and across Palms back to the office for a total travel time of three and one half minutes.

"Thanks, man," Jackson chirped as he sprang out of the door. "I still can't believe you own one of these beauties. Maybe we can drive to Malibu soon? Go up Pacific Coast Highway with the top down, beach breeze in our faces? How cool would that be?"

"Maybe someday," Paul stammered.

***

For the next three sessions, Jackson wanted to talk mostly about cars. Paul attempted to draw him back to the issues Jackson brought into therapy—his trouble trusting others, especially men, along with intense loneliness and difficulty making friends. "I try to meet new people," he would often say, "but I seem to hit up against a wall." Paul was hopeful when four sessions ago, just before he disclosed owning the BMW convertible, Jackson stated, "I think I am the one who built the wall. Others can feel it, and they move away." This was huge. The therapy would surely march forward. But now Jackson was less interested in himself than he was in Paul and his elegant car. The breakthrough Paul envisioned had slipped back below the horizon.

"Can we set a date to drive on Pacific Coast Highway?" was how Jackson ended each session. Last time he added, "We can stop for lunch at

Moonshadow afterwards. Wow, I can barely wait. I hope we can do this soon and often." Jackson clapped his hands and giggled.

Paul could no longer ignore his own error in judgment. He scorned himself for ever mentioning the BMW. He had difficulties keeping this client focused from the beginning. If Jackson learned about the car in some other way on his own, perhaps seeing Paul driving it into the parking lot, he could explain how their relationship was about tending to Jackson's needs, nothing else. Such a statement may have come across as brusque at the time, but Paul was certain things would have gone far better than what was going down now.

"Jackson," Paul said after taking a long breath, "Look. We aren't going to Malibu. I shouldn't have said anything to lead you believe it would happen. I'm sorry. Our professional relationship is about you, not my car."

Jackson's head slumped. He looked like a broken-hearted four year old upon being informed that Santa Clause was a seasonal mall employee in a fat suit and phony beard. "No Malibu?" he softly uttered.

"No Malibu. But we can do good work here if we keep ourselves focused. Let's talk about that wall you mentioned a few sessions ago."

Jackson placed his hands on the arms of the chair and lifted himself up. "I'm not feeling well. Excuse me." He looked straight at Paul with a barely veiled expression of antipathy.

"Can I do anything for you?" Paul asked as Jackson headed for the door. Jackson kept walking.

***

Dr. Paul Greenspan sat at his desk waiting for Jackson Spire's regular appointment at 2 p.m. on Fridays. He always arrived 20 minutes early. By 2:25 it became clear Jackson was a no-show.

"He might still be sick," Paul thought. Paul left a message inquiring into Jackson's health and assumed he would get back with an excuse, or at least show up the following Friday. But 2 p.m. next Friday came and went. No Jackson.

Then the certified letter arrived. Paul suspected Jackson was disappointed about the extended car ride that wasn't going to happen, but remained confident he would soon recover and return. Being hit with an ethics complaint instead was the last thing he expected.

Dear Dr. Greenspan,

Your client, Jackson Spire, wrote to us alleging a broken promise regarding a road trip you were to take together causing his condition to deteriorate. He also claims you exploited him financially. We need to discuss what transpired from your perspective and ensure that Mr. Spire's welfare was protected.

You must make an appointment with the LCP administrator, Mrs. Peggy Aldridge, to appear before the LCP Ethics Committee at its March meeting unless a compelling reason requires a postponement. Mr. Spire has signed a release allowing you to discuss the matter with us. Failure to contact us within 10 days of the receipt of this letter will constitute an act of noncompliance, which is itself an ethics violation.

Sincerely,
Victor Graham, Ph.D.
Chair, Ethics Committee
League of California Psychologists

"Road trip?" Paul cried out loud, wiping his brow. Gary Brian, a marriage and family therapist in the next office heard the outburst and rushed over to see what was going on.

"What did you say Paul? You sound riled."

"How could I have been so stupid? Gary, I can't name names, but I'm in a lot of trouble. Can you spare a few minutes?"

Paul spilled out the story, intermittingly pounding his fist on his desk.

"So, Gary, what do you think I should do? How can I explain this?"

"Your intentions were honorable enough," Gary replied. "Things can get tough when a professional boundary springs an unexpected leak. How many sessions did the two of you have?"

"Twelve."

"H'mm. The first mistake—well it turned out to be a mistake—seems like something any of us could make. Revealing a shared interest. And you're right. All might've worked out if you stopped there. The toughest one is when you said "Maybe," and you really meant "No fucking way.""

"The client seemed so overjoyed. I thought 'maybe' would keep him connected even though I made no commitments. 'Maybe' means 'not for sure,' right?"

"Not to this client," Gary said softly.

"Obviously." Paul closed his eyes for a moment. "Thanks, Gary. There's no way out besides admitting I screwed up. I hope the committee understands I never meant my client harm."

The Ethics Committee:
Paul Greenspan, Ph. D. March 17, 11:15 a.m.

Dear Ethics People,

I called your office. You said I had to write. I was treated badly by my therapist. His name is Dr. Paul Greenspan. He made promises he did not keep. We were supposed to go on a road trip, but then he called it off. I am worse than before. He only wanted my money to help pay for his expensive car.

Jackson Spire, Jr.

P.S. My father is an attorney and says you have to help me.

"This one looks sadly familiar," said Victor Graham after reading the letter aloud. "Making what clients perceive as promises with no follow-through."

"Paul's been around for a long time," said Stella Sarkosky. "I must recuse myself from this case." She rose and left the room.

Ted Bates was primed to offer his take on the matter. "We often find no solid commitment existed, but the client took a poorly worded comment and ran with it."

"Let's see what this one is about. Ted, would you locate Dr. Greenspan please?"

Ted Bates escorted a nervous but elegant-looking older man into the meeting room and ushered him to his seat. "He looks just like Walter Cronkite," Sammy Halsey leaned over and whispered to Wolf Levin.

After making quick introductions, Victor got right to the point.

"We need to better understand what Mr. Spire alleges from your perspective, starting with this road-trip that appears to be at the crux of the complaint. Can you tell us more?"

Paul cleared his throat and folded his arms on the table top.

"Jackson…Mr. Spire…is a huge fan of expensive automobiles. He can tell you everything there is to know about almost any make and model. I told him I possess one of the cars he especially admires. At the time I thought the disclosure would strengthen my connection to this isolated individual. Instead we went way off course. All he wanted to do at the end was talk about cars—mostly mine."

"Did you ever drive somewhere together in your car?" Charlotte Burroughs asked.

"Yes, once around the block the day I told him I owned that particular car. He asked if we could drive to the beach someday, and I'm afraid I gave a regrettable answer. I did not say 'yes.' But, I did say 'maybe.' Of course I should've said 'no,' and I had never had any intention even then to follow through. I was taken by the moment because at last we made a connection I thought would fortify our therapeutic partnership. I let the whole thing ride, so to speak, but his car talk began to overwhelm every subsequent session."

"I gather you kept putting him off for a period of time, over several sessions?" asked Wolf. "And, how many times all together did you see this client?"

"Twelve. And, yes, I'm afraid I did keep kicking the can down the road, again so to speak." Paul gave an uncomfortable smile as a second pun again registered only after he spoke. "I worried about losing focus with him. To tell him a trip to Malibu was never going to materialize might have made things even worse."

"Did you try to call Mr. Spire, perhaps to apologize?" asked Ted Bates.

"Not again. I'd agree to do that in a heartbeat. I want more than anything to make this right. I've been practicing for 36 years without a single complaint."

"Mr. Spire seems to also be angry, thinking you strung him along to help pay for your car, suggesting you were attempting to create a dependency."

"Ouch" Paul blurted, jerking forward in his seat. "The last thing I would do is exploit that young man or any client. I've made good investments over the years and have far more resources than I will ever need. Of course, he doesn't know anything about my finances."

"Does anyone else have any questions? Or do you want to say more, Dr. Greenspan?"

"No, except I am truly apologetic that it ever came to this. I believe I could've helped this young man had I not botched my answer to his request."

"Thanks for coming in and on time, Dr. Greenspan. You will hear from us within two weeks" said Victor with what appeared to be a sincere sympathetic smile.

***

"OK, so I'll start," said Wolf. "He screwed up. He doesn't deserve to be flogged, but his waffling caused the client considerable grief. I say a reprimand. He will know better if anything like this happens again."

"You don't think he erred when he told the client about his fancy car, that BMW whatever it was?" asked Sammy.

"That's a tough one," answered Wolf. "This client had trust issues. If the psychotherapist can get through that barrier with an appropriate disclosure, psychotherapy can move forward faster. I'm not going to slam him for revealing his ownership of a particular automobile. But he should've set the boundaries firm thereafter."

Even driving around the block?

"Yes, in my clinical judgment."

And his answer to the Malibu question? That "maybe."

"Clearly a mistake. I get it though. You hate to say anything to disappoint a client. But the mythical outing got rolling and had to be stopped. He had several chances and didn't take them." Wolf leaned back into his chair.

"Are we ready to make our judgment call?" asked Victor. "Then let's pick up lunch at Ting's and bring it back here. Somebody track down Stella after we're done."

Decision and Dispositions

The Committee decided to issue a reprimand, the least severe of any sanction, to Dr. Greenspan that would remain confidential. Mr. Spire received a letter letting him know his complaint was heard and appropriate action taken.

Dr. Greenspan reflected often on how poorly he handled the client's requests. He decided to write an apology letter and included a check for $1,000. Jackson Spire did not respond, but the check was cashed immediately.

Case Commentary

The Committee accepted the initial disclosure as a sincere, though hastily made, clinical judgment. Self-disclosures, after all, can be benign and helpful (Knapp & VandeCreek, 2006). The committee's "guilty finding" was based primarily on managing the unanticipated fallout in a timely manner. Many of us who have served on ethics committees are well aware of such consequential blunders. Uneasy feelings and doubts were ignored or pushed out of awareness, in this case for not wanting to disappoint a client (Pope and Keith-Spiegel, 2008).

The most unfortunate outcome for the client, in my opinion, was his interpretation of being strung along for the psychologist's financial gain. If clients suspect they are being exploited, harm is likely regardless of the therapists' intent (Peterson, 2002).

The point of including this story was not to give dire warnings about disclosing any personal information. However, even though becoming too relaxed when sharing one's own personal life (or ignoring unexpected client reactions to disclosures) may not result in a formal ethics charge, effective psychotherapy can be compromised (Barnett, 2011; Robertiello & Schoenwolf, 1987).

We are also reminded how clients can become overly intrusive, and psychotherapists reserve the right to consider their own level of comfort (Goldstein, 1997, Barnett, 2011). Dr. Greenspan exhibited discomfort when the client wanted to accelerate involvement with him and the car, but did not heed the red flags early enough.

Let's consider an extreme incident for comparison. A friend of mine, a psychotherapist, expressed to her own psychiatrist how angry she felt towards one of her co-workers. She asked him if he ever became enraged. He responded, "Yes, I daydream about marching one of my colleagues at gunpoint down Wilshire Boulevard before shooting him down like a dirty dog." The psychiatrist may have believed that sharing his own reverie mirrored empathy, but my friend wondered, half-jokingly, if clients had the same "duty to warn" when their psychotherapists divulge a clearly-designed plot to do someone bodily harm! Nevertheless, because she was so shaken by what she referred to as a "creepy revelation" she sought psychotherapy elsewhere.

Dr. Greenspan's story also reveals how even more experienced mental health professionals can stumble in the moment and fumble righting themselves (Koocher & Keith-Spiegel, 2008). This psychologist decided on his own to return the client's fees. Reparation cannot be dictated by an ethics committee, and one might argue that it was unnecessary.

Finally, this story illustrates an ever-present coincidence, namely that a member of an ethics committee has personal ties to the respondent. Stella Sarkosky rightly recused herself without indicating the nature of a relationship that might have influenced the other members' thinking. It is difficult to remain impartial when one is friends with (or dislikes) the accused. Stella and Paul Greenspan had been close friends for over 25 years.

Notes on Self-Disclosure

Is sharing personal information with clients about oneself beneficial to the therapeutic alliance? Or can disclosures create a boundary violation, distorting the professional nature of the therapist's role? Traditional psychoanalytic thinking viewed self-disclosure as evidence of countertransference, thus a red flag alerting a contamination of the therapeutic process (Peterson, 2002).

Although some practitioners still hold that there is no place for self-disclosures, most mental health professionals today apparently do knowingly share information about themselves, at least on occasion (Hill & Knox, 2001; Yeh & Hayes, 2011). The question, then, remains not so much "if?" as "how, when, why and what?"

Those who espouse the use of appropriate self-disclosures with clients suggest numerous benefits. Carefully measured self-disclosures motivated by the client's welfare can create a more authentic alliance, help a client understand that everyone has failings and insecurities, strengthen and deepen the therapeutic engagement, decrease anxiety, facilitate insights and new perspectives, elevate trust, and free clients to be honest and to more readily disclose difficult and shameful material (Bridges, 2001; Curtis & Hodge, 1994; Peterson, 2002; Williams, 2009; Zur, 2007).

Concerns center on intentional self-disclosures for the purpose of gratifying the needs or desires of the psychotherapist, or that burden or confuse clients, or are excessive or unwelcomed (Hill & Knox, 2001; Zur, 2007). Contextual issues are important; these include the therapist's theoretical orientation and treatment approach as well as client factors, such as culture, gender, mental health history, current treatment needs, and agreed upon goals (Barnett, 2011).

Discussion Questions

1. Would you have told Jackson Spire about owning the car? If not, what would you say if he stormed into an appointment after having spotted you driving into the parking lot, and angrily accused you of hiding something he should have been told about you?

2. Knowing a client could easily discover sensitive data about you on his or her own, should you pre-empt that possibility by sharing the information first? What factors might go into your decision?

3. Do you believe the professional role of, and confidence in, a psychotherapist is ever strengthened by sharing:
    a. a serious personal failure?
    b. your own experience of being a psychotherapy client?
    c. a difficult childhood?
    d. chronic physical illness?
    e. a recent divorce?
    f. a commission of adultery?

    If you answered "yes" to any of the above, what contextual or other factors would be helpful to the client by sharing such information?

4. What are the pros and cons of apologizing to clients who may have been unintentionally or intentionally mistreated in some way? Should therapeutic errors ever be divulged to the client? Can you think of examples?

5. The title of Cristelle's (2011) article suggests the question: "Do therapist self-disclosures violate boundaries or remove barriers?" What might differentiate one from the other?

6. How might the psychiatrist described in the author's commentary respond in a helpful way to the client's question? What might he have said instead of revealing his death wish towards his colleague?

References

Barnett, J. E. (2011). Psychotherapist self-disclosure: Ethical and clinical considerations. *Psychotherapy, 48,* 315–321.

Bridges, N. A. (2001). Therapist's self-disclosure: Expanding the comfort zone. *Psychotherapy, 38,* 21 30.

Cristelle, A. (2011). Client perspectives of therapist self-disclosure: Violating boundaries or removing barriers? *Counseling Psychology Quarterly, 24,* 85–100.

Curtis, L. C., & Hodge, M. (1994). Old standards, new dilemmas: Ethics and boundaries in community support services. *Psychosocial Rehabilitation Journal, 18,* 13–33.

Goldstein, E. G. (1997). To tell or not to tell: The disclosure of events in the therapist's life to the patient. *Clinical Social Work Journal, 25,* 41–58.

Hill, C. E., & Knox, S. (2001). Self-disclosure. *Psychotherapy, 38,* 413–417.

Knapp, S. J., & VandeCreek, L. D. (2006). *Practical ethics for psychologists*. Washington DC: American Psychological Association.

Koocher, G. P., & Keith-Spiegel, P. (2008). *Ethics in Psychology and the Mental Health Professions*. New York, NY: Oxford University Press.

Peterson, Z. D. (2002). More than a mirror: The ethics of therapist self-disclosure. *Psychotherapy*, *39*, 21–31.

Pope, K. S., & Keith-Spiegel, P. (2008). A practical approach to boundaries in psychotherapy: Making decisions, bypassing blunders, and mending fences. *Journal of Clinical Psychology*, *64*, 638–652.

Robertiello, R. C., & Schoenwolf, G. (1987). *101 common therapeutic blunders*. Northvale, N.J.: Aronson.

Williams, M. H. (2009). How self-disclosure got a bad name. *Professional Psychology*, *40*, 26–28.

Yeh, Y. J., & Hayes, J. A. (2011). How does disclosing countertransference affect perceptions of the therapist and the session? *Psychotherapy*, *48*, 322–329.

Zur, O. (2007). *Boundaries in psychotherapy: Ethical and clinical explorations*. Washington, DC: American Psychological Association.

Additional Reading

Bazerman, M. H., (2011). *Blind spots: Why we fail to do what's right and what to do about it.* Princeton, NJ: Princeton University Press.

Bloomgarden, A., & Mennuti, R. B. (Eds.). (2009). *Psychotherapist revealed: Therapists speak about self-disclosures in psychotherapy*. New York, NY: Routledge.

Farber, B. A. (2006). *Self-disclosure in psychotherapy*. New York. NY: Guilford.

Striker, G., & Fisher, M. (Eds.). (1990). *Self-disclosure in the therapeutic relationship*. New York, NY: Plenum.

eleven
MAD FAX

Given the intimate nature of psychotherapeutic relationships, clients may view their therapists as friends and even assume their fee payments can be delayed during hard times, or perhaps forgiven altogether. The psychologist in this story would have been spared an ethics hearing had she been less engrossed with her own financial concerns and more attuned to why her client failed to pay in a timely manner.

Life was unkind to Tillie Booker, and she was not adept at fighting back. Her single mother and two older sisters used her as their personal pin cushion, taking full advantage of Tillie's inability to retaliate. Early on she mastered the art of being hard to find, the only protection within her capability. She found places to hide for hours at a time—under a bed, inside the garden shed, in the back of a closet, under the porch, and up in the old plum tree. The price for self-concealment was high. She grew up lonely and sad.

As an adult she had trouble keeping a job. Her sullen demeanor hindered her performance and dampened the work environment for others. She never succeeded in landing any position requiring a certain amount of perkiness.

Tillie finally found employment taking orders for medical supplies and stayed long enough to qualify for the employees' health insurance plan. She realized a need for professional help, and now she could get it.

Medications for depression didn't work for her. She needed someone to talk to—someone to confide in. She needed to purchase a special friend who would listen and understand.

In the beginning Tillie thought psychotherapy with Dr. Lydia Savage was the best decision she ever made. She felt spurts of optimism as new ways of looking at life cast a faint glow over the gloominess that usually engulfed her mood. But when she unexpectedly lost her job in a flurry of layoffs, the darkness retuned. Dr. Savage offered to keep seeing her at a lower fee. But Tillie had saved up little and could barely manage the cost of food and rent while looking for new work.

"Well, you can pay me when you get a job," Dr. Savage chirped, assuming the problem was solved.

"You are so wonderful, Dr. Savage," Tillie responded, thankful for such a charitable offer.

It would be almost five months before Tillie found a new position. Yet with the support of Dr. Savage, Tillie continued to move forward. Dr. Savage willingly cared for her, despite Tillie's inability to pay during her employment hiatus.

Tillie called Dr. Savage with the good news about her new position in a large secretarial office pool. She liked having her own cubicle, but was also enjoying being around people.

"Hi, Dr. Savage. Leaving a message on your machine to let you know I got a job! I really love it. I am so much better now. I don't think I need more therapy. I will pay what I owe as soon as I can. Thanks. You saved my life!"

Dr. Savage immediately started sending invoices for eighteen sessions. Tillie assumed she had much more time before the debt would come due, especially after Dr. Savage had been so kind. An ally really. She put the bills in a drawer and didn't respond to Dr. Savage's subsequent attempts to reach her, letting the answering machine take all incoming calls. In fact, she began to feel like a child again, hiding out from her new tormenter. That desolate mood was stealing back into her waking hours.

One day the depression weighed so heavy that Tillie could not get out of bed. She called into work sick. By the next day she was able to drag herself to her job, and that's when her world crumbled down around her. The FAX, dated yesterday, was face-up on her desk. The other women in the office stopped what they were doing to bear witness to her reaction.

A surge of bleakness enveloped Tillie. Her body went limp. A co-worker ran over to suggest she take the day off. Tillie considered running out of the office, never to return. She stayed home for two more days, splayed like a damp rag on the living room couch. By the third day a twinge of something with substance, something sharp, came upon her. She would not slide all the way back. Not again. She would be proactive. She would stand up for herself for the very first time.

Tillie called a co-worker whose partner was an attorney and asked if her legal rights had been violated. The attorney thought not, but believed an ethical infraction had been committed, possibly a serious one. He suggested Tillie contact any professional organizations to which her psychologist belonged and request guidance.

Tillie called the League of California Psychologists and spoke with the office administrator who confirmed Lydia Savage's membership. Peggy Aldridge also gave her the information needed to construct a formal complaint about the harassment she received at the hands of Dr. Savage.

Dear Ethics People,

I have been publicly disgraced in the worst possible way. I have depression. It makes my life very hard. Medications don't help me.

I went to Dr. Lydia Savage because I was afraid I was going to lose my job. I liked her at first. We talked a lot about how my mother and sisters would always belittle me and get on my case and how I had never developed courage to stand up to them. But then I lost my job and my insurance. I told Dr. Savage I couldn't pay to her the full fee. Then she said I could pay her after I got another job.

I saw her eighteen times after I lost my job. I did get another job, but not as good as the one before, and I don't have insurance any more. I did leave a message for Dr. Savage telling her I would pay as soon as I got back on my feet.

The next month and the month after that she sent me three bills in the mail and left me many phone messages to pay her now. But I still did not have the $900 because I had borrowed from my friend who got into a car accident, and my friend needed the money back really bad.

Then Dr. Savage did the most awful thing to me. She sent a FAX to my new job. I was not at work that day because I was feeling really down. The women in the office saw the bill and the nasty message she wrote on it before they put it on my desk. When I came back I was embarrassed enough to come close to quitting.

Is this an acceptable way to treat someone who went for mental help? If so I will never see another psychologist. The FAX she sent is included.

Yours truly,
Tillie Booker

***

Dr. Lydia Savage was angry and frustrated. But she knew she made a mistake the instant she pushed the "send" button.

"I know, it wasn't the best timing for me to do anything," she wailed to her boyfriend, passing the letter from the LCP Ethics Committee to him. "This client had no insurance when she lost her job, so I offered my lowest fee. Almost half. I tried every other means possible to bill her for her unpaid sessions after she found employment again. I wasn't going to show up at her apartment."

As Jack silently read the letter his brow furrowed.

Dear Dr. Savage,

Ms. Tillie Booker, a past client, wrote to us alleging you sent a bill with an additional inappropriate message through the FAX machine at her place of work rather than to a secure address available only for her viewing. If these charges are accurate, ethical issues involve Ms. Booker's right to privacy as well as showing disrespect by including a comment based on an issue shared in a confidential session. We would further like to discuss with you the practice of allowing clients to run up a large bill.

You must make an appointment with the LCP administrator, Mrs. Peggy Aldridge, to appear before the LCP Ethics Committee at its March meeting unless a compelling reason requires a postponement. We expect you will be able to respond in detail to Ms. Booker's allegations. Ms. Booker has signed a release allowing you to discuss the matter with us. Failure to contact us within 10 days of the receipt of this letter will constitute an act of noncompliance, which is itself an ethics violation.

Sincerely,
Victor Graham, Ph.D.
Chair, Ethics Committee
League of California Psychologists

"Why didn't you use a collection agency?" Jack asked, handing the letter back.

"I don't condone their methods," Lydia snapped. "Dr. Bartoli who works in the clinic next door hired one to collect from a deadbeat client. The agency used threatening tactics, so his client thought Dr. Bartoli ordered a hit on him. The client called the police. Dr. Bartoli spent three hours in jail until they got everything sorted out."

"Did you try other ways to collect?" her boyfriend asked innocently.

"Well, duh. Of course. I'm not stupid, Jack," she snapped. "The client made a promise to pay as soon as she found work. She got a new job months ago. I sent three bills and tried to call her at least five times to talk about the outstanding debt. No response." Lydia needed to catch her breath before continuing. "She never bothered to try to explain why she couldn't pay or even suggest a monthly payment plan if she wasn't able to come up with the full amount. Nothing." With that, Lydia stomped into her bedroom.

Lydia plopped down on the bed trying to reconstruct how it all went down that day. She remembered she was doing her books. It had been a sluggish month. Her five regular paying clients did not cover her monthly bills. Tillie Booker had a job and still owed $900, enough to pay for most of her office rent coming due in a week.

"How infuriating," she thought. "This client is treating me the same way she used to handle all of her problems. Runs away from them. Hides. Takes no responsibility. That's why I scribbled the note across the face of the bill."

But now Tillie had stuck her neck out and complained to the LCP Ethics Committee.

"God, maybe I helped her too much," Lydia thought. "She would never have had the spunk to complain before she came to me. Poisoned with my own medicine!"

Lydia Savage knew the hard evidence was against her. The Ethics Committee had the actual FAX. She would have to try to explain how she made a too-hasty decision after extending extra considerations until her patience wore thin. Then she would beg for mercy.

The Ethics Committee:
Lydia Savage, Ph.D. March 17, 12:45 p.m.

"Next case!" announced Victor Graham, tapping on the table for everyone to come to order. "Wolf, what are you doing there?"

Wolf Levin had his entire head inside Sammy Halsey's briefcase. "A smell is coming from inside here. We're trying to figure out what it is."

"Well, figure it out later," said Victor, as if he were talking to preschool children.

After reading Tillie Booker's letter aloud, Victor added "Another in a growing pool of instant electronic messaging coming back to bite the sender in the ass. We need a new principle in our ethics code that reads, 'Do not send any confidential or sensitive message via email, FAX, Internet, or social media until you wait 24 hours to think through possible consequences.'"

"Agreed," said Ted Bates. "I remember an old case where the psychologist posted a message on a Yahoo! group with 300 subscribers asking if one of his prominent colleagues, a director of a clinical psychology program, was a drunk. He said he had heard a rumor to that effect and was seeking verification. The hapless director was not even on the list but was informed about the slur within an hour."

"Did the poster get into trouble?" Sammy inquired, hands clasping his cheeks.

"A law suit followed against the psychologist who posted the damning question for defamation of character. I think it was successful because no evidence confirmed that this guy was even a heavy social drinker. The poster tried to defend himself by saying the Yahoo! group was restricted to members only, so everything was confidential. Furthermore, he didn't say he actually was an alcoholic, he was just asking."

"What a thoughtless thing to do," said Stella Sarkosky. "Just because someone earned an advanced degree doesn't always mean they have common sense."

Wolf was waving a hand high in the air and sporting a wicked smile. "The even better one is the woman who hit 'reply *all*' instead of 'reply to sender' on a big list for clinical psychologists, responding to a post by an old colleague she had an affair with years earlier. She wrote something like, 'Good to know you're still alive. It's been a long time since we rolled around, so what say we meet up and go at it again?'" Wolf leaned back and slammed both hands on the table. "But I later heard her marriage broke up," he added in a more somber tone.

"How about Facebook?" said Charlotte Burroughs. "I can't believe any mental health professional would state on an open Facebook page, 'I hate my therapy clients' and imagine he wouldn't get busted. The client who found it was incensed enough to construct a blown-up poster of the message and staple it onto a long stick. Then he marched outside the psychologist's office for five days to make sure all of his other clients saw it."

"It's just plain stupid to have an open Facebook page in the first place if you are in a profession largely defined as a one-way mirror," said Stella Sarkosky. "Most of us don't want our clients to know we are divorced or play tennis every Saturday at 9 a.m. at the downtown park or have a drink every night, let alone something more enticing. Such irrelevant revelations can shift therapeutic relationships into unwanted directions. Psychotherapy isn't about our lives, it's about theirs."

"But we aren't just therapy machines," Ted Bates snapped. "I think it's fine to let our clients know we have a pulse."

"What's on your Facebook page?" Stella shot back, her eyes darting.

"Enough!" said Victor. "Let's get on with this case."

"So what did Dr. Savage write on the FAX that others in her office had access to?" Sammy asked.

"Here, I'll send it around," said Victor. "It's a standard bill for $900 for services rendered. But this hand scrawled message, all in caps, complicates things significantly."

DON'T BLAME ME FOR HOW YOUR MOTHER AND SISTERS SCREWED YOU UP!

"Totally uncalled for," snapped Stella.

"And why would she let an unemployed client run up almost a thousand dollar bill?" Charlotte added, sounding exasperated. "She doesn't seem to understand the old song *Sixteen Tons* that Tennessee Ernie Ford made famous about owing your soul to the company store. If an already depressed client feels hopelessly in debt, well, she wouldn't be the first one to do harm to herself."

"True," said Wolf, wringing his hands. "A colleague told me about a psychologist who loaned a client $2,000 because he felt so bad when his wife took off with another guy and their bank account. The client became despondent and quit his job and hit the bottle. Then he felt guilty for letting down his therapist and was ultimately suicidal. What a sorry situation."

"Let's see what she understands now," said Victor. "Sammy, would you please see if Dr. Savage is waiting for us?"

***

Sammy escorted Lydia Savage into the meeting room. She looked so fragile. A tiny woman, spindly and pale and probably not yet 30 by looks alone, seemed nothing like the sort he imagined would do such a foolhardy thing. Her face looked pinched, as if her features had been squeezed together. She wore no discernible makeup. Her light brown hair was cut short in a ragged style, making her appear to Sammy as if she had just tumbled out of bed. She wore a gray sweater, a straight gray skirt, and gray clogs. Once she sat still in her chair, Sammy thought her bland attire and ashen complexion made her almost invisible.

"Hello Dr. Savage," said Victor as he introduced her around the table. She tried to smile but couldn't manage more than a slight quiver of her lower lip.

"Do you understand the complaint against you, Dr. Savage?" asked Victor in a softer tone, attempting to ease her obvious discomfort.

"Yes, sir. I do," she replied in almost a whisper.

"Could you tell us why you decided to send the FAX?" Victor continued.

Lydia was still for a moment, looking down at her hands now folded neatly on the table. When she finally looked up she spoke slowly. "I was so frustrated with this client. I let her run up 18 sessions. She didn't respond to any of my billings or phone messages. I tried to be patient, but she would not get back to me." She stopped to clear her throat. "I'm sorry."

"Go on," said Victor softly.

"We made an agreement. She would pay when she got a job. She got a job. But months passed. I felt betrayed and, I admit, very angry at her in that moment. I called and requested the FAX number from the person in her office who answered the phone, and then I just did it. I was mad."

"Did you concern yourself with who else might view the bill and what you wrote on it?" asked Wolf.

"I wasn't thinking. You know that flash in your head right *after* you do something, and you wish it had come in *just before*? I meant it only for her, of course. I didn't stop to consider she might not be the only one to see it."

"What about the hand-printed message? You used a therapeutic issue shared in confidence against your client. How do you justify that?" asked Wolf, this time with an edge in his voice.

"I don't. I can't. I'm sorry." Her eyes filled with tears.

"I understand. Just wanted to know," said Wolf in a softer tone.

"Another matter needs to be discussed here even though it's not a part of the complaint," said Stella. "Why would you allow an unemployed client run up such a large bill?"

"I thought I was doing her a big favor. I wanted to help her out. She had no money. The amount I calculated was only half my usual fee." Dr. Savage now looked perplexed. This was yet another accusation, except this one she didn't understand.

"Here's the thing, Dr. Savage," said Stella, tapping her index finger once on the table. "If you allow a client to owe you more than he or she can reasonably expect to pay back in a timely manner, you invariably create a serious problem for the client and ultimately for yourself."

"I said she could wait until she got a job," Dr. Savage wailed, still not getting the point.

"No, see," Wolf broke in. "The client gets trapped, and whatever positive came from the therapy is lost because the once-helpful therapist is transformed into a huge bar tab."

"Odd analogy, but otherwise correct," added Stella. "The psychologist is no longer a lingering source of strength. Just one more heavy weight an already weakened client cannot lift."

"I like my analogy better," Wolf whispered to Sammy.

"Well, what should I have done instead?" asked Lydia, now sounding exasperated. "Don't I deserve to get paid at least something for my services?"

"I understand you haven't been practicing long. You seem fairly new at this," said Ted in a considerate tone. "Sometimes you have to help clients over the hump when they become unable to pay for whatever reason, or refer them to an agency or other resource willing to counsel them at little or no cost."

"Or, in your case, you might have seen this client for briefer sessions at no charge until she got a job, depending on her condition," added Charlotte. "Your client seems very despondent. As you know, of course, the risk of doing harm to oneself increases when a depressed individual feels under stress."

Lydia looked petrified. "I guess I really messed up. What's going to happen to me?"

Sammy hadn't said anything so far. He realized he was afraid of doing emotional damage to this brittle young woman. He would have to better understand the unexpected vulnerability of some offending colleagues if he was to become an effective member of the Ethics Committee. But he did have a question.

"I guess what's important at this point is how you would handle this sort of situation in the future," Sammy asked in his paternalistic voice. "You will likely have clients facing hard financial times again, given the bad economy."

"Differently. Just differently. I will be different," she answered sounding determined, even if unsure of what she meant in concrete terms.

"Just to make sure," said Victor, "you *do* understand the evidence is clear. You violated your client's right to confidentiality and did it in a most callous way, if I may be so blunt."

"Yes. I do. I'm very sorry." Her eyes filled with tears again.

"And it also sounds to me like the repayment agreement was nebulous. It's your responsibility to make fee expectations clear to clients," Victor added.

"Yes, I understand," Lydia said dutifully.

"If no one has anything else to say or any questions, we'll be in contact with you within two weeks, Dr. Savage," Victor said, passing a box of tissues in her direction.

Sammy rose up and went to assist an unsteady Lydia Savage out of the room, gently taking her arm. Sammy suggested she sit for a while before leaving and pointed out the cooler. "Can I get you some water?" he asked. "Yes, thank you" she replied.

Once again Sammy Halsey unexpectedly felt sorry for an accused psychologist who made serious ethical errors. He felt torn, almost in a fatherly way, about this young woman's plight, having to face an ethics tribunal so early in her career.

***

"I feel sorry for her. She really didn't know any better about the therapy-now-but-pay-later hitch," said Ted.

"Well, it's obvious she committed two ethical violations," Wolf said. "She failed to respect her client's privacy and, worst of all, used what transpired in therapy to berate the client."

"The ambiguous way she set up her repayment expectation and allowed a client's debt to pile up constitutes a couple more bad judgments," added Charlotte.

"We can cut her a small break for being a newbie." Suggested Ted. "She didn't try to make fancy excuses. This is no doubt her first offense."

"What do we want to do now, people?" Victor was clearly anxious to move on.

"She can use another ethics course. I can't help but think she didn't get a good dose of it while in training," said Stella. "These are not errors a psychologist with a solid grounding in our ethical principles would make, not even in anger. I say we mandate her to take one course at the very least."

"Agreed?" asked Victor Graham, scanning around the table. All heads nodded. "What else?"

"I wouldn't kick her out," said Wolf. "She still has to ripen, and I think she understands that. But her mistake is severe enough to warrant a censure. That's a more serious slap than a reprimand. We can keep it as a confidential notice to her, but she needs to fully understand her atrocious error, and, if she makes another one, things will not go easy for her."

No one objected.

Wolf started rummaging through Sammy's briefcase again, looking for the source of the strange odor. "Ah ha," he shouted as he slowly pulled out a small, cylindrical purplish object covered with grey fuzz. "I think it *was* a fig, and it's overly ripe. And that's an understatement." Sammy laughed. Victor rolled his eyes.

Decision and Dispositions

Dr. Lydia Savage was informed of a letter of censure to be placed into her file for violating a client's right to privacy and using confidential information in a harassing manner. Furthermore, she was ordered to take a continuing education ethics course at her own expense and supply verification of completion within six months to avoid a harsher sanction. A list of approved courses was included. The Committee also noted it allowed some leeway for being new to the profession, but any further ethical improprieties would offer no such advantage. Although the Committee did not have the authority to mandate forgiving a bill, it suggested that might be something to consider, and perhaps an apology as well.

Tillie Booker was informed that the matter had been appropriately handled. The Committee offered to help her find another therapist at a greatly reduced fee. Tillie called the office two weeks later extending a message of thanks to the Committee for whatever action was taken to persuade Dr. Savage to forgive the bill and to express regret for her poor judgment. Tillie concluded with, "No one who was important in my life ever apologized to me before."

Dr. Savage contacted the Committee several weeks later to say she had completed an online ethics course and would be mailing the verification form to the LCP office. In an unexpected twist, she announced that she and Tillie Booker had re-established their relationship and she was again Tillie's therapist at a reduced fee with a clear understanding about the payment schedule. She reported considerable satisfaction with their reconciliation, noting they both learned and grew from this ordeal.

Case Commentary

In my ethics committee experience the interplay of several dynamics eventually escalating to an ethical lapse is not uncommon. Dr. Savage failed to recognize how she confused her client and how her own frustration led to totally inappropriate behavior. However, and perhaps partially due to inexperience, the underlying issues involved a lack of attention to the business aspects of her practice.

Psychotherapists can have transference reactions not only to clinical issues but also to clients paying (or not) for mental health services already rendered (Barnett & Walfish, 2012). Such a reaction dominates this story and ultimately created a perfect storm, an impulsive action that any psychotherapist, even a recently licensed one, would never consider under a different set of circumstances.

Psychotherapists may offer financially troubled clients the opportunity to extend payment over a period of time, but this practice is counterproductive if the client cannot reasonably repay it (Koocher & Keith-Spiegel, 2008; Zur, 2007). In this story the client's depressive disorder returned as a direct result of pressure to bring her account current. Other ways of assisting the financially-strapped client should always be considered such as offering a sliding fee scale, more flexible scheduling (e.g., once every two weeks), or seeing them *pro bono* until their finances are stabilized (Chamberlin, 2009).

This case also illustrates how ethics committees often take situational variables into consideration during the assigned penalty phase, such as inexperience, a first offense, or a willingness to commit to no repetition of the violation. Dr. Savage hardly got off the hook, however. A censure on one's record is more serious than a reprimand, and she will have to report being sanctioned by an ethics committee whenever such information is formally requested.

Notes on Ethical Issues Involving Financial Arrangements

Making ends meet is as important to mental health professionals as it is to their clients. Those psychotherapists who are anxious about managing their own finances may have difficulty dealing with money matters, including adopting a plan for fees and billing practices that are easily explainable and understood and agreed to by clients (Gelso & Hayes, 2001; Zur, 2007). A psychotherapy practice must navigate between what Carnochan (1997) labeled "commerce and care." If these two features are disjointed, ambiguous or confusing to clients, unethical mistakes are substantially heightened.

Psychotherapists may resist, or even experience an aversion to, discussing issues associated with fees, especially with those clients who are suffering and vulnerable (Gabbard, 2005; Knapp & Vandecreek, 2008). Financial understandings are even more complicated during a declining economy when clients may become unable to pay previously agreed upon fees (Treloar 2010).

A major category of legal and ethical complaints against mental health professionals involve fee disputes and money issues (Bennett, et al., 2007; Koocher & Keith-Spiegel, 2008). Graduate training programs may not be doing an adequate job of preparing students for the business side of their careers (Barnett & Walfish, 2012).

Discussion Questions

1. Did the fact that the client broke her promise to pay, even after the psychologist offered her a lower fee, mitigate the psychologist's culpability? That is, did this psychologist deserve some sympathy for feeling that the client took advantage of her generosity?
2. Dr. Savage is newly licensed. Was it appropriate for the Ethics Committee to go easier on her than they might have had she been more experienced?
3. How would you deal with a client who still requires treatment but suddenly had no job or insurance?
4. Psychotherapists are in the business of treating vulnerable people. Do you feel torn between being compassionate and expecting full payment for your services in a timely manner? What can be done to minimize that ambivalence and still be a caring professional?
5. Did you get adequate coverage of the business side of psychotherapy in your graduate program? If not, what was missing?

References

Barnett, J. E., & Walfish, S. (2012). *Billing and collecting for your mental health practice: Effective strategies and ethical practice.* Washington, DC: American Psychological Association.

Bennett, B. E., Bricklin, P. M., Harris, E., Knapp, S., VandeCreek, L., & Younggren, J. N. (2006). *Assessing and managing risk in psychological practice: An individualized approach.* Rockville, MD: The Trust.

Carnochan, P. (1997). The therapist's fee. *Psychologist-Psychoanalyst, 17,* 14.

Chamberlin, J. (January, 2009). Offer a financial break: Six ways psychologists can help patients who can no longer afford therapy. *Monitor on Psychology*, 40–41.

Gabbard, G. O. (2005). How not to teach psychotherapy. *Academic Psychiatry, 29*, 332–338.

Gelso, C. J., & Hayes, J. A. (2001). Countertransference management. *Psychotherapy, 38*, 418–422.

Knapp, S., & VandeCreek, L. (2008). The ethics of advertising, billing, and finances in psychotherapy. *Journal of Clinical Psychology, 64*, 613–625.

Koocher, G. P., & Keith-Spiegel, P. (2008). *Ethics in psychology and the mental health professions*. New York, NY: Oxford University Press.

Treloar, H. R. (2010). Financial and ethical considerations for professionals in psychology. *Ethics & Behavior, 20*, 454–465.

Zur, O. (2007). *Boundaries in psychotherapy: Ethical and clinical explorations*. Washington, DC: American Psychological Association.

Additional Reading

Barnett, J. E., & Klimik, L. (2012). Ethical and business issues in psychology practice. In S. J. Knapp (Ed.). *APA handbook of ethics in psychology*, Vol. 1 (pp. 433–451). Washington, DC: American Psychological Association.

Mikalac, C. M. (2006). *Money and outpatient psychiatry: Practice guidelines from accounting to ethics*. New York, NY: W. W. Norton.

Norcross, J. C. (2005). Psychotherapists' fees and incomes. In G. P. Koocher, J. C. Norcross & S. S. Hill (Eds.). *Psychologists' Desk Reference* (2nd ed., pp. 662–666). New York: Oxford University Press.

twelve
THE STAR
CATCHER

In an ideal world psychotherapists perceive red flags when they first pop up and move ahead with caution and vigilance. The tragic saga of the "The Star Catcher" illustrates how impairment impedes ethical aware-ness. One is also left to wonder why this psychologist's graduate school supervisors apparently failed to pick up clues that this young man would likely make regrettable and reckless decisions. Although this story is unusual and further complicated by an obsession with success and movie stars, it also describes the more common problems arising from pushing career aspirations too fast to the neglect of acceptable profes-sional standards.

Dr. Jonathan Muscatel lay spread eagle on the carpet of his Hollywood office on Melrose Avenue as if nailed to the floor.

"This cannot be happening to me!" he yelled up at the ceiling fan. "This is unacceptable! After all I did for him, he betrays me in the worst possible way."

As of yesterday, but before the certified letter arrived, Jonathan Muscatel's grand vision, the one he designed so meticulously, had proceeded as he'd always planned. At last he was perched on the edge of glory. The prep work, almost seven years of intense intellectual effort and financial sacrifice, was finally complete when, six months ago, he received his license to practice psychotherapy.

Jonathan had already settled into a small office just a stone's throw from Paramount Studios and a cluster of smaller movie and television production companies. He chose this site quite deliberately, even though the neighborhood was hardly a location where most mental health professionals would consider setting up shop. Paramount's massive double arches and filigree iron gates stood in stark contrast to the aging single-story storefronts only a block away. But his simple one-storey office with a new outside coat of pale blue paint fit perfectly into his grand scheme. The inside walls were done in pastel yellow and were decorated with classic movie posters. *Gone with the Wind. Lawrence of Arabia. La Dolce Vita. Ben Hur. It's a Wonderful Life.* The scope of his new practice, topped by a logo of three gold stars, adorned his entrance door and business cards.

Dr. Jonathan Muscatel, Psychologist
Theatrical Performance Enhancement
Memory Improvement
Anxiety Reduction
Self-confidence Building
Psychological Counseling

Yet today his world turned upside down. As Jonathan lay there scanning the ceiling from corner to corner, he reviewed how his career was supposed to play out, just as he did almost every day growing up in a household where stress and rage were far more intense than the mayhem played out on the screen in the only movie theater in Abilene, Kansas. If his parents were not threatening bodily harm while screaming at each other or at him, the silence hung like giant icicles poised to snap and collapse on whoever was in their trajectory. Meal preparation, house cleaning and laundering were hit-and-miss. But when he slid back into the red velvet seats in the old Grand Abilene Theater, he felt comfortably invisible under the protection of the darkened auditorium. The violence portrayed on the screen felt as exciting as it was safe. The theater became his sanctuary and the actors his friends. With lights and colors flickering on the faces of the other theatergoers, none of whom ever bothered him or even noticed he was there, his body would unwind and his consciousness would fuse into the intrigue, transfixed on every character, especially the leading men.

Michael Douglas. Mel Gibson. Richard Gere. Kurt Russell. He yearned to be one of them. But he was too stoutly built and his face pocked deep with acne scars. He lacked much of a chin and his ears were so small and flat against his head that from the front it appeared as if they were missing altogether. His tiny ears contrasted sharply with his oversized nose. The bully at school called him "Toucan," followed by a vocalization sounding more like a crow.

Jonathan Muscatel was hardly leading man material, and he knew it. He would have to find another way, a means of getting up close and personal with these larger-than-life superhumans, to someday be *with* them if not *like* them.

The answer came upon him like a lightning bolt during Career Day in his sophomore year of high school. A counselor drove in from Topeka and described to students what psychologists do and the career path to becoming one. Jonathan knew right then that he would become *the* psychologist to the stars. His life took on a meaning and focus from that day forward. He would borrow to fund his education and repay his debt shortly after his practice took off.

Student loans and earnings from working on Hank Dupree's farm every harvest since he was 12 provided enough to pay his way through college and take him on to California for graduate training. Now, just months after earning his license to practice, turning his life-long aspirations into concrete reality became a single-minded fixation. He would make it convenient for the clients he wanted to attract. They would be able to get to him within minutes. They could even walk over during breaks if they worked at Paramount.

Now, so many years after his weekly escape to the Saturday matinee in Abilene, he would get personal with those who lit up the silver screen, readily disclosing their securely locked secrets and fears. He would explore what was left after stripping away the glamorous exteriors and the public relations bullshit, revealing only their naked psyches. He would mine the substance of their very souls. He imagined most of them to be haunted, scarred, and harboring dark thoughts and wicked proclivities. He alone would discover their true essences as weak and bare, like new-born mice. Then, like the Phoenix, his own unique talent would raise them up, strengthen them to achieve new heights, and in the process their spirits would become his, and his would become theirs. After their transformations, sitting in the ornate Hollywood theaters beholding their images on giant screens, he would revel in knowing what anguish once hid within these larger-than-life apparitions, truths unknown to anyone else, not even to those they held most dear. He would encounter his own consciousness in an endless stream of personas for the entire world to admire in awe. The crush of paparazzi, the screaming fans, the Emmys and the Oscars, the gold stars dotting Hollywood Boulevard. Only he would know the Divine Truth. It was all about him.

***

"He's gonna be a great actor someday," Eduardo Costa's proud father repeated to everyone he knew as well as to most strangers who paused long enough to chat. By age five, Eduardo acted out a passage from one of his favorite story books during the Sunday family meals at the Costa home, much to the delight of his parents, sisters, aunts, uncles, and cousins. In school he landed the lead role in almost every play. Yet as Eduardo matured and the material became more complex, memorizing the longer scenes was more arduous causing him to tense up and sometimes trip over his lines.

Despite his waning confidence, Eduardo remained committed to giving a career in show business a try. Acting was all he ever thought about doing, all he ever wanted to do. So, upon graduating from Tulsa Community College and with his family's blessings, he took off in his 2002 Chevy Camaro and headed west to link up with the I-40. Destination, Hollywood.

Eduardo's outgoing personality readily landed him new friends with similar aspirations. Waiting tables where the glitterati gathered was the occupation of choice among aspiring actors itching for a chance encounter leading to that first break. Eduardo worked every weekend at La Mexicana Verde and charmed enough in tips to pay his share of the rent with two other Hollywood hopefuls. Many of his new acquaintances became discouraged and returned to where they came from, only to be quickly replaced with another litter of starry-eyed optimists. But Eduardo's pride and his father's mantra kept him focused, searching for an agent and showing up at open calls, even as his confidence continued to decline. His fear of stammering and blowing his lines accelerated, creating a vicious cycle of performance anxiety.

After being excused from too many auditions and never receiving a call-back, Eduardo realized he needed help. Any form of "mental help" was foreign to his family's culture. And yet returning home with nothing to show but six months of failure to land a single part, even in equity waiver theater, was far more daunting than giving psychotherapy a try. He decided to check out a tip from a restaurant patron about a psychologist on Melrose Avenue who specialized in working with performers. Eduardo called his father to say "a producer" suggested he receive more formal acting training, and asked for a loan to pay for the expensive "lessons."

Just six weeks with Dr. Jonathan Muscatel resulted in Eduardo's ability to remember lines improving markedly. He was learning a form of self-hypnosis—messages to give himself to enhance poise and well-being—in addition to role-playing, breathing exercises, and guided imagery tours. After the third month, Eduardo landed the role as the Guardian Angel in *Pepper Street,* performed in a small theater on Magnolia Boulevard in North Hollywood, hooked up with an agent, appeared in a TV commercial for a pest control company, and received a call-back for a made-for-television movie. He didn't land the role, but he knew he was finally headed in the right direction.

The following month Eduardo's agent set him up with an audition for a minor part in a major production requiring an actor of his age and "great Latino looks." He showed up and gave it his best. Several days later Eduardo called his father with the news he had been itching to deliver since landing in California.

"Papa, I got a role in *The Bosnia Massacre.* It's already into production, has top stars, and is budgeted at 250 million dollars."

Eduardo's father let out a whoop. "I told you so! I knew you would be a great actor someday. Consuelo, come here. Good news from the boy."

"Papa, it's not one of the major roles. I play an aid to General Wesley Clark. I do have 13 lines. I get killed about half way through. The Jeep driver goes over a cliff, but I don't survive it."

"Not a problem, Son. You are on your way up. I guess those lessons really paid off."

"Yes, Dad, they did indeed." Eduardo held back telling his father the whole story that, by now, had become far more complicated.

As soon as Eduardo hung up the phone, it rang. It was Dr. Muscatel. Again. Eduardo did not answer. Instead he picked up a pad and pen and wrote out a long letter to the organization Dr. Muscatel often bragged about belonging to.

To the League of California Psychologists

I hate doing this, but I don't know where else to turn. When I called your office yesterday the lady said I had to put my problem in writing.

First I need to say I have a lot to be grateful for. Jonathan Muscatel is really good at what he does. I needed mental help in the worst way. I came to Hollywood to be an actor. But I have trouble talking under pressure. Jonathan helped me control my fears with things like role play and what he called desensitization. It worked. I got an agent. I have a great part in a movie now. I may get a shot for a recurring part in a TV series.

So you can see how I have to be desperate to write this letter asking you to get Jonathan off my back. I paid for every session but he says I owe him for curing me and have to pay him in more ways than just money. I really don't want anything bad to happen to him. I just want him to stop asking me to do stuff for him.

He says I have to get him onto the movie set and any parties I am invited to where other Hollywood stars or directors or producers are present. I also have to hand out his business cards and tell everyone how great he is and they should go see him. I tell him I really don't feel comfortable doing that but he won't stop. I did take him to one cast party and he embarrassed me by trying to sign up more clients and even pointing me out to Matt Damon as an example of what he could do for them.

I quit seeing him for counseling over a month ago, but he still calls all the time asking me to do him favors. He says I don't understand that when you help a friend as much as he helped me you have to go the extra mile in return. I like him and what he did for me but I don't see him as a friend in that way.

Please just tell him to stop bothering me. That's all I am asking. Maybe he will listen to you.

Thank you.
Eduardo J. Costa

★★★

Jonathan Muscatel held up the letter from the LCP to read again, just to make sure there was not some alternative way of interpreting it.

Dear Dr. Muscatel,

We have received a complaint from Mr. Eduardo Costa. He contends you persistently asked him to promote your practice even after he terminated your services. He states he informed you he does not wish to engage in the tasks you request of him, such as passing out your business cards at his place of work or taking you to events where potential clients may be present. He also says you disclosed his identity as your client to others.

These allegations raise ethical issues involving boundary violations, coercion, harassment, and confidentiality breeches. We ask you to respond to them.

You must make an appointment with the LCP administrator, Mrs. Peggy Aldridge, to appear before the Ethics Committee at its March meeting unless a compelling reason requires a postponement. We expect you will be able to respond to Mr. Costa's allegations. He has signed a release allowing you to discuss the matter with us. Failure to contact us within 10 days of the receipt of this letter will constitute an act of noncompliance, which is itself an ethics violation.

Sincerely,
Victor Graham, Ph.D.
Chair, Ethics Committee
League of California Psychologists

No, the letter was clear. Eduardo turned into Judas, and he, himself, was to be crucified. He thought about how Eduardo was struggling when he first signed on as a client, how he experienced acute stage fright, how he was unable to remember more than five lines at a time, how he stumbled over words with more than three syllables, and how he had a maddening stammer when he was the least bit nervous. Yet after only 18 sessions he landed a role in *The Bosnia Massacre*, a blockbuster in the making, given the status of the director and six top box office stars.

Jonathan crumpled the letter. "Does Eduardo think he could have gotten anywhere without me?" he yelled, tossing the letter up at the ceiling fan. "Instead he betrays me." He turned slowly onto his side and curled up into a tight ball. Sleep provided a merciful if only temporary sanctuary from his waking agony.

The Ethics Committee:
Jonathan Muscatel, Ph.D. March 17, 1:50 p.m.

"Here we go," said Victor Graham, pulling a letter from his briefcase. "A boundary violation with a couple of twists. This case gives a new wrinkle to the definition of payment and for how long a bill remains outstanding."

Victor read Eduardo Costa's letter aloud.

"I always admire ambition. But if Mr. Costa is telling us the truth, this guy's taken it to the next universe," said Ted Bates. "How long has he been in practice?"

"Got his license less than a year ago," answered Victor.

"Aha! A Green Menace. I knew it!" Wolf Levin yelped, clapping his hands together. "They can be hazardous to the health of our profession."

"What's a Green Menace?" Sammy Halsey innocently inquired.

"It's what we call newly licensed psychologists in a big hurry to arrive at their own end game," Wolf answered. "They don't think about getting there, just being there. Without the experience to see what can go wrong, they are vulnerable to doing stupid stuff like this."

"What was this one thinking?" Stella Sarkosky blurted out. "I mean, trying to coerce a client into becoming his sales force? And to continue even after the client is no longer a client?"

"Maybe there's another side to the story, and we can get it all straightened out" said Ted, always looking for the happiest possible ending.

"Well, let's see what Dr. Jonathan Muscatel has to say for himself," said Victor. "I think I saw him pacing the hallway."

"Yep, he's out there," said Wolf. "He looks distraught. I'll go round him up."

***

After taking one look at this strange looking young man, Sammy thought Wolf's description of Jonathan Muscatel's distress was drastically understated. His face was pale and riddled with anguish. His chunky body was trembling, as if on the verge of a full-blown panic attack.

Victor must have had the same take. "Please take a seat here," calmly waving Dr. Muscatel to the seat to his left. "Nobody here bites. We need to talk to you for a few minutes. Can we get you a glass of water?" Victor sported the engaging smile he puts on when the accused seems unusually anxious.

Jonathan stumbled into the chair and softly uttered, "Yes, thank you, I could use water." Charlotte Burroughs went to the back table and poured a cup.

Victor pointed out each member by name as Jonathan Muscatel grasped the cup with unsteady hands and took a sip, dribbling a few drops down the front of his yellow pullover sweater.

"So, let's start with your relationship with Mr. Eduardo Costa," said Victor, acting as if he didn't notice anything amiss. "You did consider him to be a therapy client, yes?"

"Yes and no," Jonathan mumbled as he fumbled to put the glass down, spilling a little more water into his lap. "I worked hard with him for almost

20 sessions, but we focused only on his performance anxiety. We didn't ever get into his childhood or anything about his past." He stopped for a few seconds and let out a deep sigh.

"We worked so well together. He's going to be a major star, you know. He couldn't get five lines out when he came to me. But now he's in a big movie and has lots of other offers. I am responsible." Jonathan almost smiled.

"Is it true you requested that he hand out your business cards and invite him to social events where Hollywood players are invited?" asked Stella, sounding like an assistant DA again.

"We became very close early on. I was asking for his help as my best buddy. Friends do those things for each other," Jonathan answered, seemingly beginning to calm down.

"Do you think Eduardo Costa also thought of you as his friend?" asked Stella, her brow furrowing slightly.

"Yes, of course he did. I am sure he did. He reached out to me as friends do, and I helped him become somebody. We were always glad to see each other. After our sessions I would offer him coffee or a soda, sometimes a beer, and we would talk about what was happening on the set, the gossip—that sort of thing. Sometimes we would talk for over an hour."

"So you saw him as your friend while you were still seeing him as a client?" Stella continued.

"Yes, of course. We hit it off right from the beginning."

"Thank you, Dr. Muscatel," Stella responded in a way the other Committee members knew she got whatever she was after.

"So, Eduardo paid you for his sessions. Is that correct?" Sammy asked, just to make sure they had not set up any bartering arrangement, trading therapy in exchange for promoting Jonathan's practice.

"Yes, he always paid me for my professional services. My fee was completely separate from our friendship."

"Did you view your request to promote your practice as exploiting him in any way?" asked Archie Wittig, trying to sound inquisitive rather than accusatory. "That is, if he paid for your services, he didn't actually owe you anything. Yet you apparently asked him to help you even after he quit seeing you professionally."

"I seem to be having trouble making myself understood," Jonathan responded, now sounding exasperated. "We became close friends, so much more than just therapist and client. We superseded a strictly therapeutic relationship early on. I would have done anything he asked of me. Anything. And I asked him to help me in a simple and straightforward way, given his many new contacts."

"So you felt maybe he owed you?" asked Charlotte, trying to be gentle and make up for Stella's harsher tone with this tense man.

"He needed me and I saved him from total failure and obscurity. He would have gone back to Oklahoma as a shamed nobody were it not for me. Now it was my turn. I needed what he could give to me," Jonathan said, as if he thought his declaration was the obvious conclusion the people seated around him should have reached on their own.

"So, I think I am hearing you say you were simply asking for what you had earned in return," continued Charlotte. "Do I understand you correctly, Dr. Muscatel?"

"I was not asking much. What I am able to do can create top performers, so why shouldn't others know and have a real life example as solid proof? So many others would be grateful for what I can offer."

"That leads me to my question," said Wolf. "Dr. Muscatel, do you have many other clients who are rising stars?"

"I do have a few clients, but none like Eduardo. I'm just starting off, you know. I counsel a graduate student who has trouble speaking up in class, a secretary who is very shy and wants help becoming more assertive, and a couple of people who want to get into show business but whose chances are slim to none, I'm sorry to say. Oh, a guy from Senegal with a shop next door to my office wants to be better understood in English. He knows the words, but his accent is too thick for most Americans to figure out what he is trying to say, even me sometimes."

"I'd also like to ask if you pointed Eduardo out to others during an event as one of your successful clients," Wolf continued.

"Yes, he had a lot to be proud of. I wanted everyone to know how much he had accomplished."

"Did Eduardo give permission for you to discuss his progress with others?" Wolf asked.

"No, but why should he? We were at a party where lots of people who could help me…him were present. The name of the game in Hollywood is to be noticed in any way possible. This was a clever way to make sure some of the important people in the room knew who he was."

"Did you not consider confidentiality issues?" Archie continued.

"As I said, we knew each other inside and out—like identical twins. He would be fine with it."

"One more question," said Wolf. "Mr. Costa wrote to us because he wanted you to stop asking him to do these favors. He claims he also told you he didn't want to promote you and your business. Did you understand his reluctance?"

"He said something once or twice, but I didn't take him seriously. He wanted us both to succeed."

"He wrote to us about it, though," Wolf continued. "Why would he have complained if he wasn't serious?"

Dr. Muscatel resumed an anguished expression. "I don't know," he said, his voice cracking. "I just don't know." His face puckered and his eyes reddened.

"We won't keep you much longer, Dr. Muscatel," said Victor. "Thank you for responding to our questions to the best of your ability."

"Does anyone else have anything?" Victor asked, hoping no one would. No one responded. "Dr. Muscatel, if you have nothing else to share with us, you are free to leave."

"No, nothing, thank you."

Charlotte rose to walk out with Dr. Muscatel. She did not come right back in.

***

"Ouch, he made me uncomfortable," said Wolf. "The fellow presented such a distressing spectacle. The good-looker tall genes didn't pause long for me, but they flashed right past him at warp speed. I have a feeling he's trying to make up for his peculiar physical appearance by attempting to attract glamorous clients and be seen with them. So far only this Eduardo fills that bill."

Stella had one of her rare puzzled expressions. "It's true, Wolf. There's something jarring about this whole case. I can't put my finger on it. But he seems to have melted into this client like butter on a hot potato. I think he sees himself in some mutual symbiotic cycle, a fusion between himself and Eduardo Costa where one cannot exist without the other. It's just my gut feeling. He didn't actually disclose anything quite that extreme."

"Let's wait for Charlotte before we go on," said Victor. "Knowing her good soul, she's trying to soothe Dr. Muscatel a little before he takes off. Get yourselves some coffee or stretch."

When Charlotte returned 10 minutes later, she looked conflicted. "Sorry," she said. "That poor man is Jello. I got him over to Ting's and waited until he ordered a sandwich and hot tea. He hadn't eaten yet today."

"Did you pick up anything we missed, Charlotte?" asked Archie.

"Not really. He's feeling defeated and now terrified of us, of course. I'm worried about him. I suggested he take some time out. Do something he likes to do. He said he only likes to go to the movies."

"It sounds like he did this Eduardo Costa a lot of good. Does he get points for that?" asked Ted, always looking for a pony in the poop pile.

"That may be true," added Stella, "but it only means he may be good at what he does therapeutically. Some mental health professionals who screwed their clients—and I am being literal—were probably also competent psychotherapists. Other variables, often their own needs overriding those of their clients, contaminated the relationship creating serious trust issues for those who thought they were in protected space. This Eduardo Costa is lucky because he only wanted to get over his specific career-related hurdles. His triumphs are less likely to backslide compared to the effects of being exploited sexually. But I'm not sure the difference should have much impact on how we evaluate Jonathan Muscatel's ethical transgressions."

"Well I'm not in favor of expelling him or sending him to the licensing board given how new he is at this, even though a case could be made for expulsion," said Wolf. "And yet he needs to get a rock solid message and maybe extended psychotherapy for depression at least, although I sense his problems go much deeper. But, frankly I am worried if we cut him loose he may call himself something else like "Star Coach" and keep doing the same thing. We can't take his doctorate away, so he will always have a legitimate diploma with Ph.D. in Clinical Psychology to hang on an office wall.

"He can even tell people he completed all of the required internships," added Archie Wittig. "He just doesn't seem to understand the importance of appropriate professional boundaries at even the most rudimentary level. You can't move right into a client's private life and stay stuck in it forever."

"This case is troubling," said Victor. "Dr. Muscatel is clearly guilty of several ethical violations. He attempted to manipulate, exploit, and harass a client even after the client left, and he violated the client's right to confidentiality. Even he doesn't deny these actions. His seeming inability to comprehend the ethical issues poses an ethical problem in and of itself."

"I like the idea of tabling this case and mandating therapy," said Charlotte. "He's such a sorry fellow. We will be able to monitor him and stipulate that he cease and desist from asking any of his other clients to do anything extra for him besides paying his fee or else there will be additional sanctions. His therapist can also let us know in general terms if he is getting anywhere with—well I can't definitively diagnose him based on what we saw today—but probably a narcissistic personality disorder with border-line features."

"OK, said Victor. Let's make those decisions."

Decision and Dispositions

The Committee was unanimous in finding Jonathan Muscatel guilty of encouraging an inappropriate multiple role relationship, exploitation, and violations of his client's right to confidentiality. Dr. Muscatel's seeming incapability to understand the gravity of his transgressions was of particular concern and the primary reason the Committee wanted to attempt to ensure that he receive proper treatment.

The Committee drafted a letter to Dr. Muscatel issuing a strong censure and a cease-and-desist order stipulating a minimum of 20 sessions of psychotherapy to explore his boundary and other issues at his expense with a mutually agreed-upon therapist. The Committee also offered the name of someone who would see him at a greatly reduced fee. Assigning an ethics class was briefly discussed but dismissed because Dr. Muscatel's issues seemed to run far deeper than what didactic instruction could reach at this time.

Jonathan Muscatel initially agreed to the Committee's mandate to attend therapy. He even accepted their suggestion of Lynn Perkins, Ph.D., an established practitioner with a reputation for having unending patience and skill in working with personality disordered clients. However, Jonathan did not show up for his first appointment. She tried to reach him several times, but without luck.

Victor Graham's subsequent attempts to contact Dr. Muscatel over the next weeks also failed. His office phone had been shut off and two letters to his office were returned as undeliverable with no forwarding address.

The Committee members had no choice at their next meeting but to recommend expulsion to the LCP Board for noncompliance with an Ethics Committee directive. The California Board of Psychology was also notified, as is routine.

Seven months after Jonathan Muscatel's original hearing, the local six o'clock news carried the story of a psychologist who died from a self-inflicted gunshot wound in a West Hollywood movie theater during a Saturday matinee showing of *The Bosnia Massacre*.

Case Commentary

Dr. Muscatel was seriously impaired, so much so that he was able to incorporate multiple ethical violations into his own grandiose delusions. As a lone practitioner far from where other professionals cluster, he was inaccessible to any source of support or intervention. Diverse aetiologies besides professional isolation likely contributed to his ethical failures; difficult childhood, inadequate training or supervision, situational-based depression as manifestations of his lifelong obsession faded, as well as a probable underlying personality disorder. Being sanctioned by an ethics committee compiled Dr. Muscatel's stress, despite the offer of monitored assistance and a chance for rehabilitation. Such options can sometimes be appropriately used as a leverage against possible delicensure (Monahan & Bonnie, 2004), although they failed in this case.

The concept of self-destructive emotional healers seems paradoxical. However, an elevated risk of suicide for health care professionals is well-established (e.g., Agerbo, Gunnel, Bonde, Mortenses, & Nordentoft, 2007; Schernhammer, 2005). Psychologists were not included in these data, but some surveys, despite methodological shortcomings, suggest that suicide rates and suicidal ideation are higher among psychologists than for the general public (Kleespies, et al., 2011). Pope and Tabachnick (1994) found that 29 percent of their national sample of 800 psychologists reported suicidal ideation, and 4 percent reported having actually attempted suicide. Possible risks are proposed, including a number of the situational factors mirroring difficulties in Dr. Muscatel's life that may have pushed him over the edge. These include social isolation, depression, impulsivity, underemployment, and access to lethal means (Kleespies, et al., 2011; O'Connor, 2001).

Dr. Muscatel's supervisors probably missed (or ignored) red flags that might predict later engagement in unprofessional behavior and client exploitation. It's as if he slipped through the cracks. Supervisors are gatekeepers of the profession (Behnke, 2005), although not all are themselves competent and ethical (Jacobs, 1991; Johnson & Huwe, 2002; Landany, Lehrman-Waterman, Molinaro, & Walgast, 1999; Landany, Mori, & Mehr, 2013). Students and interns have expressed concerns that impaired peers have been inadequately addressed (Oliver, Bernstein, Anderson, Bashfield, & Roberts, 2004;

Rosenberg, Getzelman, Arcinue, & Oren, 2005), although barriers have been described that make effective intervention difficult (Gizara & Forrest, 2004; Vacha-Haase, Davenport, & Kerewsky, 2004). Even highly problematic students can be licensed (Jensen, 2003).

Can one become "just friends" with ex-clients if both agree to this shift in their relationship (as was not the case in this story)? The APA ethics code (2010) is silent on this specific issue (whereas stated rules pertain for sex with ex-clients), except for the general provision that clients should never be exploited. Shifting from a one-way relationship with a power-differential to a shared egalitarian relationship may be difficult and even disappointing, possibly even eroding the gains from psychotherapy if the ex-client discovers that the therapist-as-a-real-person is not an idealized friend (Neale, 2010). Complications could occur if the friendship goes awry. Should the ex-client need additional services, such as a court appearance or other forms of support, things would be awkward at best (Koocher & Keith-Spiegel, 2008).

Finally, creating a narrowly defined clientele niche, as Dr. Muscatel attempted to do, is becoming commonplace. This phenomenon is likely in response to the decreased demand for traditional psychotherapy due to such factors as third-party payer session limitations and increased reliance on psychopharmacology (Gottlieb, 2012). One recent attempt to re-establish client numbers is to "brand" one's services, to focus on a specialty that will attract particular clients, and market it as a product. Gottlieb quotes a "branding consultant" who assists psychotherapists in targeting specialties as exclusive as treating tweens, military wives, video-addicted teenage boys, children with Asperger's syndrome, and repeat D.U.I. offenders. What specific training one should undertake before declaring expertise in a narrowly defined service domain remains unclear.

Notes on Impaired Psychotherapists

Despite their advanced training, psychotherapists are not immune from serious emotional problems (Barnett, 2008; Gizara & Forrest, 2004; Guy, Poelstra, & Stark, 1989; Johnson & Barnett, 2012). Sadly, however, their likelihood of seeking assistance may be low (O'Connor, 2001). Because decision-making and other elements of competence can be compromised, emotionally distressed and impaired profes-sionals may be at greater risk for engaging in unethical behavior (Good, Khairallah, & Mintz, 2009; Hendricks. Bradley, Brogan, & Brogan, 2009). Ethical violations often involve psychotherapists whose professional judgment and actions were clouded by addiction, marital discord, physical difficulties, and, most frequently, emotional problems (Katsavdakis, Gabbard, & Athey, 2004; O'Connor, 2001). The classic survey conducted by the APA Task Force on Distressed Psychologists found that almost 70 percent of the sample had personal knowledge of therapists experiencing serious emotional difficulties (reported in VandenBos & Duthie, 1986). In another classic and large scale survey, almost three quarters of the survey respondents reported dealing with personal distress during the previ-ous three years, and a third of these admitted a decrease in the quality of the care they delivered (Guy, Poelstra, & Stark, 1989).

The ethics codes of most mental health professional organizations mandate the limitation or suspension of services when emotional or physical problem diminish competency. Also, many ethics codes encourage collegial intervention when a colleague is suspected of being incompetent due to mental illness (e.g., American Psychiatric Association, American Association of Marriage and Family Therapists, National Association of Social Workers).

Yet the question remains; "How impaired to too impaired?" Such a decision may involve a subjective and imperfect process (Williams, Pomerantz, Segrist, & Pettibone, 2010). Furthermore, it is unclear whether professionals experiencing personal difficulties are capable of being forthcoming when assessing their own competence (Zeddies, 1999; Zerubavel & Wright, 2012).

Discussion Questions

1. What features of maintaining solo practice with no ongoing communications with other mental health professionals enhance the potential for making ethical errors?
2. A dilemma is created when graduate students are doing compe-tent academic work but also display behaviors that could

compromise their ability to deliver sound professional services. How do you think such students should be evaluated in a way that is fair and preserves due process?

3. How impaired is too impaired? Generally speaking, how do you feel about the practitioners described below? What would you say to each if you knew the facts and the psychotherapist is a close friend?

   a. A social worker has five alcoholic drinks a day after work to help deal with the stresses of working with people with difficult and sometimes seemingly unsolvable problems.

   b. A psychiatrist uses cocaine on her off days. She defines herself as a "harmless recreational user."

   c. A counselor is so depressed that he has trouble getting out of bed in the morning.

   d. A psychologist's wife committed suicide a week ago, and he is back in the office.

   e. A marriage and family counselor is experiencing a bitter divorce and custody battle.

   f. A psychologist's auto accident has left her in such intense pain that she requires very high dosages of a Schedule II controlled painkiller. Even still, she has to cancel several sessions a week.

   g. A social worker is battling stage 4 melanoma, and his life expectancy is unclear.

4. Can having a diagnosable mental condition (e.g., a depressive or anxiety disorder) actually facilitate effective psychotherapy? How or why not? What if the problem occurred in the past but is now either under control or resolved? Might that past experience be helpful now?

5. Most ethics codes admonish mental health professional to assess for themselves whether they are competent to work with clients. Do you think it is possible to make an accurate assessment if one is already troubled? What factors mitigate against seeing oneself as sufficiently impaired to require psychotherapy and to suspend seeing clients?

6. Do you think it is all right to become friends with an ex-client, assuming both parties are in agreement and no exploitation appears apparent? Why or why not?

References

Agerbo, B. S., Gunnel, D., Bonde, J. P., Mortenses, P. B., & Nordentoft, M. (2007). Suicide and occupation: The impact of socio-economic, demographic and psychiatric differences. *Psychological Medicine, 37,* 1131–1140.

American Psychological Association (2010). Ethical principles of psychologists and code of conduct. Retrived from http://www.apa.org/ethics/code/index.aspx

Barnett, J. E. (2008). Impaired professionals: Distress, professional impairment, self-care, and psychological wellness. In M. Hersen, & A. M. Gross (Eds.). *Handbook of clinical psychology,* Vol. 1 (pp. 857–884). Hoboken, NJ: Wiley.

Behnke, S. (May, 2005). The supervisor as gatekeeper: Reflections on Ethical Standards 7.02, 7.04, 7.05, 7.06, and 10.01. *Monitor on Psychology,* 90–91.

Good, G. E., Khairallah, T., & Mintz, L. B. (2009). Wellness and impairment: Moving beyond noble us and troubled them. *Clinical Psychology, 16,* 21–23.

Gottlieb, L. (2012). What brand is your therapist? *New York Times* retrieved from http://www.nytimes.com/2012/11/25/magazine/psychotherapys-image-problem-pushes-some-therapists-to-become-brands.html?pagewanted=1&_r = 2&partner = rss&emc = rss&

Gizara, S. S., & Forrest, L. (2004). Supervisors' experiences of trainee impairment and incompetence at APA-accredited internship sites. *Professional Psychology, 35,* 131–140.

Guy, J. D., Poelstra, P. L., & Stark, M. J. (1989). Personal distress and therapeutic effectiveness: National Survey of psychologists practicing psychotherapy. *Professional Psychology, 20,* 48–50.

Hendricks, B., Bradley, L. J., Brogan, W. D., & Brogan, C. (2009). Shelly: A case study focusing on ethics and counselor wellness. *The Family Journal: Counseling and Therapy for Couples and Families, 17,* 355–359.

Jacobs, C. (1991). Violations of the supervisory relationship: An ethical and educational blind spot. *Social Work, 36,* 130–135.

Jensen, D. G. (Nov./Dec., 2003). Dealing with unqualified, incompetent, or dishonest interns. *The Therapist,* 30–33.

Johnson, W. B., & Barnett, J. E. (2012). When illness strikes you. *Monitor on Psychology, 43,* 52–56.

Johnson, W. B., & Huwe, J. M. (2002). Toward a typology of mentorship dysfunction in graduate school. *Psychotherapy, 39,* 44–55.

Katsavdakis, K., Gabbard, G. O., & Athry, G. I. (2004). Profiles of impaired health professionals. *Bulletin of the Menninger Clinic, 68,* 60–72.

Kleespies, P. M., Van Orden., K. A., Bongar, B., Bridgeman, D., Bufka, L. F., Galper, D. I., Hillbrand, D., & Yufit, R. I. (2011). Psychologist suicide: Incidence, impact, and suggestions for prevention, interventions, and postvention. *Professional Psychology, 42,* 244–251.

Koocher, G. P., & Keith-Spiegel, P. (2008). *Ethics in psychology and the mental health professions.* New York, NY: Oxford University Press.

Landany, N., Lehrman-Waterman, D., Molinaro, B., & Wolgast, B. (1999). Psychotherapy supervisor ethical practice: Adherence to guidelines, the supervisory working alliance, and supervisee satisfaction. *The Counseling Psychologist, 27,* 443–475.

Landany, N., Mori, Y., & Mehr, K. E. (2013). Effective and ineffective supervision. *The Counseling Psychologist, 41,* 28–47.

Monahan, J. & Bonnie, T. J. (2004). License as leverage: Mandating treatment for psychologists. *International Journal of Forensic Mental Health, 3,* 131–138.

Neale, S. (2010). Why you can't be friends with your therapist—Ever! Retrieved from http://blogs.psychcentral.com/unplugged/2010/01/why-you-cant-be-friends-with-your-therapist-ever/

O'Connor, M. F. (2001). On the etiology and effective management of professional distress and impairment among psychologists. *Professional Psychology, 32,* 345–350.

Oliver, M. N. I., Bernstein, J. H., Anderson, K. G., Bashfield, R. K., & Roberts, M. C. (2004). An exploratory examination of student attitudes toward "impaired" peers in clinical psychology training programs. *Professional Psychology, 35,* 141–147.

Pope, K. S., & Tabachnick, B. (1994). Therapists as patients: A national survey of psychologists' experiences, problems, and beliefs. *Professional Psychology, 25,* 247–258.

Rosenberg, J. L., Getzelman, M. A., Arcinue, F., & Oren, C. Z. (2005). An exploratory look at students' experiences of problematic peers in academic professional psychology programs. *Professional Psychology, 36,* 665–673.

Schernhammer, E. (2005). Taking their own lives: The high rate of physician suicide. *New England Journal of Medicine, 352,* 2473–2476.

Vacha-Haase, T., Davenport, D. S., & Kerewsky, S. D. (2004). Problematic students: Gatekeeping practices of academic professional psychology programs. *Professional Psychology, 35,* 115–122.

VandenBos, G. R., & Duthie, R. F. (1986). Confronting and supporting colleagues in distress. In R. R. Kilburg, P. E. Nathan, & R. W. Thoreson (Eds.). (1986). *Professionals in distress: Issues, syndromes, and solutions in psychology.* (pp. 211–231). Washington, DC: American Psychological Association.

Williams, B. E., Pomerantz, A. M., Segrist, D. J., & Pettibone, J. (2010). How impaired is too impaired? Ratings of psychologist impairment by psychologists in independent practice. *Ethics & Behavior, 20,* 149–160.

Zeddies, T. J. (1999). Becoming a psychotherapist: The personal nature of clinical work, emotional availability and personal allegiances. *Psychotherapy, 36,* 229–235.

Zerubavel, N., & Wright, M. O. (2012). The dilemma of the wounded healer. *Psychotherapy, 49,* 482–491.

Additional Reading

Barnett, J. E., & Hilgard, D. (2001). Psychologist distress and impairment: The availability, nature, and use of colleague assistance programs for psychologists. *Professional Psychology, 32,* 205–210.

Freudenberger, H. J. (1990). Hazards of psychotherapeutic practice. *Psychotherapy in Private Practice, 8,* 31–34.

Kilburg, R. R., Nathan, P. E., & Thoreson, R. W. (1986). *Professionals in distress.* Washington, DC: American Psychological Association.

Landany, N., Friedlander, M. L., & Nelson, M. L. (2005). Addressing problematic emotions, attitudes, and behaviors. *Critical events in psychotherapy supervision.* Washington, DC: American Psychological Association.

Rothchild, B., & Rand, M. L. (2006). *Help for the helper.* New York, NY: Norton.

Thomas, J. T. (2010). *The ethics of supervision and consultation: Practical guidance for mental health professionals.* Washington, DC: American Psychological Association.

thirteen
VAMPIRE

Out of touch with how his own challenging home life is impacting his professional work, a psychologist struggles to maintain control with a new client who pierces a sore spot. Although most countertransference episodes are not of such rapid onset, self-care measures, including seeking counseling for himself, may have saved this psychologist from facing an ethics committee.

After thrashing about in bed most of the night Mora Slocum still could not decide what she would say to the man she had yet to meet, the man who would surely concur about the worthlessness and depravity of her soon-to-be ex-husband. What image of her would this man find impressive, maybe even alluring? How would she present her case to ensure gaining a formidable ally against Raymond?

With extra cosmetic boosts, the face and body once assuring Mora's election as homecoming queen at Chatsworth High School matured gracefully. Surgery around her large brown eyes and under a slightly drooping chin coupled with bimonthly visits to Imelda's Salon where Imelda herself converted the threads of silver to match Mora's thick black hair, held the clock almost still. Biweekly Pilates sessions and a strict diet further decelerated the inevitable changes normally assaulting the body of a 49-year-old woman.

"I married Mora for her mind-blowing figure," Raymond used to quip when recounting their courtship to friends. But Mora knew he wasn't kidding, keeping her on an unrelenting but ultimately futile mission to preserve herself as a 22-year-old bride. Raymond was not interested in fathering more children as he already had two teenagers from a previous marriage. Remaining childless was quite acceptable to Mora, given the priority to maintain her appearance.

Raymond had been a catch to be sure—a litigation attorney who always had as many clients as he could manage. He knew the people in town who needed to be known. Except for a few disgruntled ex-clients, everyone loved Raymond. He wasn't as handsome as he was exciting in bed. Still, he had grown more distant as the years passed, with sex now reduced to a once or twice a month routine, leaving Mora empty and wanting.

After a quick cup of green tea and a dish of fat-free lemon yogurt, Mora cautiously approached her closet as if she was unsure of what she would find when she slid open the door.

"I should have planned this sooner," she thought to herself. But, she hadn't committed until yesterday to going through with today's appointment.

Mora had already abandoned presenting herself modestly in favor of appearing fashionable and advantaged to this stranger she was counting on to soothe her ravaged psyche and partner in an assault against Raymond. She pulled out, but then rejected, a black jersey dress with long sleeves and a deep V front. Even though it showed off her contour better than any other outfit she owned, it wasn't right for a sunny day. The red linen suit and white silk blouse with a floppy bow at the neck was hastily returned to the rack. She wondered why she had ever purchased an outfit that made her look like a strawberry sundae. Facing tightening time pressure, Mora settled on a lime green sleeveless jersey shift and a long string of simulated pearls. A white loose-knit shawl would complete the ensemble close enough to her goal of looking smart without appearing affluent, thus avoiding the possible risk of being charged more than the fee quoted over the phone.

Now staring into the bathroom mirror, Mora cursed herself for not getting a better night's sleep. The thinning skin under her eyes had slightly discolored to a pale bluish gray. Repair would require extra makeup and an application of a product promising to firm any sags. (Her best friend Michele had scoffed upon learning a tiny bottle of Define-Eye with its bold admonition to "Keep Refrigerated" cost $35. According to Michele, it was likely just egg whites.)

After applying a light shade of make-up, soft black eyeliner, a hint of lime green shadow, and one careful swipe of mascara to each eye, she looped her long, thick hair into a loose bun secured with a beret edged with pearly beads. She slipped on a pair of white leather strapped sandals with three inch heels, tossed a comb, lipstick, and wallet into a white purse with a long strap, flung it over her shoulder and headed for the front door.

Mora paused to glance at herself once again in the entry hall mirror. She whisked a rogue hair back into place before locking her gaze onto the reflection of her own eyes. How deeply they were set now she thought, with dark and drooping lids despite her attempt to camouflage them with the pale green shadow. "*He* did this to you," she screamed at her image. Thoughts of the other women over the course of 27 years of marriage, the lies and humiliation, brought on a rush of desolation. Mora stood up tall and took a deep breath to restore a more powerful feeling by recapturing a mind-set filled with rage and resentment. She gave herself a toothy faux smile, yanked the car keys from her purse, and with renewed resolve walked briskly out the door.

The drive to the office of Dr. Jared Dominion in downtown Van Nuys took 23 minutes. Close enough to Chatsworth to be convenient, yet far enough away to feel anonymous. Turning into the parking lot Mora now wished she had accepted Michele's offer to accompany her. A month ago, after a particularly disquieting evening, Michele extracted the promise responsible for bringing her to this day and place. Upon witnessing Mora vacillating between wailing threats to slice her own wrists with a pair of sewing scissors and hollering wrathful plots to put Raymond into an early grave, Michele struck a deal. If Mora would enter counseling within four weeks, Michele wouldn't call 911 right then and there.

Mora relented, despite her belief that seeking therapy was yet another victory for her soon-to-be ex-husband. One more disgrace. One more sign of weakness, imperfection and undesirability. She fought back impending tears, welcoming instead a bolt of thick rage. A focus on settling the score with Raymond sustained her far better than self-contempt.

Dr. Dominion's modest location was not what she anticipated. Michele had found his name in the directory of the League of California Psychologists, and Mora expected that anyone associated with such an elegant-sounding organization would practice in a sleek structure encircled by lush, manicured greenery. Dr. Dominion's single-story stucco building was small and boxy, painted a yellowish tan and set behind a print shop. Mora parked her silver Mercedes towards the back of the lot, just in case anyone she knew came to this part of town and recognized the

"Hillary Clinton for President, 2008" bumper sticker she steadfastly refused to remove. Thoughts of backing out and driving somewhere else, anywhere else, swept through her. But, she had gotten this far. Despite the disappointing ambience, this professional man, this member of a notable professional society, this *Dr.* Dominion, was going to make her stronger and capable of gaining an upper hand on Raymond.

Mora locked her car and stood between it and a dilapidated wooden fence to smooth out the front of her dress before walking haltingly towards the small building. The scrawny hedges standing guard on the cement pathway at three foot intervals were in obvious need of water. An uneven crack almost caused her to stumble. The rusting handle on the thick, wooden entry door needed tightening. As she opened it, an irritating buzzer announced her arrival.

The small, empty waiting area with two mismatched arm chairs and a brown tweed love seat with saggy cushions felt dark and closed in. She decided on the orange armchair because it looked to be the cleanest and was next to a table with magazines, although she had no intention of picking one up. Her eye caught a small sign by the door presumably leading to an inner office where Dr. Dominion's conducted his sessions. Mora got up to read it.

Please have a seat. I will come get you soon.

"*Get* me? That sounds vaguely ominous." She felt a shiver.

The clock on the dark walnut-paneled wall informed Mora she was a few minutes early. She squelched an urge to change her mind, to run out the door, jump into her car and take off. Instead, she settled into the orange chair, tapping her fingers gently on its scratched wooden arms. She looked around nervously, despite little to see. Chagall's *Bella with White Collar* on the wall across from her was among her favorites, although she had seen prints of far superior quality. The other framed print was unfamiliar to her. It was in black with dark greens and purples. Two shadowy and intertwined human figures were in what could be a dense forest or a jagged cave, and it was unclear what they were doing. Mora thought the image quite intimidating, though she was also strangely drawn into it. Two people—probably a man and a woman—clasping each other in a dark and possibly precarious place.

As her attention fixated on the enigmatic poster, the door from the inner office burst open. Startled, Mora turned abruptly to face the man she was about to trust to remove her bottomless ache and replace it with authentic bravado. Her heart was pounding so hard that she was sure the man at the door could hear it.

Mora's preconceived visual image of Dr. Dominion bore no resemblance to the stunning vision standing before her. His deep but gentle voice on the phone led Mora to expect a pleasant-looking, middle-aged individual of average height. Instead she stared straight into the dark eyes of a breathtakingly striking man, perhaps 15 years her junior with the physique of a competitive swimmer. His tanned, rugged face and sleek black hair brought back Mora's images of Rudolph Valentino at last year's silent film festival. Dr. Dominion was well over 6 feet tall, and dressed in a long-sleeved black silk shirt, black dress slacks, and a thin black leather belt with a gold buckle containing three small jade stone insets. Rings adorned two of the long fingers on his right hand. They, too, were heavy gold with deep green jade stones. No wedding ring. Perhaps he was one of the figures in the unfamiliar poster on the reception office wall she thought, as a tingle surged through her. Mora tried to smile, but wasn't sure what her mouth actually did.

"Come in Mrs. Slocum, and let's see what's going on and how I might be of service." Dr. Dominion ushered Mora towards a brown suede lounge chair. A quick glance around the office revealed a nicely appointed and spacious room quite unlike the waiting area or the building's exterior. Mora lowered herself delicately into the chair, but preferred a stiff pose on the edge of the seat with her hands neatly folded on her lap. If she leaned back she thought she would tumble into the upholstery and disappear altogether.

"I'll just ask you a couple of questions and we'll see if we think we can work together," Dr. Dominion said in reassuring tones, settling into a high-backed, black leather office chair placed only a few feet away from Mora's crossed legs. He swiveled around to look her squarely in the face.

"So, then, Mrs. Slocum. What brings you here today?"

At first, Mora's mind felt blank. She just then realized she had spent the morning preoccupied with her outfit and makeup, forgetting to create and memorize an initial presentation of her unpleasant circumstance. Instead she was looking into Dr. Dominion's dark eyes and felt herself being pulled right into them. Her thoughts were like debris in the wind.

"Umm. Yes." She paused for a few seconds trying to gather up her words.

"Well, I am getting a divorce. It is very hard, you know. I guess everybody says that, don't they?" She laughed nervously. "My husband—his name is Raymond—has turned, well, into quite the monster, I would say. I used to love him, of course, or I would not have married him." She giggled weakly.

Mora looked down at her folded hands, thinking she was already coming off all wrong. She could get out what she needed to say if she didn't look directly at this stunning man, this accidental Adonis.

"How do you think I could help you with your angry feelings towards your husband?" This time Dr. Dominion's tone had a slight edge to it. Mora looked up. She detected a flash in his eyes now fixed on her. Her gaze shifted back to her folded hands. She would have to justify herself, to gain his sympathy and understanding.

"To be honest, Dr. Dominion, Raymond is dirt. A human stain, really. A horrible, horrible human being. He wants a divorce and I am not going to make things easy for him."

Mora felt her voice break up. She would have to make it stronger. "He made my life miserable with his lies. He's never home until late, smelling like cheap perfume and marijuana," she continued. "He's a cheat and a liar. He needs to be brought down."

"And, I repeat, Mrs. Slocum, what would you want me to do?" Dr. Dominion sounded irritated. She looked up again. His dark eyes had narrowed, his brow slightly crinkled.

Mora glanced down again, feeling flustered. She was not making her case. She would have to speak even louder with more confidence.

"Well, I need you to help me deal with this man. He victimized me with his insults and verbal abuse while flaunting his whores. I want him to know how it feels to be rejected. I need to get stronger to retaliate. I want to take him for all he is worth in this divorce, to show him two can play his dirty game. You do understand, don't you, Dr. Dominion?"

Mora waited for a response, still looking down, but there was only silence. She glanced up and was taken aback by the look on Dr. Dominion's face. His eyes were like slits now, his forehead rippled with creases. His upper lip almost completely covered his bottom lip. His body was rigid and his hands were clutching the arms of his chair.

Finally Dominion spoke. "I'm not sure I do."

Now his voice was much deeper, almost gruff. She looked down into her lap again to gain focus.

"Well, he has no sensitivity. Everything is all about him. He is a selfish ass…a jerk. He wants to do what he wants to do when he wants to do it. He ignores me. He treats me like a piece of—well, badly. He doesn't care how much he hurts me. He is fuck…well, you know, seeing yet another one of his sluts."

Mora now heard her own voice as shrill and uncontrolled. She would have to watch her language.

"I am an extreme victim," she blurted, "and I need to be strong to deal with what he has done to me." There. She had answered his questions. She had clearly stated her purpose for coming to him today.

She inhaled and glanced up slowly. Her face blanched in horror. Dr. Dominion's face was flaming red with tiny beads of sweat seeping from the deep ridges of his forehead. His sharp, white teeth protruded, and blood streamed from his mouth and trickled down his chin. Mora put her hands to her face and screamed. She struggled up from the chair, stooped to grab her purse from the floor, and darted from the room. Dr. Dominion bounded out after her.

Dear Esteemed Members of the League of California Psychologists,

It is with great urgency that I must write to you. Women must be protected from a person, or I should say a being that looks human, listed as a member of your organization.

While under great stress I sought help from Dr. Jared Dominion who operates out of a lair-like office in a seedy area of Van Nuys. I poured out my soul to this "psychologist," to help me deal with my husband who I am divorcing. At first Dr. Dominion appeared to be nice enough, but that is the trick he uses to ensnare victims. Shortly after I started answering his unnerving questions, without provocation he showed his fangs and blood gushed from his mouth. I screamed and ran out as fast as I could. He chased after me. Thankfully, he tripped and fell, allowing me to get to my car and escape with my life.

So, I must inform you of something quite shocking. One of your members is a vampire. I heard they existed but was not sure until now. I was lucky. He has probably killed many women and will likely kill again. I cannot call the police because my awful husband plays poker with the Van Nuys police chief every Wednesday night.

Very sincerely yours,
Ms. Mora Slocum

***

Three weeks had passed since Mora Slocum dashed out of his office. Dr. Jared Dominion now thought about it less often, although during quiet times the bizarre and puzzling incident would invade his thoughts. He considered trying to call her, but decided that would only complicate matters. He had too little information to contact a family member or friend. Getting in touch with her husband would be an obvious error in judgment. Still, he did not expect the certified letter from the League of California Psychologists.

Dear Dr. Dominion,

This letter is to inform you of Mrs. Mora Slocum's communication with our office about her single, partial session with you. Her assertions are unusual, but it is our duty to ensure Mrs. Slocum was treated with respect and her well-being was protected.

Mrs. Slocum claims you asked her inappropriate questions and did not respond in a helpful way to her purpose for seeking counseling. She stated she left the session after only about 10 minutes feeling very frightened and, for reasons we seek to better understand, described you as a vampire. She also claims you chased after her with intent to do her bodily harm.

We are asking to hear your account of what happened during the session with Mrs. Slocum and any subsequent contact you may have had with her. Please make an appointment with the LCP administrator, Mrs. Peggy Aldridge, to appear before the Ethics Committee at its March meeting unless a compelling reason requires a request for a postponement. Mrs. Slocum has signed a release allowing you to discuss the matter with us. Failure to contact us within 10 days of the receipt of this letter will constitute an act of noncompliance, which is itself an ethics violation.

Sincerely,
Victor Graham, Ph.D.
Chair, Ethics Committee
League of California Psychologists

Jared Dominion grasped the sides of his head with both hands. *A vampire? Intent to do harm?* Mrs. Slocum was a strange one to be sure. The few minutes spent in his office were insufficient to competently diagnose this out-of-control, manipulative woman. He first thought she was under the influence of some substance, perhaps the more serious side effects of an antidepressant. In any event, he knew she would not be coming back, and that was fine with him. Her abrupt departure felt like a blessing.

He tried to merge this unanticipated burden of facing an ethics committee with his own chaotic circumstances. Sharon, his wife of 11 years, had moved herself and their two young sons to her mother's house two months ago. The split was volatile. Even more distressing than their year-long yelling fest over anything qualifying as a difference of opinion was being separated from his boys. Reading to them before bedtime had become his sole source of joy after long hours of listening to other people's troubles, many being far more benign than his own, and coming home to Sharon who was always poised to start accusing him of sins, only a few of which he actually committed. The day before Mora Slocum's appointment, he learned the identity of his wife's attorney. Abe Zicker, known in and around the San Fernando Valley as "Legal Jaws," would be representing Sharon in family court. He could lose everything, including access to his sons.

Over the course of the next few days Jared Dominion considered what he would say to the LCP Ethics Committee. Upon consulting his notes and carefully recreating the incident, he reconstructed what happened and why.

The Ethics Committee:
Jared Dominion, March 17, 3:00 p.m.

"Our last case. Mora Slocum versus Dr. Jared Dominion, VAMPIRE!" announced Victor Graham with twinkling eyes. The others chuckled softly. The Ethics Committee members were familiar with occasional allegations likely arising from the delusions of seriously troubled clients.

"Mrs. Slocum is accusing Dr. Dominion of extremely unusual behavior," Victor continued. "It appears to have no rational explanation. I first thought Mrs. Slocum was in the throes of decompensation, but things are not always as they seem."

Victor read Mora Slocum's neatly hand-penned letter. Sniggles and head shaking soon ensued.

"This reminds me of that case where a woman accused her psychologist of co-opting the soul of her canary," said Wolf Levin, pointing his index finger to his head.

"Or what about the time a guy claimed his psychologist was riding a motorcycle back-and-forth in front of his house all night, every night, making it impossible for him to get any sleep?" added Charlotte Burroughs.

"Or the one where the client wanted us to call the police because she said her psychologist was living in the freezer compartment of her refrigerator," said Archie Wittig, wincing.

"Now, now," scolded Victor. "Let's not get into a pissing contest as to who can recall the weirdest allegation. And before judging Mrs. Slocum, don't forget the incident involving the fellow who thought his boss was trying to kill him, and his psychologist put him on 72-hour hold in the UCLA Neuropsychiatric Unit. Then we learned the boss actually *was* trying to kill him."

"Victor, are you agreeing with Mrs. Slocum that vampires exist?" asked Wolf, with a wink. Victor ignored the question.

Sammy still wanted to make a positive impression on his new colleagues before everyone went home. He decided to cut to the chase by stating what he saw as the obvious answer.

"It seems this woman exhibits pathology besides the problems she is having with her husband," Sammy offered in a sober tone. "I cannot imagine any plausible response to neutralize the hallucinatory nature of this complaint. I suspect she is schizophrenic, or maybe bipolar. Do we know if she is on meds?" Sammy leaned back in his chair, raised up his arms and laced his fingers behind his neck, feeling confident about his succinct assessment bringing needed focus to the discussion.

"Well, let's just learn what Dr. Dominion has to say," said Victor. "Wolf, please escort him into the room."

***

Dr. Dominion's head almost touched the transom. A paranormal energy seemed to accompany him; an unreadable something was palpable. He could be on the cover of GQ magazine, strikingly handsome with dark eyes and jet black hair. His attire was all black from a raw silk shirt to lizard loafers, save for a jade green silk tie. He appeared to be in his mid-to late thirties. To Sammy he looked like a younger George Clooney, but more solemn, more angular, more inscrutable. Charlotte's wide eyes confirmed an enthrallment with the tall, dark man who just graced the room.

"Good day, Dr. Dominion," said Victor, gesturing him to the chair next to his. "Thank you for joining us. Let me introduce you to our members." Dr. Dominion's dark eyes locked with those of each member, just a little longer on Charlotte's, as they were introduced around the table, but displayed no discernible expression.

"The first thing we would ask is your recounting of what happened in the office the day of Mora Slocum's appointment. Take us through it as best you can recall," Victor continued as if nothing was unusual about this mysterious man.

"Yes, I do recall the incident very well," replied Dr. Dominion in a respectful but edgy voice. "Mrs. Slocum is a middle-aged woman who came to see me, as far as I could tell, about problems she was having with her husband and their impending split. She was extremely angry and vindictive. In shrill, whiny, wrathful terms, she defiled the man she married. I found her to be quite scary."

"I gather things started to go poorly between the two of you right from the start," Victor interjected. "How did it come to pass?"

"Well, I found her difficult to listen to as I am going through a divorce myself. In fact, Mrs. Slocum, though older, reminds me of my wife Sharon. Sharon is also challenging to deal with, very spiteful. She is putting me through hell."

"Did your own situation impact any of your reactions to Mrs. Slocum?" Stella Sarkosky asked.

"Probably to some extent," Dominion replied in a somber tone, leaning back in his chair. "As Mrs. Slocum spewed a barrage of loathing and profanity I found myself becoming apprehensive. Maybe I would have been more sensitive if a loving family greeted me at home every night, although I would respond poorly to any client who is so hateful. Without warning or provocation, Mrs. Slocum let out a shriek and bolted from the room. I assumed she fell ill and followed her outside to help. But I wasn't being careful and tripped on a crack in the walkway and fell, injuring my left knee. I watched her back up and take off in a fancy Mercedes, tires screeching and kicking up gravel."

"So why would she characterize you as a vampire?" asked Ted Bates. All eyes fixated intently on Dr. Dominion.

"Well, here's what happened." Dr. Dominion's voice sounded more apprehensive, as if wary of how this would play out with those about to stand in judgment of him. "At one point, I bit down on my lip to keep from showing my irritation over her incessant, insufferable shouting. After she left I limped back into the office washroom to tend my wounded knee and splash my face with cold water. I looked up into the mirror and realized I had bitten down on my bottom lip hard enough to draw blood."

The room hushed. There it was! The vampire connection. Sammy felt chagrined for so quickly labeling the client as psychotic. Now the image of Dr. Dominion all dressed in black and drooling blood down his chin seemed rather comical, although Sammy stifled an urge to smile. The other members appeared to be similarly beguiled, judging by the impish glint in their eyes.

Victor asked if anyone had additional questions for Jared Dominion. No one even stirred.

Dr. Dominion was politely excused. He thanked the Committee for their time as he walked toward the door, now a little stooped and appearing far less imposing.

***

"Well, *that* was interesting," said Victor with an uncharacteristically wide smile. "What say you?"

Sammy, still embarrassed for being too quick to label Mora Slocum's mental status spoke first. "I have to admit I am a little remorseful for being tickled by the misadventures of two such unhappy people. I guess I need to hear from the rest of you to understand where this fits as an ethics matter."

"Well, it isn't an ethics matter," said Charlotte in a brusque tone. "Here's a guy going through his own stuff and trying to hold it together as best he can. He didn't purposely hurt himself. He didn't yell at her like the first case we heard yesterday, that Dr. Pegoris."

"You just think he's hot," said Wolf, mocking Charlotte by panting like a thirsty dog.

"Put a sock in it, Levin," snapped Charlotte. "His looks have nothing to do with what happened with his client. I am able to think objectively." Charlotte folded her arms and frowned.

"Technically speaking, she wasn't ever a client. She never paid him anything," said Ted.

"That point isn't always clear," said Victor. "If a person believes herself to be a client, regardless of whether money changes hands, a presumption of a client/therapist relationship exists. This woman went to Dr. Dominion's office for the purpose of engaging his professional services."

"Should he have stopped her sooner when he realized how much she upset him?" Sammy asked. "It sounds like she gored his ox right from the beginning."

"Fair question," answered Charlotte in a brisk tone while unfolding her arms. "But what would you expect him to say to her? 'Oh, let's stop. My wife is a spiteful bitch just like you so you need to find someone who can stomach your vitriol?' How ethical would that be?"

"He probably had a few minutes warning that things were going badly before he drew his own blood," said Wolf. "Couldn't he have stopped her with something like, 'I hear you are upset, Mrs. Whatever-her-name-is, but I'm going through a divorce myself so I am sensitive to this topic. I think you would be wise to see someone else, and I will be happy to recommend a couple of good ones to you and will not charge you for today, of course.' What's wrong with this simple solution?"

Charlotte jumped in. "That would be fine if he hadn't been so upset. Psychologists are human, you know, and our thinking is affected when we are upset."

"Here's what I think," said Ted. "Had Dr. Dominion not bitten his lip and the session continued it would have gone badly. I also think it is likely he would have referred to her someone else soon enough, although we can never know for sure. But this session lasted for how long? Ten minutes before turning into a dark circus with neither performer in control."

"I basically agree with you," said Stella in her sterner voice, which meant she was about to disagree. "But here's the thing. If Dominion had not been so weakened by his own stressors, this drama would have never played out.

I also thought his characterizations of this woman he barely knew exposed his own anger towards women in general, at least at this point in his life. Maybe she was angry, but she wasn't upset with him until he sprang a capillary. Now I am not saying he is unfit to practice. I do say we should keep him and any new female clients presenting relationship issues from linking up. Can we do that?"

Victor thought for a moment before speaking. "Unless we find him responsible ethically for his behavior, we can't mandate anything. Nothing stops us, however, from suggesting he refrain from seeing certain kinds of clients for now. He may not nibble on himself again, but I doubt any other woman having a problem with a man would receive capable counsel from him at this point. Coming from us, such a suggestion should carry weight," answered Victor. "We can word it authoritatively."

"Are you OK with this, Charlotte?" asked Wolf, with a wink.

"Sounds fine," said Charlotte bluntly, although it was clear she was still pouting.

"Maybe we should ask Dr. Dominion to write Mora Slocum some sort of explanation and offer an apology?" asked Ted. "I mean, it might be a gracious thing to do."

Sammy recalled Ted's desire for the most pleasant possible outcomes all around, even though a fair resolution was usually the more realistic goal. "Ted," Sammy replied, "I'm not sure a communication would work right now, unless we had access to the content. Dr. Dominion appears to have some control problems when his buttons are pushed." Sammy smiled kindly at Ted, not wanting to come off as challenging his optimistic perspective.

"I agree," said Stella. "He would just stir the pot again. I think we have a better chance communicating the outcome ourselves."

"Anyone disagree or have anything to add?" asked Victor, eyes scanning around the table. "OK then, it's done. We will ask Dr. Dominion to voluntarily refer any female clients seeking help for relationship problems elsewhere and forget about asking for an apology letter. Vampire indeed! That's one for the books."

Decision and Dispositions

No formal charges were filed against Dr. Jared Dominion for violating any specific principle of the LCP Ethics Code. However, the Committee expressed its concern that his own problems at home could be affecting his professional performance. He was advised to refrain from accepting new female clients who were experiencing difficulties with significant others until his own life was in order. It was gently suggested that he, himself, may benefit from counseling.

Upon receiving the letter, Jared Dominion felt relief and gratitude. He was unexpectedly thankful to the Committee. He needed this fear-provoking experience of being examined by his peers to appreciate how his unruly personal life could be leaking into and polluting his professional work. He even sensed a renewed energy to move ahead with dissolving his marriage in the most constructive possible way, not only for himself and the boys, but for all of his clients who would benefit from a therapist who was emotionally well-settled.

Dr. Dominion wrote a note of thanks to the Committee for not finding him guilty of an ethics violation and promised to refrain from taking on new female clients until his personal affairs had improved. He acknowledged the value of their advice and offered the name of a colleague, Abby Hashfield, Ph.D., as his referral for women fitting the criteria suggested by the Committee. He also informed the Committee of his own entry into psychotherapy to weather his own rough period.

Mora Slocum received a calming letter briefly addressing the "vampire matter," noting Dr. Dominion had inadvertently bitten his lip. She was gently encouraged to seek counseling with someone else during this trying time in her life and recommended three female therapists practicing in the San Fernando Valley. The Committee also assured her of its appropriate handling of her complaint, even though they shared, as is the usual protocol, no details as to what "dealt appropriately" entailed.

Although Mora Slocum did not respond to the letter, at the next meeting Wolf told the others about Dr. Barbara Persoff, a colleague who practiced down the hall from his office. She stopped in to ask him to thank the Ethics Committee members for the referral. Wolf assumed the client was Mora Slocum, given that Dr. Persoff was one of the three recommended therapists.

Case Commentary

Some readers may think Dr. Dominion should have received a reprimand for not realizing that certain clients at this juncture of his life were unsuited for his care. The tumultuous first few minutes with Mrs. Slocum was too short to judge how he might have managed the session better. Had he not bitten himself and continued to work with Mrs. Slocum, more serious problems could have ensued. No one will ever know for sure, not even Dr. Dominion.

Although we may refer to Dr. Dominion's response as a rapid onset of negative countertransference, it stems not from unconscious resistance as Freud (1910) conceived of the phenomenon. More recent iterations arising from research-based findings suggest countertransference stems from interactions between what material the client brings and the psychotherapists own unresolved conflicts, which may be conscious or unconscious (Gelso & Hayes, 2002; Hayes, 2004). Winnicott (1949) acknowledged the potential for countertransference stemming from hate and anger and argued that such feelings must not be denied lest the therapy become adapted to the needs of the therapist as opposed to the needs of the client. Dr. Dominion's fervent though unsuccessful attempts to cover his reactions to Mrs. Slocum's tirade auger against suggesting that disclosure on his part would set both of them on a positive course.

An admission of family discord in his own home and its relevance to explaining the incident was appreciated as an honest response to the committee's questioning. A more devious respondent might have discounted the bleeding lip as a shaving mishap or the client's hallucination.

Dr. Dominion's acceptance of seeking counseling for himself was also viewed favorably, especially since he could have refused the Committee's suggestion. Self-care during times of personal crisis is not only healing for the psychotherapist but may mitigate against ethical errors (Pope & Vasquez, 2005; Wise, Hersh, & Gibson, 2012). The stress model put forth by the APA Board of Professional Affairs Advisory Committee on Colleague Assistance (n.d.) reveals a slippery slope if stress if not effectively managed; Stress spirals downward to distress, then impairment, and finally improper behavior that could often involve ethical violations.

Notes on Personal Stressors and Self-Care

Mental health professionals are trained to treat the stressed and troubled; however they may be doing so at the neglect of their own mental health. As Norcross (2009) put it in his article on the paradox of self-care, "The self-defeating situation is so easy to see and diagnose in other people; it is so hard to get off the treadmill ourselves." We fail to follow the very advice we give to others.

A survey of psychologists by Bridgeman and Gelper (cited in APA's Advisory Committee on Colleague Assistance, 2010) expressed concerns that some psychologists may be disregarding their own stress levels to the point of damaging their health and their practice. Half of the respondents admitted to facing challenges that impacted their professional functioning. Those who failed to take coping and constructive self-care measures cited lack of time, denial, and privacy/confidentiality issues. Bearce and her colleagues (2013) studied barriers that deter psychologists from seeking professional help. Impediments included difficulty in finding the right therapist, lack of time or finances, privacy concerns, and, more rarely, professional or personal stigma. Nevertheless, 86 percent of their sample indicated that they had received psychotherapy at some point in their lives.

In *Tips for Self Care*, APA's Advisory Committee on Colleague Assistance (2010) advises clinicians to remain self-aware of their life stressors, strengthen relationships with colleagues, readjust their caseloads and schedules, tend to their physical needs, and seek consultation or psychotherapy—all common sense to those paying adequate attention to their personal well-being.

Discussion Questions

1. If you felt within the first few minutes that you were the wrong psychotherapist for a client, what would you do? What exactly would you say?
2. How could Dr. Dominion have managed this situation better, given his immediate negative reactions to this client? Or does he get a pass for trying to hold it together?
3. Do you think it is wise to speak with a prospective client on the phone briefly about their reasons for seeking therapy? Might that avoid what happened in this story? Or do you think face-to-face in the initial session is a better way to evaluate the client's suitability to your practice?

4. Do you have any preconceived ideas about what kinds of clients you should *not* work with because of your own personal values or issues?

5. Do you agree with the Committee that Dr. Dominion did not commit an ethical violation? Why or why not?

6. What do you do to take good care of yourself? How do you manage the endemic stress accompanying a career in mental health?

References

Advisory Committee on Colleague Assistance (n.d.). *The stress-distress impairment contin-uum for psychologists*. Retrieved from the American Psychological Association, Practice Organization website: http://www.apapracticecentral.org/ce/self-care/colleague-assist. aspx? − utma = 12968039.1402018276.1335218668.1362424812.1362432875.160& − utmb = 12968039.1.10.1362432875& − utmc = 12968039& − utmx = -& − utmz = 12968039.1362432875.160.105.utmcsr = apapracticecentral.org|utmccn = (referral) |utmcmd = referral|utmcct = /404-error.aspx& − utmv = -& − utmk = 263085196

APA's Advisory Committee on Colleague Assistance (July, 2010). Tips for self-care. Practice Central. Retrieved from http://www.apapracticecentral.org/ce/self-care/acca-promoting.aspx? − utma = 12968039.1402018276.1335218668.1362424812.136243287 5.160& − utmb = 12968039.2.10.1362432875& − utmc = 12968039& − utmx = -& − utmz = 12968039.1362432875.160.105.utmcsr = apapracticecentral.org|utmccn = (referral)|utmcmd = referral|utmcct = /404-error.aspx& − utmv = -& − utmk = 192233386

Freud, S. (1910). Future prospects of psychoanalytic therapy. In J.Strachey (1962). (Ed.). *The standard edition of the complete psychological works of Sigmund Freud* (pp.139–151). London: Hogarth Press.

Gelso, C. J., & Hayes, J. A. (2002). Countertransference management: The empirical status of an inherently relational construct. In J. Norcross (Ed.). *Psychotherapy relationships that work* (pp. 267–283). London: Oxford University Press.

Hayes, J. A. (Fall, 2004). Therapist know thyself: Recent research on countertransference. *Psychotherapy Bulletin, 39*, 6–12.

Norcross, J. C. (Fall, 2009). Psychologist self-care in a workaholic nation. *The Clinical Psychologist, 62*, 1–5.

Pope, K. S., & Vasquez, M. J. T. (2005). *How to survive and thrive as a therapist: Information, ideas, and resources for psychologists in practice*. Washington, DC: American Psychological Association.

Practice Research & Policy Staff (August, 2010). *Survey findings emphasize the importance of self-care for psychologists*. Practice Central. Retrieved from http://www.apapractice central.org/update/2010/08−31/survey.aspx

Winnicott, D. W. (1949). Hate in the counter-transference. *International Journal of Psychoanalysis, 30*, 69–74.

Wise, E. H., Hersh, M. A., & Gibson, C. M. (2012). Ethics, self-care and well-being for psychologists: Reenvisioning the stress-distress continuum. *Professional Psychology, 43*, 487–494.

Additional Reading

Baker, E. K. (2003). *Caring for ourselves: A therapist's guide to personal and professional well-being.* Washington, DC: American Psychological Association.

Barnett, J. E., Baker, E. K., Elman, N. S., & Schoener, G. R. (2007). In pursuit of wellness: The self-care imperative. *Professional Psychology, 38*, 603–612.

Giovacchini, P. L. (1989). *Countertransference triumphs and catastrophes.* Northvale, NJ: Jason Aronson.

Gorkin, N. (1987). *The uses of countertransference.* Northvale, NJ: Jason Aronson.

Hedges, L. E. (1992). *Interpreting the countertransference.* Northvale, NJ: Jason Aronson, 1992.

Hedges, L. E., Hilton, R., Hilton, V. W., & Caudill, O. B. (1997). *Therapists at risk.* Northvale, NJ: Jason Aronson.

Kaslow, F. W. (Ed.). (1984). *Psychotherapy with psychotherapists.* New York, NY: Haworth Press

Manning, E. A. (2005). Wrestling with vulnerability: Countertransference disclosure and the training therapist. *Psychotherapy Bulletin, 40*, 5–11.

Robertiello, R. C., & Schoenewolf, G. (1987). *101 common therapeutic blunders.* Northvale, NY: Jason Aronson.

Schaeffer, J. A. (2007). *Transference and countertransference in non-analytic therapy: Double-edged swords.* Lanham, MD: University Press of America, 2007.

Strean, H. S. (2001). *Controversies on countertransference.* Northvale, NJ: Jason Aronson.

Wishnie, H. A. (2005). *Working in the countertransference: Necessary entanglements.* New York: Jason Aronson.

Epilogue

"We'll see you all back here in June," chirped Victor Graham. "Good work people. Have a safe trip home."

Farewells abounded during a flurry of hugs and gentle backslaps. Sammy, normally uneasy with California's social touching rituals, found himself comfortably participating. Something whole, an entity with its own character and purpose, would now break into six parts and scatter until the time came to reunite again.

It was a balmy Sunday afternoon and traffic was light on the 405 South. Wolf drove Sammy all the way to Los Angeles International Airport to catch Sammy's 5:45 p.m. flight. He smiled recalling how Wolf had to stand on his toes to give him a final hug.

Once inside the plane, Sammy eased back into his seat for the short flight into Monterey. What a weekend! A remarkable assembly of seemingly mismatched characters somehow managing to reach decisions with both merit and heart.

Had someone told him before this weekend that he would feel sorry for a colleague who committed a serious ethical error with an impulsive and cruel communication, or feel compassion for a cross-dressing psychologist who hung out on the streets at night, or remain concerned about the welfare of a prostitute, or feel empathy for a colleague who lost his temper with a client, he would have scoffed at such a possibility. He also didn't expect it possible for serious, well-educated violators to miss obvious signs of trouble looming ahead or to be totally out of touch with the gravity of their actions, seemingly unable to perceive their own failings. Then there were those forced to endure the trepidation of an ethics hearing even though they did nothing seriously wrong, or in one case, did everything almost as right as possible under emergency circumstances.

Only one of the accused came close to fitting his preconceived stereotype of a malicious and premeditated wrongdoer. The others should have known better. Some simply screwed up without intention. Or their actions were impulsive and otherwise uncharacteristic. These were the mistakes any mental health professional could make, including himself, if looming needs were not blocked at the gate separating psychotherapy from something else.

For the first time Sammy admitted he had his own possible near misses, especially with Ava Gordon, a lovely and delicate client from his practice in Indiana towards whom he had special yet not fully identifiable feelings. This intelligent young woman from a large farming family who wanted to do more with her life than her community's culture was willing to support became his favorite client. She was languishing in an emotional cage and desperately needed help breaking out. Sammy sensed something vivid inside her, and he delighted in supporting her struggle to escape to freedom. He even found himself dressing more elegantly and paying more attention to how he combed his thinning hair on her appointment days. Then she was gone, off to college over her family's objections. He recalled tsunami-sized wave of pride when seven years later he learned she graduated from the University of Indiana Law School.

But, what would have happened if he and Elizabeth were not getting along when he first started seeing Ava Gordon? Or, if the hole left in his life when both sons moved to California resulted in unrelenting despair? Or, if he had been burning to explore more exciting horizons when he realized his life was comfortable but otherwise unremarkable? Would he have ventured into perilous territory with Ava Gordon? Was he, the newest member of the League of California Psychologists Ethics Committee, actually capable of disrupting and possibly destroying a client's life as well his own, saved only by a gauzy boundary perhaps having less to do with the values he held dear than fragile external circumstances?

It would take hours of reflection for Sammy to process the shifts brewing in his reflections on so many dimensions. Good, evil. Right, wrong. Premeditated, accidental. Major, minor. Understanding, ignorance. Rules, situational convenience. Opposing poles no longer dictated his previous way of sorting behaviors and the motivations behind them. He would have to revisit them all.

But, for now, he looked forward to landing in Monterey and taking the short drive north into Santa Cruz. Elizabeth and their two sons would be waiting to go out for their traditional Sunday Thai dinner at Bangkok West. One of the boys had a new girlfriend. He would be bringing her along. That part of his life, at least, would return to normal.

Appendix A
Selected Ethics Resources for Mental Health Professionals and Consumers

American Psychological Association (APA)

- Current Ethics Code http://www.apa.org/ethics/code/index.aspx
- Current Reporting Procedure http://www.apa.org/ethics/complaint/index.aspx
- What clients should know http://www.apa.org/topics/ethics/potential-violations.aspx
- Rules and procedures for dealing with ethics complaints http://www.apa.org/ethics/code/committee.aspx

American Association for Marriage and Family Therapy (AAMFT)

- Code of Ethics
  http://www.aamft.org/imis15/content/legal_ethics/code_of_ethics.aspx
- Ethics Complaint Process http://www.aamft.org/imis15/content/legal_ethics/Ethics_Complaint_Process.aspx

American Counseling Association (ACA)

- Code of Ethics http://www.counseling.org/Resources/CodeOfEthics/ TP/Home/CT2.aspx
- Policy and Procedures for Processing Complaints of Ethical Violations (PDF file) http://www.counseling.org/Resources/CodeOfEthics/TP/ Home/CT2.aspx

American Psychiatric Association (APA)

- The Principles of Medical Ethics With Annotations Especially Applicable to Psychiatry http://www.psych.org/MainMenu/PsychiatricPractice/ Ethics/ResourcesStandards.aspx
- Procedures for Handling Complaints of Unethical Conduct included in above document.

National Association of Social Workers (NASW)

- Code of Ethics (in English and Spanish) http://www.naswdc.org/pubs/code/default.asp
- Procedures for Professional Review http://www.naswdc.org/pubs/code/default.asp

National Board for Certified Counselors (NBCC)

- Code of ethics (2005) http://www.nbcc.org/Ethics
- Ethics Case Procedures www.nbcc.org/Assets/Ethics/nbcc-caseprocedures.pdf

National Association of School Psychologists (NASP)

- Professional Standards (2010) http://www.nasponline.org/standards/ 2010standards.aspx
- Resolution of Ethical Concerns and Complaints http://www.nasponline.org/standards/ethics/resolution-of-ethical-concerns.aspx

Association of State and Provincial Psychology Boards

- Code of Conduct (2005)
  http://asppb.org/publications/model/conduct.aspx

American Group Psychotherapy Association and National Registry of Certified Group Psychotherapists (AGPA and NRCGP)

- Guidelines for Ethics (2002)
  http://www.agpa.org/group/ethicalguide.html
- Complaints to be registered with the complainant's state licensing board

Canadian Psychological Association (CPA)

- Code of Ethics for Psychologists (2000)
  http://www.cpa.ca/aboutcpa/committees/ethics/codeofethics/
- Rules and Procedures for Dealing with Ethical Complaints
  http://www.cpa.ca/aboutcpa/committees/ethics/rulesandproce-
  duresfordealingwithethicalcomplaints/

California Board of Psychology

- Laws and Regulations Relating to the Practice of Psychology (2009)
  http://www.psychboard.ca.gov/lawsregs/index.shtml
- Complaint Information
  http://www.psychboard.ca.gov/consumers/complaints.shtml

California Board of Behavioral Sciences (BBS)

- http://www.bbs.ca.gov/
- (The BBS is responsible for consumer protection through the regulation of Marriage and Family Therapists (MFT); Licensed Clinical Social Workers (LCSW); Licensed Educational Psychologists (LEP); Licensed Professional Clinical Counselors (LPCC); MFT Interns

(IMF); Associate Clinical Social Workers (ASW); and Professional Clinical Counselor Interns (PCCI) in the State of California)
- Complaint Information
  http://www.bbs.ca.gov/consumer/complaint_process.shtml

Appendix B
Actions Available to the Ethics Committee of the American Psychological Association

The American Psychological Association Ethics Committee Rules and Procedures issued four sanctions that can be assigned (or referred to the Board to Directors) when the Ethics Committee issues a finding. Part II, Section 11 of the Rules and Procedures (2001) reads:

> On the basis of circumstances that aggravate or mitigate the culpability of the member, including prior sanctions, directives, or educative letters from the Association or state or local boards or similar entities, a sanction more or less severe, respectively, than would be warranted on the basis of the factors set forth below, may be appropriate.
>
> *11.1 Reprimand.* Reprimand is the appropriate sanction if there has been an ethics violation but the violation was not of a kind likely to cause harm to another person or to cause substantial harm to the profession and was not otherwise of sufficient gravity as to warrant a more severe sanction.
>
> *11.2 Censure.* Censure is the appropriate sanction if there has been an ethics violation and the violation was of a kind likely to cause harm to another person, but the violation was not of a kind likely to cause substantial harm to another person or to the profession and was not otherwise of sufficient gravity as to warrant a more severe sanction.

11.3 Expulsion. Expulsion from membership is the appropriate sanction if there has been an ethics violation and the violation was of a kind likely to cause substantial harm to another person or the profession or was otherwise of sufficient gravity as to warrant such action.

11.4 Stipulated Resignation. A stipulated resignation may be offered by the Committee following a Committee finding that the respondent has committed a violation of the Ethics Code or failed to show good cause why he or she should not be expelled, contingent on execution of an acceptable affidavit and approval by the Board of Directors…

In addition, directives of required actions may satisfy part or all of the Committee's decision. Part II, Section 12 reads:

12.1 Cease and Desist Order. Such a directive requires the respondent to cease and desist specified unethical behavior(s).

12.2 Other Corrective Actions. The Committee may require such other corrective actions as may be necessary to remedy a violation, protect the interests of the Association, or protect the public. Such a directive may not include a requirement that the respondent make a monetary payment to the Association or persons injured by the conduct.

12.3 Supervision Requirement. Such a directive requires that the respondent engage in supervision.

12.4 Education, Training, or Tutorial Requirement. Such a directive requires that the respondent engage in education, training, or a tutorial.

12.5 Evaluation and/or Treatment Requirement. Such a directive requires that the respondent be evaluated to determine the possible need for treatment and/or, if dysfunction has been established, obtain treatment appropriate to that dysfunction.

12.6 Probation. Such a directive requires monitoring of the respondent by the Committee to ensure compliance with the Ethics Committee's mandated directives during the period of those directives.

Reference

Access full Rules and Procedures (October, 2001) at http://www.apa.org/ethics/code/committee.aspx or Ethics Committee of the American Psychological Association (2002). Rules and procedures: October 1, 2001. (2002). *American Psychologist, 57,* 626–645.

INDEX

39538485R00148

Made in the USA
Middletown, DE
18 January 2017